HANDBOOK OF
WORLD MYTHOLOGY

APOLLO

HANDBOOK OF
WORLD MYTHOLOGY

ALEXANDER S. MURRAY

Notes, Revisions and Additions by
WILLIAM H. KLAPP

DOVER PUBLICATIONS, INC.
Mineola, New York

Bibliographical Note

This Dover edition, first published in 2005, is an unabridged republication of *Manual of Mythology: Greek and Roman, Norse and Old German, Hindoo and Egyptian Mythology,* published by Tudor Publishing Company, New York, 1935.

Library of Congress Cataloging-in-Publication Data

Murray, A. S. (Alexander Stuart), 1841-1904.
  [Manual of mythology]
  Handbook of world mythology / Alexander S. Murray ; notes, revisions, and additions by William H. Klapp.—Dover ed.
    p. cm.
  Originally published: Manual of mythology. New York : Tudor Pub. Co., [1935].
  Includes index.
  ISBN-13: 978-0-486-44374-4 (pbk.)
  ISBN-10: 0-486-44374-4 (pbk.)
  1. Mythology. I. Klapp, William H. (William Henry), 1849-1924. II. Title.

BL310.M85 2005
201'.3—dc22

2005051794

Manufactured in the United States by Courier Corporation
44374402   2013
www.doverpublications.com

PREFACE.

THE rapid sale of the first edition of *The Manual of Mythology* was so signal an assurance of public favor, that in preparing the second edition, which is now called for, every effort has been made to render it efficient as a standard text-book. The descriptions of the Greek deities have been largely re-written, and at the end of each has been added, in smaller type, an account of the most memorable works of art in which each deity is or was represented. Among the legends of the Greek heroes, those of the labors of Hercules have been re-written and greatly enlarged. The chapters on the Eastern and Northern Mythology are entirely new, and have been further made more readily comprehensible by the addition of new illustrations.

With these alterations, it is hoped that the *Manual* will now justify its claims to be a trustworthy and complete class-book for Mythology. This much it may also claim : to be no longer described as founded on the works of Petiscus, Preller, and Welcker. Not that in its new form it owes less to the splendid researches of Preller and Welcker. On the contrary, it owes more than ever to them, but this time as masters whose works have rather been an assistance which it is a pride to acknowledge, than models to copy with exactness.

AMERICAN EDITOR'S PREFACE.

IT seems hardly necessary to offer an apology in present-- ing a new edition of Murray's *Manual of Mythology* to the public. The work itself is an invaluable one to whoever would understand the religions of antiquity, and of equal importance to the student of our own literature, and, indeed, to any one who expects thoroughly to enjoy the accepted English classics. Though widely known through- out Great Britain, it has had but a limited circulation in America, and this sphere it is now designed to enlarge by presenting a revised and handsomely illustrated text.

Naturally the religions of Greece and Rome play a more prominent part than the Asiatic, Egyptian, or Norse, and consequently more space is devoted to them. Additions have been made when necessary, but nothing has been omitted ; *the whole text has been thoroughly revised.*

Here arose a question as to the spelling of the Greek proper names—whether, following the movement initiated by Grote and amplified by Gladstone and the purists, the proper names should be transliterated, or whether the old spelling derived through the Latin should be adopted? Personally, transliteration is preferred, but the difficulty of reproducing certain sounds and the unfamiliarity of the general reading public with the Greek forms were powerful

(v)

factors against it. It was finally determined to adopt the Latin spelling throughout the book. Almost all the Greek names can be found in some Latin author, and consistency at least is thereby obtained. The book is not intended for profound scholars, who are as familiar with the Greek as with the Latin forms, but for the younger students and for those who wish to familiarize themselves with the grand and interesting myths of antiquity, which have had unbounded influence on the literature of Greece and Rome, and in no less degree upon our own.

The editor desires to express his obligations for many valuable suggestions to Professors John William White, of Harvard University ; Bernadotte Perrin, of Yale University ; B. L. Gildersleeve, of Johns Hopkins University ; and W. A. Lamberton, of the University of Pennsylvania.

The engravings have been prepared with great care, and, it is believed, will prove a valuable and artistic aid to the proper understanding and enjoyment of the text. A full and careful index has been prepared, without which a book like this is practically useless, and especial attention has been paid to the orthography.   **W. H. K.**

PUBLISHERS' NOTE.

MURRAY'S *Manual of Mythology* has been known to the American public thus far only through the English edition. As originally published, the work was deficient in its account of the Eastern and Northern Mythology ; but with these imperfections it secured a sale in this country which proved that it more nearly supplied the want which had long been felt of a compact hand-book in this study than did any other similar work. The preface to the second English edition indicates the important additions to, and changes which have been made in, the original work. Chapters upon the Northern and Eastern Mythology have been supplied, the descriptions of many of the Greek deities have been re-written, accounts of the most memorable works of art in which each deity is or was represented have been added, and a number of new illustrations have been inserted. This American edition has been reprinted from the perfected work. Every illustration given in the original has been carefully reproduced ; and the new chapters upon Eastern and Northern Mythology were thoroughly revised by Prof. W. D. Whitney, of Yale College, who corrected some minor inaccuracies which had escaped observation in the

(vii)

English edition.   The volume in its revised form is without a rival among manuals upon this interesting subject.
For the purpose of a text-book in high schools and colleges,
and a guide to the art student or general reader, it will be
found invaluable.

The Acropolis of Athens.

CONTENTS.

(ix)

Capitol and Temple of Jupiter.

LIST OF ILLUSTRATIONS.

FULL PAGE PLATES.

ALPHABETICAL LIST OF TEXT ILLUSTRATIONS.

(xi)

A TABLE OF DESCENT OF THE GODS.

(xv)

ARES, OR MARS.

INTRODUCTION.

THERE is a charm in the name of ancient Greece; there is glory in every page of her history; there is a fascination in the remains of her literature, and a sense of unapproachable beauty in her works of art; there is a spell in her climate still, and a strange attraction in her ruins. We are familiar with the praises of her beautiful islands; our poets sing of her lovely genial sky. There is not in all the land a mountain, plain, or river, nor a fountain, grove, or wood, that is not hallowed by some legend or poetic tale. The names of her artists, Phidias, Praxiteles, Apelles, and Zeuxis; of her poets, Homer, Pindar, Aeschylus, Sophocles, Euripides; of her philosophers, Socrates, Plato, Epicurus; the names of her statesmen and orators, Pericles and Demosthenes; of her historians, Herodotus, Thucydides, and Xenophon; of her mathematicians, Archimedes and Euclid, are familiar to us as household words. We look back over a period of more than two thousand years with feelings of wonder at her achievements on the battle-field and in the arts of peace. We emulate her in many ways, but always confess to failure ; and when we have no desire of emulation, we are still ready in most cases to admire.

How far we may find just cause for admiration or the contrary with regard to her religion remains to be seen. But whichever way it be, we shall at any rate find abundant evidence of the intense hold it had upon the great mass of the people, and of the important influence it was calculated to exercise on their civilization. For it was in the firm belief of his interests being the special care of a deity that the husbandman sowed his seed, and watched the vicissitudes of its growth; that the sailor and trader entrusted life and property to the capricious sea. The mechanic traced the skill and handicraft which grew unconsciously upon him by practice to the direct influence of a god. Artists ascribed the mysterious evolution of their ideas, and poets the inspiration of their song, to the same superior cause. Daily bread and daily life, the joy and gladness that circulated at festal gatherings, were duly acknowledged as coming from the same high source. Everywhere in nature was felt the presence of august invisible beings : in the sky, with its luminaries and clouds; on the sea, with its fickle, changeful movements; on the earth, with its lofty peaks, its plains, and rivers. It seemed that man himself, and everything around him, was upheld by Divine power; that his career was marked out for him by a rigid fate which even the gods could not alter, should they wish it on occasion. He was indeed free to act, but the consequences of all his actions were settled beforehand.

These deities to whom the affairs of the world were entrusted were, it was believed, immortal, though not eternal in their existence, as we shall see when we come to read the legends concerning their birth. In Crete there was even a story of the death of Zeus, his tomb being pointed out; and, further, the fact that the gods were believed to sustain their existence by means of nectar and ambrosia, is sufficient proof of their being usually deemed subject to the infirmities of age. Being immortal, they were next, as a consequence, supposed to be omnipotent and omniscient. Their physical strength was extraordinary, the earth shaking sometimes under their tread. Whatever they did was done speedily. They moved through space almost without the loss of a moment of time. They knew all things, saw and heard all things with rare exceptions. They were wise, and communicated their wisdom to men. They had a most strict sense of justice, punished crime rigorously, and rewarded noble actions, though it is true that they were less conspicuous for the latter. Their punishments came quickly, as a rule; but even if late, even if not till the second generation, still they came without fail. The sinner who escaped retribution in this life was sure to obtain it in the lower world; while the good who died unrewarded enjoyed the fruit of their good actions in the next life. To many this did not appear a satisfactory way of managing human affairs, and hence there frequently arose doubts as to the absolute justice of the gods and even the sanctity of their lives. These doubts were reflected in stories, which, to the indignation of men like the poet Pindar, represented this or that one of the gods as guilty of some offence or other, such as they were believed to punish. Philosophers endeavored to explain these stories, some as mere fictions of the brain, others as allegories under which lay a profound meaning. But the mass of the people accepted them as they came, and nevertheless believed in the perfect sanctity of the gods, being satisfied that human wickedness was detested and punished by them.

Whether the gods were supposed to love the whole of mankind, or only such as led good lives, is not certain. It would seem, however, from the universal practice of offering sacrifice and expiation on the occasion of any wrong, that they were believed to be endowed with some deep feeling of general love, which even sinners could touch by means of atonement. At all events they were merciful. They hated excessive prosperity among individual men, and would on such occasions exercise a Satanic power of leading them into sin. They implanted unwritten laws of right and wrong in

the human breast.   Social duties and engagements were under
their special care, as were also the legislative measures of
states.

There were tales of personal visits and adventures of the
gods among men, taking part in battles, and appearing in
dreams.   They were conceived to possess the form of human
beings, and to be, like men, subject to love and pain, but
always characterized by the highest qualities and grandest
form that could be imagined.   To produce statues of them
that would equal this high ideal was the chief ambition of
artists; and in presence of statues in which success had been
attained, the popular mind felt an awe as if in some way the
deity were near.   But while this was the case with regard
to the renowned examples of art, such as the statue of Zeus
at Olympia, by Phidias, it was equally true with regard to
those very ancient rude figures of deities which were believed
to have fallen from heaven, and were on that account most
carefully preserved in temples, the removal or loss of such a
figure being considered an equivalent to the loss of the favor
of the deity whose image it was.   This was idolatry.   At the
same time, owing to the vast number of beautiful and grand
statues of gods, there gradually arose a feeling of the deification of man and a struggle to become more and more like
these beings of nobler human form and divine presence.   For
it is one of the advantages of having gods possessed of
human form that mankind can look up to them with the feeling of having something in common, and the assurance of
pity and favor.   This was a powerful element in the Greek
religion, and led more than any other to the extraordinary
piety of the Greek race, in spite of all the awkward stories
which we are accustomed to ridicule.

It would seem that the gods were not looked on, at any
rate popularly, as having created the world.   Perhaps the
mass of the people cared nothing for speculation as to the
origin of what actually existed, their chief thoughts being
concentrated in the changes that took place in what existed

and directly affected their interests. In this spirit they looked on the gods as only maintaining and preserving existing order and system of things according to their divine wisdom. Hence it was that the Greeks never arrived at the idea of one absolute eternal God, though they very nearly approached that idea in the case of Zeus, who occasionally exercised control or sovereignty over the other gods who presided in particular departments in the management of the world. Their natural tendency to polytheism may have been further aggravated by the peculiar circumstances of their early history as a race. It has been suggested with much plausibility that a number of their deities, as Dione, Hera, Gaea, and Demeter, resemble each other so much as to warrant the reasonableness of the conclusion that their separate existence in the mythology was due to a coalescence at some remote early time of distinct tribes of the Greek race, each possessing beforehand a god or gods of their own, with separate names and slightly different attributes, though in the main capable of identification and a common worship. It is probable that, in consequence of such amalgamation, some of the earliest gods have disappeared altogether; while others, who in after times, as in the case of Dione, held subordinate positions, may have originally been deities of the first order.

At the time with which we are here concerned, the Greek nation inhabited the country still known by the name of Greece, though its present population has small claim to be descendants of the ancient race. It was spread also in colonies over the islands of the Archipelago and Mediterranean, along the coasts of Asia Minor and the Black Sea, in the Crimea, on the north coast of Africa, and on the south coast of France. In many of its features the mainland of Greece may be compared with England, both having the same comparatively vast extent of sea coast, very few parts of the country being out of sight of the sea. Both are well supplied with mountains that invigorate the climate and stir the spirit of adventure. In both cases it may be that this proximity of the greater part of the population to the sea, with its horizon tempting young minds to penetrate beyond its ever-receding line, was the main cause of the general desire of commerce and distant colonization. At any rate, the natural features of Greece, her beautiful bays, the vivid lines of her mountain peaks, her delightful groves and valleys, made a deep impression on the people; and colonists, wherever they spread, retained the warmest recollection of them; of snow-clad Olympus, where the gods lived; of the lovely vale of Tempe; of the smiling banks of the Peneus; of the sacred grove at Delphi; of peaceful Arcadia, with its pastoral life; of the broad plain of Olympia, with its innumerable temples, statues, and treasure-houses of costly presents to the gods; of Corinth, with its flag that ruled the sea; of Athens; of Thebes, with its ancient citadel founded by Cadmus; of Eleusis, and many other places.

We propose now to examine more particularly the religious belief of the Greeks and Romans, with the view of preparing the way for the descriptions that follow of the gods individually. But first of all let us explain the meaning of the word "mythology." According to its derivation from the Greek *mythos*, a tale, and *logos*, an account, it would mean "an account of tales," the tales in this case being confined to the origin, character, and functions of the ancient gods, to the origin of mankind, and the primitive condition of the visible world. To understand these stories we must try to understand the circumstances under which they were invented, and must endeavor to comprehend the condition and circumstances of a nation in the early stage of its existence. For this purpose we can compare the early tales relating to the gods of other nations, of the Indian on the one hand, and the German on the other; or we may also compare the condition of races at present in an uncivilized state. From these sources it would seem that the youth of a nation, like that of an individual, is the period at which the activity of imagination and fancy is greatest in proportion as knowledge is least. The mystery of surrounding nature strikes forcibly on the mind, its phenomena on the senses. There is a feeling of alarm when thunder crashes on the ear, of gladness in the warm light of day, of terror in the darkness of night, and of a strange dread at the darkness of death. The accidents of daily life bind men together, and repel the rest of the animal creation, over which the human superiority soon becomes known. Men learn to know each other when as yet they know nothing else. They know their own passions and instincts. They measure everything by themselves, by feet, paces, palms, and ells; and when they seek to fathom or measure the cause of the phenomena of nature they have no standard to employ at hand, except themselves. They might, it is true, imagine the cause of the thunder under the form of a great invisible lion; but in that case they could not commune with and implore the thunderer for pity, as they are moved to do. He must, therefore, be conceived as fashioned like a man, endowed with the highest imaginable qualities of a man. As knowledge and civilization advance, those qualities become higher and higher. It seems probable that the first phenomena that appealed to the mind were those of the change of weather, of seasons, the revolving day and the revolving year. At any rate, the earliest deities, as well as we can trace them, appear to be those who presided over the movements of the celestial sphere.

We seem to recognize the influence of such phenomena in the chief characteristics of mankind in a primitive stage of existence—the sense of order and regularity, the feeling of fatality, the conviction that whatever temporary disturbances might arise, the course of human life obeyed some fixed law, coming with bright light, and departing in darkness, but only to commence another day of happy life elsewhere. We know that the name of the highest god of the ancients signified the "light of the world," in a literal sense. In time, as the perceptive faculties expanded and the wants of men multiplied, the other phenomena of the world became the subject of inquiry, and were, as usual, ascribed to the direct influence of deities. The singular part, however, of this process of inventing deities is, that having, at the commencement, obtained one great powerful god, they did not simply extend his functions to all the departments of nature, instead of finding a new god to preside over each. It may be that the apparent conflict frequently observed between the elements of nature was hostile to such an idea, while on the contrary nothing was more readily imaginable than a quarrel among different gods as the cause of such phenomena. By a similar process the combination of different elements, as, for example, warmth and moisture, was appropriately described from the human point of view as a prolific union or marriage of two deities. The sun and moon were called brother and sister.

Another opinion, somewhat at variance with this, is, that the primitive stage of all religions is a universal belief in one great god—such a belief, it is said, being as natural to man as the use of his arms and legs. But this earliest and pure form of belief became, they say, in course of time debased into a belief in the existence of many gods, originating in such a method of explaining the phenomena of nature as we have described.

On the other hand, the oldest religious records we know of—the Vedas—speak of hosts of divine beings: while in the primitive religion of the American Indians the Great Spirit is surrounded by a crowd of lesser spirits, who represent the various phenomena of nature. It would seem that when the notion of one god did arise, it was of the one true God as opposed to the other and false gods, and this did not take place till a high stage of civilization was reached. In the best times of Greece, no doubt, thinking men acknowledged but one supreme being, and looked on the crowd of other gods as merely his servants, and in no sense really different from our idea of angels.

In due time the religion of the ancients became a polytheism on a very extensive scale; every phase of nature, sky, sea, and earth, every phase of human life, its habits, accidents, and impulses, being provided with a special guardian and controlling deity. In all the varying circumstances of life men turned to one or other of these divine persons in gratitude or for help. Temples, sanctuaries, altars, were erected to them everywhere, one being worshipped with special favor here, and another there; one with special favor at one season of the year, another at another season. Many of them were only known and worshipped in particular localities; as, for instance, marine deities among people connected with the sea. Others belonged to particular periods of the national history. This limitation, however, with regard to local differences, applies only to the vast number of minor deities whose names and attributes have come down to our times; for a belief in the superior order of gods was the common property of the whole nation, whether learned or unlearned, and of whatever occupation. The mysteries of Eleusis united the people in honor of Demeter; the national festivals united them in honor of other gods, as of Zeus at Olympia. Every one believed in the oracular power of Apollo, in the might of Poseidon, in the grim character of Hades, that Hera was the wife of Zeus, that Athene was his daughter, that Aphrodite was the goddess of love, Artemis of the moon, and Ares the god of war.

It was believed that these higher deities inhabited Olympus, living together in a social state which was but a magnified reflection of the social system on earth. Quarrels, love passages, mutual assistance, and such incidents as characterize human life, were ascribed to them. It must, however, be borne in mind that these human attributes, and the stories connected with them, whether they represent admirable qualities or the reverse, were not in the first instance ascribed to the gods out of a desire to make their resemblance to man more complete, but were the natural result of identifying the gods with the elements of nature over which they were supposed to preside, of conceiving and representing the combi-

nation or conflict of elements visible in nature as the result
of the combination of invisible beings of human form.   In
later times of higher civilization and greater refinement, when
the origin of the gods as personifications of natural phenomena was lost sight of, many of these stories came to be viewed
as disgraceful, and by being made the subject of public ridicule in plays tended largely to uproot the general faith in the
gods.   Philosophers attempted to explain them as allegories.
Others, who did not themselves see their way to believing
them, yet advised that the popular faith in them should not
be disturbed.   But we who live in other times, having no
need of a religion that has long since passed away, and desiring only to trace its origin and the source of its long and
deep influence on a great nation, may look at them in a
calmer mood.   It is our part to admire as far as possible,
and not to condemn without first taking into account every
extenuating circumstance.

Turning now to the rites and ceremonies by which the
Greeks and Romans expressed their belief in and entire dependence on the gods, we would call attention first to the
offering of sacrifices.   These were of two kinds, one consisting of fruits, cakes, and wine; the other of animals, which
were led to the altar decked with garlands and ribbons, after
various ceremonies slain, and part of the flesh consumed upon
the altar fire, the smell of it being supposed to rise agreeably
to the gods.   It was necessary that the animals selected for
this purpose should be spotless and healthy, that the persons
participating in the ceremony should be cleanly in person and
in mind; for no costliness could make the offering of a sinner
acceptable to the gods.   The color, age, and sex of the animal
were determined by the feeling of appropriateness to the
deity for whom it was slain.   The time chosen for the ceremony was the morning in the case of the gods of heaven, the
evening in the case of the gods of the lower world.   To these
latter deities the victim was always offered entire, as it was
not deemed possible that they could share in a feast in com-

pany with men. The fire on the altar was considered holy, and special care was taken that it should be fed with wood that gave a pure flame. In early times it would seem that even human beings were offered as sacrifices to certain gods, the victims in such cases being occasionally, to judge from the instance of Iphigenia, closely connected by ties of blood and affection with the person required to make the sacrifice. But these were, perhaps, mostly cases in which the will of the gods was specially communicated through a seer or prophet; whereas sacrifice generally was a spontaneous gift to the gods, either for the purpose of expressing gratitude for the blessings bestowed by them, or of atoning for some sin of which the person sacrificing was conscious. Sacrifices were not presented intermittently and at mere pleasure, but regularly when occasion offered, as at harvest time, when the fruits of the fields and garden were gathered in. The herdsman sacrificed the firstlings of his flock, the merchant gave part of his gain, and the soldier a share of his booty in war. The gods to whom all prosperity and worldly blessings were due expected such offerings, it was thought, and punished every instance of neglect.

There was, however, another class of sacrifices, springing from a different motive, and with a different object in view; for example, to obtain by means of an examination of the entrails of an animal an augury as to the issue of some enterprise—a form of sacrifice which was held of great importance at the commencement of a battle; or to sanctify the ratification of a treaty, or some important bargain between man and man; or to obtain purification for some crime. In this last case it was supposed that the victim took the sin upon its own head, and that both perished together. Hence no part of such victims was eaten.

How the gods were supposed to partake of the share of sacrifices allotted to them is not always clear, though in the case of burnt offerings they may be imagined to have been satisfied with the smell that rose in the air, and in the case of libations with the aroma of the wine. With regard to the sacrifices in honor of the deities of the lower world, it seems to have been the belief that the blood of the victim, if poured into a hole in the ground, would sink down to them, and be acceptably received. In the same hole, or near by, were buried the ashes that remained on the altar on which the victim was consumed. The portions assigned to marine or river deities were sunk in deep water.

It was the duty of the priests to perform the ceremony of offering up the sacrifices brought to the gods in whose service they were. The first part of the ceremony was to take a basket containing the sacrificial knife, some corn, and perhaps also flowers, and to pass it, along with a vessel containing water, round the altar from left to right. The water was next purified by dipping a brand from the altar in it. Thereupon the people who had brought the sacrifice sprinkled themselves and the altar, and taking a handful of corn from the basket, scattered it on the head of the victim as it approached. The priest then, after shearing a lock of hair from the head of the animal, and distributing it among the bystanders to be thrown on the altar fire, commanded silence, prayed that the offering might be acceptable to the god, and slew the victim. The blood, except in the case of the deities of the lower world, as has been observed, and the entrails, were mixed with wheat, wine, and incense, and placed upon the fire.

The strong feelings of piety, gratitude, dependence, or consciousness of guilt, which gave rise to such offerings, gave rise also to a universal habit of prayer, and a desire to frequent on all possible occasions the temples and altars of the gods. Morning and evening, at the beginning of meals, at the opening of business in the courts of justice and public assemblies, a prayer was offered up, now to one god, now to another, or, if no particular deity appeared to be an appropriate guardian for the time and occasion, to the gods generally. There was this peculiarity in the Greek prayers, which we must not omit to mention, that after calling on a deity by his usual name a clause was added to save the suppliant from any possible displeasure of the deity at the name employed; for how could man know the true name of a god? We have an example of such a prayer in Aeschylus: " Zeus, whoever thou art, and by whatever name it please thee to be named, I call on thee and pray." In praying to the gods above it was the custom of the Greeks to lift the hands and turn the face toward the east; of the Romans, to turn toward the north. A suppliant of the sea gods stretched out his hands toward the sea, and a suppliant of the gods of the lower world beat the earth with his hands. When a prayer was offered up in a temple the rule was to turn toward the sacred image. In cases of great distress the suppliant would carry an olive branch, or a rod with wool twined round it, throw himself on the ground before the sacred image, and embrace its feet. Pythagoras, the philosopher, taught his followers to pray with a loud voice; but loud prayers do not appear to have been customary. On the contrary, it happened not unfrequently that the prayers were written on tablets, sealed, and deposited beside the image of the god, that no human being might be aware of the request contained in them. Here is a specimen of what seems to have been the usual form: " Zeus, our lord, give unto us whatever is good, whether we ask it of thee or not; whatever is evil keep far from us, even if we ask it of thee."

Besides sacrifice and prayer there is still another class of ceremonies, in which we recognize the deep piety of the Greeks : first, the custom of consulting oracles, especially that of Apollo at Delphi, in times of great perplexity; and secondly, the universal practice, in cases of less or more sudden emergency, of trying to interpret the will of the gods by means of augury or divination in a vast variety of ways. Sometimes the augury was taken from the direction in which birds were observed to fly overhead. If to the right of the augur, who stood with his face to the north, good luck would attend the enterprise in question; if to the left, the reverse.

At other times an animal was slain, and its entrails carefully examined, the propitiousness of the gods being supposed to depend on the healthy and normal condition of these parts. But the gods were also believed to communicate their will to men in dreams, by sending thunder and lightning, comets, meteors, eclipses, earthquakes, prodigies in nature, and the thousand unexpected incidents that occur to men. As few persons were able to interpret the bearing of these signs and wonders, there was employment for a large class of people who made this their particular business.

Finally, we must not forget to mention as a proof of the wide-spread religious feelings of the Greeks the national festivals, or games, as they are called, established and maintained in honor of certain gods. While these festivals were being celebrated it was necessary to suspend whatever war might be going on between separate states, and to permit visitors to pass unmolested even through hostile territory. These festivals were four in number: the *Olympian, Pythian, Nemean,* and *Isthmian.*

The first mentioned was held in honor of Zeus, on the plain of Olympia, in Elis. It occurred every fifth year, and the usual method of reckoning time was according to its reoccurrence, by Olympiads, as we say. The games with which it was celebrated consisted of running, wrestling, boxing, a combination of the two latter, horse-racing, either with chariots or only with riders. The prize of victory was simply a wreath of olive, and yet athletes trained themselves laboriously and travelled great distances to compete for it. Kings sent their horses to run in the races, and counted a victory among the highest honors of their lives. The fellow-townsmen of a victorious athlete would raise a statue in his honor. Occasionally writers, as we are told of Herodotus, took this occasion of a vast assemblage of their countrymen to read to them part of their writings. The Pythian games were held in honor of Apollo, in the neighborhood of Delphi, and occurred every fifth year, there being competition in music as well as in athletics. The prize was a wreath of laurel. At the Nemean games, which were held in honor of Zeus, the prize was a wreath of ivy. The Isthmian games were held in honor of Poseidon, on the Isthmus of Corinth, and occurred every third year; the prize was a wreath of pine.

It is remarkable and surprising, that with all the piety and religious ceremonies of the ancients, there existed among them no established means of instruction for the mass of the people, as to the character and functions of the gods whom they worshipped. There was, indeed, a regular priesthood, whose duty it was to conduct the public ceremonies, to offer up sacrifices, and to perform other offices peculiar to the god in whose service they were. But there their duties ceased. These ceremonies had been handed down from time immemorial, and that was perhaps sufficient guarantee of their importance to make the ordinary Greek assiduous in his observance of them. At any rate, this assiduity is not traceable to a clear and explicit knowledge of the character of the gods derived from public instruction. In regard to that, whatever unanimity existed was unquestionably due in the first instance to the influence of poets like Homer and Hesiod, and in the second, to the exertion of the persons connected with the oracle at Delphi. The effect of this state of things was a great amount of confusion in the popular mind, and not only in the popular mind but also in the minds of men like Socrates, who confessed that he did not know whether there was one Aphrodite or two, and wondered why Zeus, who was believed to be one god, had so many names.

The preceding remarks, it should be here observed, apply for the most part only to the mythology of the Greeks, and do not extend to that of the Romans, except so far as they refer to the most primitive class of myths, such as those concerning the origin of the world. For the practice of identifying the mythologies of those two nations has no foundation in fact. Both races, it is true, belonged to one and the same great branch of the human family, and from that source derived a common kernel of religious belief. But before this kernel had developed far the two nations parted, and formed for themselves distinct and isolated settlements in Europe. In the long period of isolation that followed, the common seed of religious belief with which both started grew up, was propagated under quite different circumstances and assumed a very different aspect. The Romans—in the early periods of their history a pastoral, agricultural, simple, and more or less united people—had no need of a various multitude of deities, such as the Greeks found necessary, scattered and separated as they were into a variety of tribes with a variety of occupations.

From this, among other casues, it happens that many, even of the very early Greek myths, were quite foreign to the Romans. To this class belong, for instance, the myths that describe the conflict between Uranus and his sons: Cronus devouring his children to escape, as he thought, being dethroned by them, and Zeus placing his father, Cronus, in durance in Tartarus. No less strictly peculiar to the Greeks were those accounts of quarrels among the gods, wounds, and occasionally the banishment of certain gods to a period of service on earth. To these we may add the carrying off of Persephone by Pluto, and several other stories. With regard to the ceremonies which accompanied the worship of certain gods, we observe the same great difference between the two nations, and would cite as an example the wild unrestrained conduct of those who took part in the festivals of Dionysus, remarking that when in later times of luxury a festival of this kind was introduced into Italy in honor of Bacchus, the Roman equivalent for the Greek Dionysus or Bacchus, the new festival was forbidden, and those who took part in it were viewed as persons of unbridled desires. Nor did Mercury ever obtain the widespread worship and honor paid to Hermes in Greece; and even Saturnus, in spite of the Roman poets, was a very different god from the Greek Cronus.

At the time when the Roman poets began to write, "Greece

captured was leading her captor captive." Greek literature was the usual means of education; Greek philosophy, Greek art—everything pertaining to the Greeks—constituted the principal pursuit of educated men. Many would rather employ the Greek than their own language in writing. Poets, constructing their poems often in close imitation of Greek models, replaced the names of gods that occurred in the Greek originals by names of native deities possessing some similarity of character, and told a Greek story of a native Italian god; or, failing such, employed the Greek name in a Latin form. At the same time no real adaptation or coalescence of the two religious systems ever took place. The Roman ceremonies and forms of worship remained for the most part distinct from the Greek, and peculiar to the race. In modern times, however, the literature (especially the poetry) of the ancient Romans was more familarly known than the facts relating to their ceremonies and forms of worship. It was more early and familiarly known than the literature of Greece, and instead of upon the latter, the modern notions of Greek mythology were founded on the statements of the Roman poets. Hence arose a confusion which our own poets, especially those of the last century, only made worse confounded. To meet this confusion we shall give the accredited Roman equivalent by the side of the Greek gods, throughout our descriptions, and point out as far as possible the differences between them.

Thus far our observations have been confined to the mythology and religious ceremonies of the Greeks and Romans, especially of the former. We have had very little to say of the Romans, because, though equal perhaps to the Greeks in their piety and trust in the gods, they appear to have been very deficient in that quality of imagination which could readily invent some divine personification for every phenomenon of nature that struck the mind. As, however, it is our intention to include a description, even if very brief, of the mythology of the Indian and Teutonic or Germanic races, it

may be well to call attention here to the fact, now clearly
ascertained, that these races are sprung from the same common family or human stock to which the Greeks and Romans
belonged, and that at least certain ideas concerning the origin
and primitive condition of the world are common to the
mythologies of them all. From this it is reasonable to con-
clude that these ideas were arrived at previous to the separation of this great Indo-Germanic family, as it is called, and
its development into distinct and isolated nations, as we find
it at the dawn of historical times. From the Ganges to
Iceland we meet with traces of a common early belief that
the wild features of the earth had been produced by some
long past convulsive conflict of Titanic beings, whom, though
invisible, the stormy elements of nature still obeyed. We
find that everywhere, within these limits of space and time,
there existed among men the same sensitiveness to the phenomena of nature—to light and darkness, to heat and cold,
to rain and drought, to storms and peacefulness—and the
same readiness and power of imagining invisible beings of
human form, but loftier attributes, as the cause of these phenomena. To these beings actions and habits of life were
ascribed, such as were suggested by the phenomena which they
were supposed to control; and in no case, it should be borne
in mind, was any feeling of morality or immorality intended to
be conveyed. For instance, when we find the natural process
by which the clouds pour out their rain upon the earth, and
are again filled from the sea, described as Hermes (the god of
rain) stealing the cattle (clouds) of Apollo, we cannot attach
to the story the idea of criminality which it at first suggests.
Similar interpretations we must be prepared to see throughout
the mythologies of the Indo-Germanic races.

It may now be asked, from what source is this knowledge
derived of the mythology of the ancients? To this we
reply, from the works of ancient writers, poets, historians,
philosophers, and others, to whom the religious belief of their
countrymen was a subject of great importance, and whose

writings have survived to our times; in the second place, from the representations of gods and mythological scenes on the immense number of ancient works of art that still exist, whether in the form of statues in marble and bronze, painted vases, engraved gems, or coins. These are the sources of our knowledge, and without becoming more or less familiar with them it is perhaps impossible to understand fully the spirit of these ancient myths; and contrariwise, to be able to appreciate at its real worth the beauty of ancient works, whether in literature or in art, it is necessary to become acquainted with the mythology and the religious spirit which guided their authors; and if that be not sufficient temptation to follow our descriptions of the various deities and heroes of ancient times, we can still appeal to this—that a great part of our grandest modern poetry and works of art can only be intelligible to those who know the ancient mythology.

Drawing near, as we are now, to the details of our subject, we become anxious to guard against all feelings of impropriety in what we may have occasionally to relate. We would, therefore, remind the reader of the principles of interpretation which we have endeavored to explain in the preceding pages. We would also repeat that we have here to do with a system of religious belief which, whatever its apparent or real shortcomings may have been, exercised enormous influence on the education of at least two of the most civilized nations of the earth.

Olympus.

THE CREATION OF THE WORLD.

In thinking of the origin of the world in which they lived, the Greeks for the most part, it would appear, were satisfied with the explanation given by the poet Hesiod—that in the beginning the world was a great shapeless mass or *chaos*, out of which was fashioned first the spirit of love, Eros (Cupid), and the broad-chested earth, Gaea; then Erebus, darkness, and Nox, night. From a union of the two latter sprang Aether, the clear sky, and Hemera, day. The earth, by virtue of the power by which it was fashioned, produced in turn, Uranus, the firmament which covered her with its vault of brass, as the poets called it, to describe its appearance of eternal duration, the mountains, and Pontus, the unfruitful sea. Thereupon Eros, the oldest and at the same time the youngest of the gods, began to agitate the earth and all things on it, bringing them together, and making pairs of them. First in importance of these pairs were Uranus and Gaea, heaven and earth, who peopled the earth with a host of beings, Titans, Giants, and Cyclopes, of far greater physical frame and energy than the races who succeeded them.

(20)

It is a beautiful idea, that of love making order out of chaos, bringing opposite elements together, and preparing a world to receive mankind.

Another apparently older, and certainly obscure notion, is that expressed by Homer, which ascribes the origin of the world to Oceanus, the ocean. How the earth and heavens sprang from him, or whether they were conceived as co-existing with him from the beginning, we are not told. The numerous ancient stories, however, concerning floods, after

Gaea.

which new generations of men sprang up, and the fact that the innumerable fertilizing rivers and streams of the earth were believed to come from the ocean, as they were seen to return to it, and that all the river gods were accounted the offspring of Oceanus, suggest the prevalence of such a form of belief with regard to the origin of the world in times previous to Hesiod. We are told that the ocean encircled the earth with a great stream, and was a region of wonders of all kinds; that Oceanus lived there, with his wife **Tethys**;

that there were the islands of the blest, the gardens of the gods, the sources of the nectar and ambrosia on which the gods lived. Within this circle of water the earth lay spread out like a disk with mountains rising from it, and the vault of heaven appearing to rest on its outer edge all around. This outer edge was supposed to be slightly raised, so that the water might not rush in and overflow the land. The space

Eros of Praxiteles.

between the surface of the earth and the heavens was seen to be occupied by air and clouds, and above the clouds was supposed to be pure ether, in which the sun, moon, and stars moved. The sun rising in the eastern sky in the morning, traversing the celestial arch during the day, and sinking at evening in the west, was thought to be under the guidance of a god in a chariot drawn by four splendid horses. After sinking into Oceanus, it was supposed that he took ship and

sailed during the night round to the east, so as to be ready
to begin a new day.

In the region of air above the clouds moved the higher
order of gods; and when, for the sake of council or intercourse they met together, the meeting place was the summit
of one of those lofty mountains whose heads were hid in the
clouds, but chief of all, the inaccessible Olympus in Thessaly.
Round the highest point of it was the palace of Zeus, with the
throne on which he sat in majesty to receive such visits as
those of Thetis (Iliad i. 498) when she came to plead for her
son. On plateaus or in ravines lower down were the mansions of the other gods, provided, as was thought, with the
convenience of store-rooms, stabling, and all that was usual
in the houses of princes on earth. The deities who thus
inhabited Olympus, and for that reason were styled the
Olympian deities, were twelve in number. We do not, it is
true, always find this number composed of the same gods,
but the following may be taken as having been the most
usual : Zeus (Jupiter), Hera (Juno), Poseidon (Neptune),
Demeter (Ceres), Apollo, Artemis (Diana), Hephaestus
(Vulcan), Pallas, Athene (Minerva), Ares (Mars), Aphrodite (Venus), Hermes (Mercury), and Hestia (Vesta).
Though allied to each other by various degrees of relationship, and worshipped in many places at altars dedicated to
them as a united body, they did not always act together in
harmony, a most memorable instance of their discord being
that (Iliad viii. 13-27) in which Zeus threatened to hurl the
others into Tartarus, and challenged them to move him from
Olympus by letting themselves down with a golden chain
and pulling with all their might. Should they try it, he
said, he could easily draw them up with earth and sea to the
bargain, fasten the chain to the top of Olympus, and let the
whole hang in mid air. The name of Olympus was not
confined to the Thessalian mountain, though it may have had
the earliest, as in after times it had the principal, claim to
the title, but was applied to no less than fourteen mountains

in various parts of the Greek world, each of which appears to have been regarded as an occasional meeting place, if not a permanent seat of the gods. Finally, the word was used to designate a region above the visible sky, from which, to express its height, it was said that once a brazen anvil fell nine days and nine nights before it reached the earth. At an equal distance beneath the surface of the earth was Tartarus, a vast gloomy space walled in with brass, where the Titans lived in banishment.

The lower order of deities, having naturally no place in Olympus, were restricted to the localities on earth where they exercised their powers—as, for instance, the **Naiades**, or Nymphs of fountains, to the neighborhood of fountains and springs; the **Oreades**, or mountain Nymphs, to the mountains and hills; and the **Dryades**, or Nymphs of trees, to trees. With regard to the place of residence of the heroes or semi-divine beings after their translation from earth, there existed considerable variety of opinion, of which we shall afterward have occasion to speak.

Representations of the deities assembled in Olympus for a particular occasion—as at the birth of Athene from the head of her father Zeus—occur not unfrequently on the Greek painted vases. This was the subject chosen by Phidias for the sculptures in one of the pediments of the Parthenon now in the British Museum. The loss, however, of many of the figures renders it impossible to say now who were the deities he selected, or whether he even adhered to the usual number of twelve. At one end of the pediment the sun rises in his chariot from the sea, at the other the moon rides away. The event must, therefore, have taken place at the break of day. The same fact is to be observed in the scene at the birth of Aphrodite, in presence of the assembled deities, with which Phidias adorned the base of his statue of Zeus at Olympia, and of which we have still the description in Pausanias (v. 403). At one end was the Sun stepping into his chariot, next to him Zeus and Hera, then Hephaestus (?) and Charis, then Hermes and Hestia. In the centre was Eros receiving Aphrodite as she rises from the sea, and Peitho crowning Aphrodite; then Apollo and Artemis, next Athene and Hercules, then Poseidon and Amphitrite, and lastly the Moon (Selene) riding away. The deities are thus grouped in pairs of male and female, those of greater importance being toward either end of the composition.

Council of the Gods.

DEITIES OF THE HIGHEST ORDER.

URANUS

Is a personification of the sky as the ancients saw and understood its phenomena, and with him, according to the version of mythology usually accepted by the Greeks, commences the race of gods. Next succeeded Cronus, and lastly, Zeus (Jupiter). With regard to this triple succession of supreme rulers of the world, we should notice the different and progressive signification of their three names, Uranus signifying the heavens viewed as husband of the earth, and by his warmth and moisture producing life and vegetation everywhere on it; Cronus, his successor, being the god of harvest, who also ripened and matured every form of life; while in the person of Zeus (Jupiter), god of the light of heaven, as his name implies, culminated the organization and perfectly wise and just dispensation of the affairs of the universe. Uranus, as we have already observed, was a son of Gaea (the earth), whom he afterward married, the fruit of that

(25)

union being the Titans, the Hecatoncheires, and the Cyclopes.

The Hecatoncheires, or Centimani, beings each with a hundred hands, were three in number : Cottus, Gyges or Gyes, and Briareus, and represented the frightful crashing of waves and its resemblance to the convulsion of earthquakes. The Cyclopes also were three in number : Brontes with his thunder, Steropes with his lightning, and Arges with his stream of light. They were represented as having only one eye, which was placed at the juncture between nose and brow. It was, however, a large flashing eye, as became beings who were personfications of the storm-cloud, with its flashes of destructive lightning and peals of thunder. From a similarity observed between the phenomena of storms and those of volcanic eruptions, it was usually supposed that the Cyclopes lived in the heart of burning mountains, above all, in Mount Aetna, in Sicily, where they acted as apprentices of Hephaestus (Vulcan), assisting him to make thunderbolts for Zeus, and in other works. Uranus, it was said, alarmed at their promise of fierceness and strength, had cast the Hecatoncheires and Cyclopes at their birth back into the womb of the earth from which they had sprung.

The Titans were, like the Olympian deities, twelve in number, and grouped for the most part in pairs : Oceanus and Tethys, Hyperion and Thia, Crius and Eurybia, Coeus and Phoebe, Cronus and Rhea, Japetus and Themis. Instead of Eurybia we find frequently Mnemosyne. Their names, though not in every case quite intelligible, show that they were personifications of those primary elements and forces of nature to the operations of which, in the first ages, the present configuration of the earth was supposed to be due. While Themis, Mnemosyne, and Japetus may be singled out as personifications of a civilizing force in the nature of things, and as conspicuous for having offspring endowed with the same character, the other Titans appear to represent wild, powerful, and obstructive forces. In keeping with this character we find them rising in rebellion first against their father and afterward against Zeus.

In the former experiment the result was that Uranus, as we learn from the poetic account of the myth, threw them into Tartarus, where he kept them bound. But Gaea, his wife, grieving at the hard fate of her offspring, provided the youngest son, Cronus, with a sickle or curved knife, which she had made of stubborn adamant, and told him how and when to wound his father with it irremediably. The enterprise succeeded, the Titans were set free, married their sisters, and begat a numerous family of divine beings, while others of the same class sprang from the blood of the wound of Uranus as it fell to the ground. Of these were the Giants, monsters with legs formed of serpents; the Melian nymphs, or nymphs of the oaks, from which the shafts used in war were fashioned; and the Erinys, or Furiae, as the Romans called them—Tisiphone, Megaera, and Alecto—creatures whose function it was originally to avenge the shedding of a parent's blood. Their form was that of women, with hair of snakes and girdles of vipers. They were a terror to criminals, whom they pursued with unrelenting fury.

The whole of these divine beings, however, with the exception of the Erinys, who were worshipped at Athens under the name of the "venerable deities," were excluded from the religion of the Greeks, and had a place only in the mythology, while among the Romans they were unknown till later times, and even then were only introduced as poetic fictions, with no hold upon the religious belief of the people.

CRONUS,

"The ripener, the harvest god," was, as we have already remarked, a son of Uranus. That he continued for a long time to be identified with the Roman deity, Saturnus, is a mistake which recent research has set right, and accordingly we shall devote a separate chapter to each. Uranus, deposed from the throne of the gods, was succeeded by Cronus, who married his own sister Rhea, a daughter of Gaea, who bore him Pluto, Poseidon (Neptune), and Zeus (Jupiter), Hestia (Vesta), Demeter (Ceres), and Hera (Juno). To prevent the fulfilment of a prophecy which had been communicated

Cronus and Rhea.

to him by his parents, that, like his father, he too would be dethroned by his youngest son, Cronus swallowed his first five children apparently as each came into the world. But when the sixth child appeared, Rhea, his wife, determined to save it, and succeeded in duping her husband by giving him a stone (perhaps rudely hewn into the figure of an infant) wrapped in swaddling clothes, which he swallowed, believing he had got rid of another danger.

While the husband was being deceived in this fashion, Zeus, the newly born child, was conveyed to the island of Crete, and there concealed in a cave on Mount Ida. The nymphs Adrastea and Ida tended and nursed him, the goat Amalthea supplied him with milk, bees gathered honey for him, and in the mean time, lest his infantile cries should reach the ears of Cronus, Rhea's servants, the Curetes, were appointed to keep up a continual noise and din in the neighborhood by dancing and clashing their swords and shields.

The Curetes Guarding Zeus.

When Zeus had grown to manhood he succeeded by the aid of Gaea, or perhaps of Metis, in persuading Cronus to yield back into the light the sons whom he had swallowed and the stone which had been given him in deceit. The stone was placed at Delphi as a memorial for all time. The liberated gods joined their brethren in a league to drive their father from the throne and set Zeus in his place. This was done; but the change of government, though acquiesced in by the principal deities, was not to be brooked by the Titans, who with the exception of Oceanus proceeded to war. The seat of war was Thessaly, with its wild natural features suggestive of a conflict in which huge rocks had been torn from mountain sides and shattered by the violence with which they had been thrown in combat. The party of Zeus had its position on Mount Olympus, the Titans on Mount Othrys. The struggle lasted many years, all the might which the Olympians could bring to bear being useless until, on the advice of Gaea, Zeus set free the Cyclopes and Hecatoncheires, of whom the former fashioned thunderbolts for him, while the latter advanced on his side with force equal to the shock of an earthquake. The earth trembled down to the lowest Tartarus as Zeus now appeared with his terrible weapon and new allies. Old Chaos thought his hour had come, as from a continuous blaze of thunderbolts the earth took fire and the waters seethed in the sea. The rebels were partly slain or consumed, and partly hurled into deep chasms, with rocks and hills reeling after them, and consigning them to a life beneath the surface of the earth. The cause of Cronus was thus lost forever, and the right of Zeus to rule established for all time.

The island of Crete, where civilization appears to have dawned earlier than elsewhere in Greece, and where the story of the secret up-bringing of Zeus was made the most of, was the principal centre of the worship of Cronus. Here, however, and in Attica, as well as in several other districts of Greece, it was less as the grim god who had devoured his children that he was worshipped than as the maturer and ripener, the god of the harvest, who sends riches and blessings, prosperity and gladness. So it happened that his festivals in Greece, the Cronia, and the corresponding Saturnalia in Italy, were of that class which imposed no restraint on the mirth and pleasure of those present, and seemed like a reminiscence of an age when under the rule of Cronus there had been a perpetual harvest time on earth.

As the devourer of his children Cronus bears some resemblance to the Phoenician Moloch, and it is highly probable that this phase of his character originated in Crete, where the influence of Phoenician settlers had been felt from very remote times. It is also to be noted that his wife Rhea enjoyed a very early and widespread worship in Asia Minor.

The scene where Rhea presents the stone carefully wrapped up to her husband as he sits on his throne, was the subject of a sculpture executed for Plataea by Praxiteles (Pausanias ix. 2, 7), from which it is possible that the relief may have been made which is represented in our illustration, and is now in the Capitoline Museum, Rome. The thoughtful attitude of Cronus, and especially the veiled head, seem to indicate a plotting mind, while the sickle in his left hand is emblematical of his function as god of the harvest, and at the same time a memorial of the deed he wrought upon his father Uranus. The war with the Titans (Titanomachia) was superseded in popular estimation as early as the time of Euripides by the Gigantomachia, or war of Giants, which will be described in connection with Zeus. Artists following the popular taste neglected the former altogether as a source of subjects.

SATURNUS,

According to the popular belief of the Romans, made his first appearance in Italy at a time when Janus was reigning king of the fertile region that stretches along the banks of the Tiber on either side. Presenting himself to Janus, and being kindly received, he proceeded to instruct the subjects of the latter in agriculture, gardening, and many other arts then quite unknown to them: as, for example, how to train and nurse the vine, and how to tend and cultivate fruit-trees. By such means he at length raised the people from a rude and comparatively barbarous condition to one of order and peaceful occupations, in consequence of which he was everywhere held in high esteem, and in course of time was selected by Janus to share with him the government of the kingdom, which thereupon assumed the name of Saturnia, " a land of seed and fruit." The period of Saturn's government was in later times sung of by poets as a happy time when sorrows and cares of life were unknown, when innocence, freedom, and gladness reigned throughout the land, in such a degree as to deserve the title of the golden age. Greek

mythology also has its golden age, said to have occurred during the reign of **Cronus**, and this, perhaps, more than any other circumstance, led to the identification of Saturnus and Cronus, in spite of the real difference between the two deities. The name of Saturn's wife was **Ops.**

Once a year, in the month of December, the Romans held a festival called **Saturnalia** in his honor. It lasted from five to seven days, and was accompanied by amusements of all kinds. During those days the ordinary distinctions were done away with between master and servant or slave. No assemblies were held to discuss public affairs, and no punishments for crime were

Saturnus.

inflicted.   Servants or slaves went about dressed like their masters, and received from them costly presents.   Children received from their parents or relatives presents of pictures, probably of a gaudy type, purchased in the street where the

HERA. OR JUNO.

picture dealers lived. Mommsen has shown that even during
the Empire the Saturnalia proper was a single day, December 19th. It was the great holiday of the Roman year, not
unlike our Christmas, and people greeted each other with the
words " bona Saturnalia." Lucian tells us that the receiver
of a book at that time was in honor bound to read it, no
matter how long or uninteresting it might be.

There was a temple of Saturn in Rome, at the foot of the
Capitoline Hill, containing a figure of him with his feet
wrapped round with pieces of woollen cloth, which could only
be removed during the festival of the Saturnalia. In one
hand he held a curved garden-knife, as a sign of his having
been the first to teach the people how to trim the vine and
olive. In this temple were preserved the state chest and the
standards of the army.

RHEA.

As Uranus, the representative of the fertilizing force in
nature, was superseded by Cronus, the representative of a
ripening force, so Gaea, the primitive goddess of the earth
with its productive plains, gave way to Rhea, a goddess of
the earth with its mountains and forests. Gaea had been
the mother of the powerful Titans. Rhea was the mother
of gods less given to feats of strength, but more highly gifted:
Pluto, Poseidon (Neptune), and Zeus (Jupiter), Hera (Juno),
Demeter (Ceres), and Hestia (Vesta). Her titles—as, for
example, Dindymene and Berecynthia—were derived for
the most part from the names of mountains in Asia Minor,
particularly those of Phrygia and Lydia, her worship having
been intimately associated with the early civilization of these
countries. There her name was Cybele or Cybebe, which
also, from its being employed to designate her sanctuarie
(Cybela) in caves or mountain sides, points to her character a
a mountain goddess.

The lofty hills of Asia Minor, while sheltering on their

cavernous sides wild animals, such as the panther and lion, which it was her delight to tame, also looked down on many flourishing cities which it was her duty to protect.   In this

Rhea.

latter capacity she wore a mural crown, and was styled **Mater tur-rita.**   But though herself identified with peaceful civilization, her worship was always distinguished by wild and fantastic excitement, her priests and devotees rushing through the woods at night with torches burning, maiming and wounding each other, and producing all the din that was possible from the clashing of cymbals, the shrill notes of pipes, and the frantic voice of song. To account for this peculiarity of her worship, which must have been intended to commemorate some great sorrow, the story was told of how she had loved the young Phrygian shepherd, Attis, whose extraordinary beauty had also won the heart of the king's daughter of Pessinus; how he was destined to marry the princess, and how the goddess, suddenly appearing, spread terror and consternation among the marriage guests. Attis escaped to the mountains, maimed himself, and died beside a pine tree, into which his soul transmigrated, while from his blood sprang violets like a wreath round the tree. The goddess implored Zeus to restore her lover.   This could not be.   But so much was granted that his body should never decay, that his hair should always grow, and that his little finger should always move.   The pine was a symbol of winter and sadness, the violet of spring and its hopeful beauty.

The first priests of Rhea-Cybele were the Curetes and Corybantes, for whom it was also claimed that they had been

the first beings of mere human form and capacity that had
appeared on the earth, having sprung from the mountain side
like trees. The great centre of her worship was always at
Pessinus in Phrygia, under the shadow of Mount Dindymon,
on which was a cave containing what was believed to be the
oldest of her sanctuaries. Within this sanctuary was the
tomb of Attis, and an ancient image of the goddess in the
shape of a stone, which was said to have fallen from heaven.
The first temple at Pessinus had been erected, it was said,
by King Midas. Successive rulers of Phrygia maintained
and endowed it so liberally that it continued to be a place
of importance long after Phrygian civilization had sunk.
Spreading from this centre, the worship of Cybele took hold
first in the neighboring towns of Sardis, Magnesia, Smyrna,
Ephesus, Lampsacus, and Cyzicus; thence to Athens, and in
later times to the moun-
tainous district of Arca-
dia, where it was locally
believed that Zeus had
been born and that the
creation of mankind had
taken place. The worship
of Cybele was introduced
into Rome during the
second Punic war, because
the Sibylline fates had an-

Rhea.

nounced that if her image was brought to Rome a foe would
be expelled; this was done in the shape of the small black
stone, mentioned above, which was placed in the Temple of
Victory. The Megalesia began on April 4th and lasted six
days.

In art Rhea appears as the goddess of mountain tops, riding on a
lion, and holding a sceptre in one hand and a cymbal in the other;
beside her the moon and a star. At other times she is seated on a
throne with a lion in her lap, or with a lion at each side, or in a
chariot drawn by lions or panthers.

ZEUS, OR JUPITER.

Third and last on the throne of the highest god sat Zeus,
The fertile imagination of early times had, as we have seen,
placed his abode on Mount Olympus in Thessaly.   But a
later and more practical age usually conceived him as inhabiting a region above the sky, where the source of all light was
supposed to be.   He was god of the broad light of day, as

Zeus, or Jupiter,

his name implies, had control of all the phenomena of the
heavens, and accordingly sudden changes of weather, the
gathering of clouds, and, more than all, the burst of a thun-
der-storm made his presence felt as a supernatural being
interested in the affairs of mankind.   Hence such titles as
" cloud-gatherer," " god of the murky cloud," " thunderer," and " mighty thunderer," were those by which he
was most frequently invoked.   On the other hand, the seren-
ity and boundless extent of the sky, over which he ruled,

combined with the never-failing recurrence of day, led him to be regarded as an everlasting god : "Zeus who was and is and shall be." To indicate this feature of his character he was styled **Cronides** or **Cronion**, a title which, though apparently derived from his father Cronus, must have assumed even at a very early time a special significance; otherwise we should expect to find it applied also to his two brothers, Poseidon (Neptune) and Hades (Pluto).

Jupiter.

The eagle soaring beyond vision seemed to benefit by its approach to Zeus, and came to be looked on as sacred to him. Similarly high mountain peaks derived a sanctity from their nearness to the region of light, and were everywhere in Greece associated with his worship, many of them furnishing titles by which he was locally known — as, for instance, **Aetnaeus**, a title derived from Mount Aetna in Sicily, or **Atabyrius**, from a mountain in Rhodes. Altars to him and even temples were erected on hill tops, to reach which by long toiling, and then to see the earth spread out small beneath, was perhaps the best preparation for approaching him in a proper spirit. In contrast with this, and as testimony to the saying of Hesiod that Zeus Cronides lived not only in the pure air but also at the roots of the earth and in men, we find the low ground of Dodona in Epirus viewed with peculiar solemnity as a spot where direct communion was to be enjoyed with him. A wind was heard to rustle in the branches of a sacred oak when the god had any communication to make, the task of interpreting it devolving on a priesthood called Selli. A. spring rose at the foot of the oak, and sacred pigeons rested among its leaves, the story being that they had first drawn attention to the oracular powers of the tree. It should here be noted that the real importance of this worship of Zeus at Dodona belonged to exceedingly early times, and that in the primitive religion of the Italian, German, and Celtic nations the oak was regarded with similar reverence.

As the highest god, and throughout Greece worshipped as such, he was styled the father of gods and men, the ruler and preserver of the world. He was believed to be possessed of every form of power, endued with wisdom, and in his dominion over the human race partial to justice, and with no limit to his goodness and love. Zeus orders the alternation of day and night, the seasons succeed at his command, the winds obey him ; now he gathers, now scatters the clouds, and bids the gentle rain fall to fertilize the fields and meadows. He watches over the administration of law and justice in the state, lends majesty to kings, and protects them in the exercise of their sovereignty. He observes attentively the general intercourse and dealings of men—everywhere demanding and rewarding uprightness, truth, faithfulness, and kindness; everywhere punishing wrong, falseness, faithlessness, and cruelty. As the eternal father of men, he was believed to be kindly at the call of the poorest and most forsaken. The homeless beggar looked to him as a merciful guardian who punished the heartless, and delighted to reward pity and sympathy. To illustrate his rule on earth we would here give a familiar story:

Philemon and Baucis, an aged couple of the poorer class, were living peacefully and full of piety toward the gods in their cottage in Phrygia, when Zeus, who often visited the earth, disguised, to inquire into the behavior of men, paid a visit, in passing through Phrygia on such a journey, to these poor old people, and was received by them very kindly as a weary traveller, which he pretended to be. Bidding him welcome to the house, they set about preparing for their guest, who was accompanied by Hermes (Mercury), as excellent a meal as they could afford, and for this purpose were about to kill the only goose they had left, when Zeus interfered; for he was touched by their kindliness and genuine piety, and that all the more because he had observed among the other inhabitants of the district nothing but cruelty of disposition and a habit of reproaching and despising the gods. To punish this conduct he determined to visit the country with a destroying flood, but to save Philemon and Baucis, the good aged couple, and to reward them in a striking manner. To this end he revealed himself to them before opening the gates of the great flood, transformed their poor cottage on the hill into a splendid temple, installed the aged pair as his priest and priestess, and granted their prayer that they might both die together. When after many years death overtook them they were changed into two trees, that grew side by side in the neighborhood—an oak and a linden.

While in adventures of this kind the highest god of the Greeks appears on the whole in a character worthy of admiration, it will be seen that many other narratives represent him as laboring under human weaknesses and error. The first wife of Zeus was Metis (Cleverness), a daughter of the friendly Titan Oceanus. But as Fate, a dark and omniscient being, had predicted that Metis would bear Zeus a son who should surpass his father in power, Zeus followed in a manner the example of his father Cronus, by swallowing

Metis before she was delivered of her child, and then from his own head gave birth to the goddess of wisdom, Pallas Athene (Minerva). Next he married, it is said, but only for a time, **Themis** (Justice), and became the father of **Astraea** and the **Horae.** His chief love was, however, always for **Hera** (Juno), with her many charms, who, after withstanding his entreaties for a time, at length gave way, and the divine marriage took place amid great rejoicing, not on the part of the gods of heaven alone, for those other deities also, to whom the management of the world had been in various departments delegated, had been invited, and went gladly to the splendid ceremony.

Hera became the mother of **Hebe, Ares** (Mars), and **Hephaestus** (Vulcan). Zeus did not, however, remain constant and true to the marriage with his sister, but secretly indulged a passion for other goddesses, and often, under the disguise of various forms and shapes, approached even the daughters of men. Hera gave way to indignation when she found out such doings. From secret intercourse of this kind **Demeter** (Ceres) bore him **Persephone** (Proserpina); **Leto** (Latona) became the mother of **Apollo** and **Artemis** (Diana); **Dione**, the mother of **Aphrodite** (Venus); **Mnemosyne**, of the Muses; **Eurynome**, of the **Charites** (Graces); **Semele**, of **Dionysus** (Bacchus); **Maia**, of **Hermes** (Mercury); **Alcmene**, of **Hercules**; several of the demigods, of whom we shall afterward speak, being sons of Zeus by other and different mothers.

These numerous love passages of Zeus (and other gods as well), related by ancient poets, appear to us, as it is known they appeared to the right-thinking men amongst the ancients themselves, unbecoming of the great ruler of the universe. The wonder is how such stories came into existence; unless, indeed, this be accepted as a satisfactory explanation of their origin—that they are simply the different versions of one great myth of the marriage of Zeus, peculiar in early times to the different districts of Greece, each version representing him as having but one wife, and being constant to her. Her name and the stories connected with their married life would be more or less different in each case. In after-time, when the various tribes of the Greeks became united into one people, and the various myths that had sprung up independently

The Marriage of Zeus and Hera.

concerning Zeus came, through the influence of poets and by other means, to be known to the whole nation, we may imagine that the only way that presented itself of uniting them all into one consistent narrative was by degrading all the wives, except Hera, to the position of temporary acquaint-

ances. It is, however, unfortunate that we cannot now trace
every one of his acquaintances of this sort back to a primitive position of sufficiently great local importance. At the
same time, enough is known to justify this principle of interpretation, not only with regard to the apparent improprieties
in the conduct of Zeus, but also of the other deities wherever
they occur. Properly Zeus could have but one wife, such
being the limit of marriage among the Greeks.

Of the several localities in Greece where the worship of
Zeus was conducted with unusual ceremony and devotion, the
two most deserving of attention are Athens and Olympia.
In Athens the change of season acting on the temperament
of the people seemed to produce a change in their feelings
toward the god. For from early spring and throughout the
summer they called him the friendly god (**Zeus Meilichius**),
offered public sacrifices at his altars, and on three occasions
held high festival in his honor. But as the approach of
winter made itself felt, thoughts of his anger returned, he
was called the cruel god (**Zeus Maemactes**), and an endeavor
was made to propitiate him by a festival called **Maemacteria**.
At Olympia, in Elis, a festival, which from an early period
had assumed national importance, was held in his honor in
the month of July (Hecatombaeon) every fifth year—that
is, after the lapse of four clear years. It lasted at least five
and perhaps seven days, commencing with sacrifice at the
great altar of Zeus, in which the deputies from the various
states, with their splendid retinues, took part. This ceremony over, a series of competitions took place in foot-racing,
leaping from a raised platform with weights (*halteres*) in the
hands to give impetus, throwing the disk (a circular plate of
metal or stone weighing about eight pounds), boxing with
leather thongs twisted around the arm and sometimes with
metal rings in the hands, horse-racing, chariot-racing with
two or four horses, and lastly, a competition of musicians and
poets. The lists were open to all free-born Greeks, except
such as had been convicted of crime, or such as had entailed

in former contests the penalty of a fine and had refused to pay it. Intending competitors were required to give sureties that they had gone through a proper course of training, and that they would abide by the decision of the judges. Slaves and foreigners might look on, but the presence of married women was forbidden. The entire management of the festival was in the hands of a board elected from their own number by the people of Elis. The plain of Olympia, where this national meeting in honor of Zeus was held, is now a waste; but some idea may still be gathered from the description of Pausanias of its magnificent temple and vast number of statues that studded the sacred grove. Within the temple was a statue of the god, in gold and ivory, the work of Phidias, the most renowned of ancient sculptors. It was forty feet in height, and for its beauty and grandeur was reckoned one of the Seven Wonders* of the ancient world.

As some would have it, these games had been established by Zeus himself to commemorate his victory over the Titans, and even the gods in early times are said to have taken part in the contests. The people of Elis maintained that the festival had been founded by Pelops, while others ascribed that honor to Hercules. The usual method of reckoning time was by the interval between these festivals, one Olympiad being equal to four years. The first festival from which the reckoning started, as ours does from the birth of Christ, occurred in the year 776 B. C.

The birth and early life of Zeus, up to the period, when, after a long and fierce war around Olympus, he defeated the Titans and established his right to reign in the place of his

---

* The seven wonders of the ancient world were (1) The Pyramids of Egypt; (2) The Walls of Babylon; (3) The Hanging Gardens of Babylon; (4) The Temple of Diana at Ephesus; (5) The Statue of Zeus at Olympia; (6) The Mausoleum at Halicarnassus; (7) The Colossus at Rhodes; all monuments of art of extraordinary beauty or stupendous dimensions. In statues of gold and ivory, such as that of Zeus at Olympia, and many others, the face and nude parts of the body were made of ivory, while the hair and drapery were reproduced in gold, richly worked in parts with enamel. We obtain an idea of the expense of such splendid statues, from the statement that a single lock of the hair of Zeus at Olympia cost about $1250.

father Cronus, has already been related. That his two brothers, to whose assistance he had been greatly indebted during the war, might have a share in the management of the world, lots were cast; and to Poseidon (Neptune) fell the control of the seas and rivers, while Hades (Pluto) obtained the government of the world under the earth. Opposition, however, on the part of the kindred of Cronus had not yet ceased, and the new dynasty of gods had to encounter a fresh outbreak of war even more terrible than had been that of the Titans, the enemy being in this case the Giants, a race of beings sprung from the blood of Uranus. The Giants took up their position on the peninsula of Pallene, which is separated from Mount Olympus by a bay. Their king and leader was Porphyrion, their most powerful combatant Alcyoneus, against whom Zeus and Athene took up arms in vain. Their mother Earth had made the Giants proof against all the weapons of the gods—not, however, against the weapons of mortals; and knowing this Athene brought Hercules on the scene. Sun and moon ceased to shine at the command of Zeus, and the herb was cut down which had furnished the Giants with a charm against wounds. The huge Alcyoneus, who had hurled great rocks at the Olympians, fell by the arrows of Hercules; and Porphyrion, while in the act of seizing Hera, was overpowered. Of the others, Pallas and Enceladus were slain by Athene, the boisterous Polybotes fled, but on reaching the island of Cos was overtaken by a rock hurled at him by Poseidon (Neptune) and buried under it, while Ephialtes had to yield to Apollo, Rhoetus to Dionysus, and Clytius to Hecate or Hephaestus (Vulcan). To the popular mind this war with the Giants had a greater interest than the Titanomachia. Ultimately the two were confounded with each other.

These wars over, there succeeded a period which was called the Silver Age on earth. Men were rich then, as in the Golden Age under the rule of Cronus, and lived in plenty; but still they wanted the innocence and contentment which

were the true sources of human happiness in the former age;
and, accordingly, while living in luxury and delicacy, they
became overbearing in their manners to the highest degree,
were never satisfied, and forgot the gods, to whom, in their
confidence of prosperity and comfort, they denied the reverence they owed. To punish them, and as a warning against
such habits, Zeus swept them away and concealed them under

Interior of the Temple of Zeus in Olympia.

the earth, where they continued to live as demons or spirits,
not so powerful as the spirits of the men of the Golden Age,
but yet respected by those who came after them.

Then followed the **Bronze Age,** a period of constant quar-
relling and deeds of violence. Instead of cultivated lands
and a life of peaceful occupations and orderly habits, there
came a day when everywhere might was right; and men, big
and powerful as they were, became physically worn out, and

sank into the lower world without leaving a trace of their
having existed, and without a claim to a future spiritual life.

Finally came the **Iron Age**, in which enfeebled mankind
had to toil for bread with their hands, and, bent on gain,

Astraea.

did their best to overreach each other.   **Dike** or **Astraea,**
the goddess of justice and good faith, modesty, and truth,
turned her back on such scenes, and retired to Olympus,
while Zeus determined to destroy the human race by a great

flood. The whole of Greece lay under water, and none but Deucalion and his wife Pyrrha were saved. Leaving the summit of Parnassus, where they had escaped the flood, they were commanded by the gods to become the founders of a new race of men —that is, the present race. To this end, it is said, they cast around them, as they advanced, stones, which presently assumed the forms of men, who, when the flood had quite disappeared, commenced to cultivate the land again, and spread themselves in all directions; but being little better than the race that had been destroyed, they, too, often drew down the displeasure of Zeus and suffered at his hands.

Among the Romans Jupiter held a place of honor corresponding in some degree to that held by Zeus among the Greeks. His favorite title was Optimus Maximus. His name being of the same derivation as that of Zeus, indicates his function as god of the broad light of day and armed with the weapon of lightning. Temples and altars were erected for the purpose of his worship, statues were raised, and public festivals held in his honor. As to sacrifice, both he and Zeus delighted most in bulls. To both the eagle, the oak, and the olive were sacred.

The growth of religious feeling precedes the development of artistic faculty in man, and accordingly we find that in the earliest ages the presence of a god was symbolized only by some natural object. In the case of Zeus this was an oak-tree, while in the case of Rhea-Cybele it was, as we have seen, a stone which was believed to have fallen from heaven. The first artistic efforts to reproduce the image of a god were called **xoana**, and consisted of a pillar rudely shaped like a human figure seen at a distance, the artist's attention being mostly directed to the head. Of this kind was the figure of Zeus Labrandeus as represented on the coins of Caria, the figure of Zeus with three eyes at Argos, and the figure of him without ears at Crete. Piety caused those rude and strange images to be retained till long after the art of sculpture had become equal to the production of imposing figures. The gold and ivory statue of Zeus at Olympia, of which mention has already been made, represented him seated on his throne, and some small idea may still be gained of it from what is no doubt a copy of it on the coins of Elis. The bust known as the Zeus of Otricoli is perhaps the best existing example of the face of

Zeus as conceived by the Greek sculptors. The attributes of Zeus are the eagle, a sceptre, a thunderbolt, and, in the case of an ancient image in Caria, an axe. He is represented sometimes with Hera by his side, sometimes with Athene, or with both, or with Athene and Hercules. When he leaves his throne it is generally to rise in might against an enemy such as the Giants, and in these cases he is always armed with the thunderbolt, and either stands in the act of hurling it, or drives in a chariot attended by other gods, as he is frequently to be seen on the ancient painted vases. Another favorite subject on these vases is the birth of Athene from the head of Zeus. In works of art no distinction is made between Zeus and Jupiter, for this reason, that Rome had no distinctive sculpture of its own.

HERA, OR JUNO,

Was a divine personification of what may be called the female power of the heavens—that is, the atmosphere, with its fickle

and yet fertilizing properties; while Zeus represented those properties of the heavens that appeared to be of a male order. To their marriage were traced all the blessings of nature, and when they met, as on Mount Ida, in a golden cloud, sweet fragrant flowers sprang up around them. A tree with golden apples grew up at their marriage feast, and streams of ambrosia flowed past their couch in the happy island of the west. That marriage ceremony took place, it was believed, in spring, and to keep up a recollection of it, an annual festival was held at that season in her honor. Like the sudden and violent storms, however, which in certain seasons break the peaceful-

Hera, or Juno.

ness of the sky of Greece, the meetings of this divine pair often resulted in temporary quarrels and wrangling, the

ZEUS, OR JUPITER.

blame of which was usually traced to Hera; poets, and most of all Homer, in the Iliad, describing her as frequently jealous, angry, and quarrelsome, her character as lofty and proud, cold, and not free from bitterness. Of these scenes of discord we have several instances, as when (Iliad i. 586) Zeus actually beat her, and threw her son Hephaestus (Vulcan) out of Olympus; or (Iliad xv. 18) when, vexed at her plotting against Hercules, he hung her out of Olympus with two great weights (earth and sea) attached to her feet, and her arms bound by golden fetters—an illustration of how all the phenomena of the visible sky were thought to hang dependent on the highest god of heaven; or again (Iliad i. 396) when Hera, with Poseidon (Neptune) and Athene, attempted to chain down Zeus, and would have succeeded had not Thetis brought to his aid the sea giant Aegaeon. As goddess of storms, Hera was consistently described as the mother of Ares (Mars), herself taking part in war occasionally, as against the Trojans, and enjoying the honor of festivals, accompanied by warlike contests, as at Argos, where the prize was a sacred shield.

Her favorite companions, in periods of peace, were the Charites (Graces) and the Horae (Seasons), of which the latter are also found in company of her husband. Her constant attendant was Iris, goddess of the rainbow. The peacock, in its pride and gorgeous array, and the cuckoo as herald of the spring, were sacred to her. In the spring-time occurred her principal festival, at which the ceremony consisted of an imitation of a wedding, a figure of the goddess being decked out in bridal attire, and placed on a couch of willow branches, while wreaths and garlands of flowers were scattered about, because she loved them. Another singular festival was held in her honor every fifth year at Olympia in Elis, the ceremony consisting in the presentation of a splendidly embroidered mantle (*peplus*) to the goddess, and races in which only girls and unmarried women took part, running with their hair streaming down, and wearing short dresses—the judges on the occasion being sixteen married women.

The character, however, in which Hera was most generally viewed was that of queen of heaven, and as the faithful wife of Zeus claiming the highest conceivable respect and honor. Herself the ideal of womanly virtues, she made it a principal duty to protect them among mortals, punishing with severity all trespassers against her moral law—but, naturally, none so much as those who had been objects of her husband's affections—as, for instance, Semele, the mother of Dionysus, or Alcmene, the mother of Hercules. Her worship was restricted for the most part to women, who, according to the various stages of womanhood, regarded her in a different light: some as a bride, styling her Parthenia; others as a wife, with the title of Gamelia, Zygia, or Teleia; and others again in the character of Ilithyia, as helpful at childbirth. Of these phases of her life that of bride was obviously associable with the phenomena of the heavens in spring-time, when the return of dazzling light and warmth spread everywhere affectionate gaiety and the blooming of new life. As queen of heaven and wife of Zeus she will be found, in connection with the legends of Argos and its neighborhood, possessed, from motives of jealousy, of a hatred toward the nocturnal phenomena of the sky, and especially the moon, as personified by the wandering Io, whom she placed under the surveillance of Argus, a being with innumerable eyes, and apparently a personification of the starry system.

The town of Argos, with its ancient legends, which clearly betray some powerful sensitiveness to the phenomena of light, was the oldest and always the chief centre of this worship of Hera. There was her principal temple, and within it a statue of the goddess by Polyclitus, which almost rivalled in grandeur and beauty the Zeus at Olympia, by Phidias. Next came Samos, with its splendid temple erected for her by Polycrates. In Corinth also, in Euboea, Boeotia, Crete, and even in Lacinium, in Italy, she had temples and devotees.

Juno, the Roman equivalent of Hera, was mostly regarded from the maternal point of view, and in accordance with that frequently styled Lucina, the helper at childbirth. Temples were erected and festivals held in her honor—of the festivals that called Matronalia being the chief. It was held on March 1 of each year, and could only be participated in by women, who went with girdles loose, and on the occasion received presents from husbands, lovers, or friends, making presents in turn to their servants. The spirits that guarded over women were called in early times Junones.

The image of Hera is said to have consisted at first of a long pillar, as in Argos, and in Samos of a plank, and to have assumed a human form only in comparatively late times. The statue of her by Poly-clitus, mentioned above, was of gold and ivory and of colossal size. It represented her seated on a throne, holding in one hand a pome-granate, the symbol of marriage, and in the other a sceptre on which sat a cuckoo. On her head was a crown ornamented with figures of the Charites (Graces) and Horae. We can still in some measure recall the appearance of the statue from the marble head known as the Juno Ludovisi, from the coins of Argos, and from several ancient heads in marble of great beauty. Praxiteles made a colossal statue of her in the character of the protectress of marriage rites, and also a group of her seated, with Athene and Hebe standing beside her. On the painted vases the scene in which she most frequently occurs is that where she appears before Paris to be judged of her beauty.

POSEIDON, OR NEPTUNE.

It has already been told how, when all resources had failed which the Titans could bring to bear for the restoration of Cronus to the throne, the government of the world was divided by lot among his three sons, Zeus, Poseidon, Hades. To Zeus fell, besides a general supremacy, the control of the heavens; and we have seen how he and his consort Hera, representing the phenomena of that region, were conceived as divine persons possessed of a character and performing actions such as were suggested by those phenomena. To Poseidon (Neptune) fell the control of the element of water, and he in like manner was conceived as a god, in whose character and actions were reflected the phenomena of that element, whether as the broad navigable sea, or as the cloud which gives fertility to the earth, growth to the grain and vine, or as the fountain which refreshes man, cattle, and horses. A suitable symbol of his power, therefore, was the horse, admirably adapted as it is both for labor and battle, whilst its swift springing movement compares finely with the advance of a foaming wave of the sea. "He yokes to the chariot," sings Homer in the Iliad, "his swift steeds, with feet of brass and manes of gold, and himself clad in gold, drives over the waves. The beasts of the sea sport around him, leaving their lurking places, for they know him to be their lord. The sea rejoices and makes way for him. His horses speed lightly, and never a drop touches the brazen axle."

It may have been to illustrate a tendency of the sea to encroach in many places on the coast, as well as to show the importance attached to a good supply of water, that the myth originated which tells us of the dispute between Poseidon and Athene for the sovereignty of the soil of Attica. To settle the dispute, it was agreed by the gods that whichever of the two should perform the greatest wonder, and at the same time confer the most useful gift on the land, should be entitled to rule over it. With a stroke of his trident Poseidon caused a brackish spring to well up on the Acropolis of Athens, a rock 400 feet high, and previously altogether without water. But Athene in her turn caused the first olive tree to grow from the same bare rock, and since that was deemed the greatest benefit that could be bestowed, obtained for all time sovereignty of the land, which Poseidon thereupon spitefully inundated.

A similar dispute, and ending also unfavorably for him, was that which he had with Hera concerning the district of Argos. But in this case his indignation took the opposite course of causing a perpetual drought. Other incidents of the same nature were his disputes with Helios for the pos-

session of Corinth, with Zeus for Aegina, with Dionysus
for Naxos, and with Apollo for Delphi. The most obvious
illustrations, however, of the encroaching tendency of the
sea are the monsters which Poseidon sent to lay waste coast
lands, such as those which Hesione and Andromeda were
offered to appease.

In the Iliad Poseidon appears only in his capacity of ruler
of the sea, inhabiting a brilliant palace in its depths, traversing its surface in a chariot, or stirring the powerful billows
till the earth shakes as they crash upon the shore. This

Poseidon, or Neptune.

limitation of his functions, though possibly to be accounted
for by the nature of the poem, is remarkable for this reason,
that among the earliest myths associated with his worship
are those in which he is represented in connection with well-
watered plains and valleys. In the neighborhood of Lerna,
in the parched district of Argos, he had struck the earth
with his trident, and caused three springs to well up for love
of Amymone, whom he found in distress, because she could
not obtain the water which her father Danaus had sent her
to fetch. In Thessaly a stroke of his trident had broken

through the high mountains, which formerly shut in the whole country and caused it to be frequently flooded with water. By that stroke he formed the pleasant vale of **Tempe**, through which the water collecting from the hills might flow away. A district well supplied with water was favorable to pasture and the rearing of horses, and in this way the horse came to be doubly his symbol, as god of the water of the sea and on the land.   In Arcadia, with its mountainous land and fine streams and valleys, he was worshipped side by side with **Demeter**, with whom, it was believed, he begat that winged and wonderfully fleet horse **Arion**.   In Boeotia, where he was also worshipped, the mother of Arion was said to have been **Erinys**, to whom he had appeared in the form of a horse. With **Medusa** he became the father of the winged horse **Pegasus**, which was watered at springs by Nymphs, and appeared to poets as the symbol of poetic inspiration.   And again, as an instance of his double capacity as god of the sea and pasture streams, the ram, with the golden fleece for which the Argonauts sailed, was said to have been his offspring by **Theophane**, who had been changed into a lamb.   Chief among his other offspring were, on the one hand, the giant **Antaeus**, who derived from his mother Earth a strength which made him invincible, till Hercules lifting him in the air overpowered him, and the Cyclops, **Polyphemus** ; on the other hand, **Pelias**, who sent out the Argonauts, and **Neleus**, the father of **Nestor**.

To return to the instances of rebellious conduct on the part of Poseidon, it appears that after the conclusion of the war with the Giants a disagreement arose between him and Zeus, the result of which was that Poseidon was suspended for the period of a year from the control of the sea, and was further obliged during the time to serve, along with Apollo, **Laomedon** the King of Troy, and to help to build the walls of that city.   Some say that the building of the walls was voluntary on the part of both gods, and was done to test the character of Laomedon, who afterward refused to give Poseidon the reward agreed upon. Angry at this, the god devastated the land by a flood, and sent a sea monster, to appease which Laomedon was driven to offer his daughter Hesione as a sacrifice. Hercules, however, set the maiden free and slew the monster. Thus defeated, Poseidon relented none of his indignation toward the Trojans, and would have done them much injury in after times, when they were at war with the Greeks, but for the interference of Zeus.

Though worshipped generally throughout Greece, it was in the seaport towns that the most remarkable zeal was displayed to obtain his favor. Temples in his honor, sanctuaries, and public rejoicings were to be met with in Thessaly, Boeotia, Arcadia, at Aegae, and Helice, on the coast of Achaea, at Pylos in Messenia, at Elis, in the island of Samos, at Corinth, Nauplia, Troezen, in the islands of Calauria, Euboea, Scyros, and Tenos, at Mycale, Taenarum, Athens, and on the Isthmus—that belt of land which connects Peloponnesus with the rest of Greece. In the island of Tenos an annual festival was held in his honor, at which he was worshipped in the character of a physician. People crowded to the festival from neighboring islands, and spent the time in banquets, sacrifice, and common counsel. But chief of all the gatherings in his honor was that held on the Isthmus of Corinth in the autumn, twice in each Olympiad—a festival which had been established by Theseus, and in reputation stood next to the Olympian games, like them also serving the purpose of maintaining among the Greeks of distant regions the consciousness of their common origin. The Corinthians had the right of arranging and managing them, the Athenians having also certain privileges. It was in his double capacity of ruler of the sea and as the first to train and employ horses that the honors of this festival were paid to him. His temple, with the other sanctuaries, stood in a pine grove, a wreath from which was the prize awarded to the victors. The prize had originally been a wreath of parsley. In this sacred pine grove was to be seen the Argo, the ship of the

Argonauts, dedicated to Poseidon as a memorial of the earliest enterprise at sea; and there also stood the colossal bronze statue of the god, which the Greeks raised to commemorate the splendid naval victory gained over the Persians at Salamis. Horses and bulls were sacrificed to him, the method of performing the sacrifice being to throw them into the sea. It was the practice of fortunate survivors of shipwreck to hang up some memento of their safety in one of his temples. The Temples of Isis in particular, whom they worship in Greece as Pelagia, were thus adorned in Rome, even in Republican times. Horace, Vergil, and other poets make frequent mention of hanging their wet garments, in which they had been saved when shipwrecked, as a votive offering, usually accompanied by a tablet with perhaps name and date.

The Romans, living mostly as herdsmen and farmers in early times, had little occasion to propitiate the god of the sea, and it was probably, therefore, rather as the father of streams that they erected a temple to Neptunus in the Campus Martius, and held a festival in his honor attended with games, feasting, and enjoyment like that of a fair.

Between Zeus and Poseidon there is, in works of art, such likeness as would be expected between two brothers. But Poseidon is by far the more powerful of the two physically—his build, like that of Hercules, expressing the greatest conceivable strength. But unlike Hercules, his attitudes and especially his head, are those of a god, not of an athlete. His features, one by one, resemble those of Zeus, but his hair, instead of springing from his brow, falls in thick masses over his temples, and is matted from the water. His attributes are a trident and dolphin. Possibly the sacred figures of him in his temples represented him seated on a throne, and clad in the Ionian chiton. But in the colossal statues of him erected on promontories and in harbors, to secure his favor, he was always standing wearing only a slight scarf, which concealed none of his powerful form, holding out a dolphin in his left, and the trident in his right hand, often with one foot raised on the prow of a vessel. In works of art not connected directly with his worship he was figured traversing the sea in a car drawn by Hippocampi, or other fabulous creatures of the sea. In one of the pediments of the Parthenon the dispute between him and Athene was represented.

AMPHITRITE,

The rightful wife of Poseidon (Neptune), was the goddess of the sea, had the care of its creatures, could stir the great waves, and hurl them against rocks and cliffs. She was the daughter of Oceanus and Tethys, or, according to another report, of Nereus and Doris. Usually she was represented with flowing hair and the toes of a crab protruding from her

Amphitrite.

temples; sometimes seated on the back of a triton or other creature of the deep, alone among sea-animals and seaweed, or accompanying Poseidon. She may be compared with the sea-goddess of the Romans, Salacia, Neverita, and Venilia.

HADES, OR PLUTO.

We have seen how Zeus, Hera, and Poseidon came to be conceived as the three great deities who between them controlled the elements of heaven, sky, and sea, and how a character came to be ascribed to each of them such as was most naturally suggested by the phenomena of the provinces of

the world in which they respectively ruled.   But there still
remained a region which could not escape the observation of
people like the Greeks, gifted with so keen a sense of the
various operations of nature.   That region was, however,
itself invisible, being under the surface of the earth.   The
growth of vegetation was seen to be steadily upward, as if
impelled by some divine force below.   The metals which
experience showed to be most precious to mankind could only
be obtained by digging into that dark region under the earth.
Thither returned, after its day on earth was spent, every
form of life.   In conceiving a god who should be supreme
in the management of this region, it was necessary to attribute a double character to him : first, as the source of all the
treasures and wealth of the earth, as expressed in his name
Pluton (Pluto); and secondly, as monarch of the dark realm
inhabited by the invisible shades of the dead, as expressed
in his name of Aides (Hades).

While by virtue of his power of giving fertility to vegetation, of swelling the seed cast into the furrows of the earth,
and of yielding treasures of precious metal, he was justly
viewed as a benevolent deity and a true friend of man, there
was another and very grim side to his character, in which
he appears as the implacable, relentless god, whom no cost of
sacrifice could persuade to permit any one who had once passed
his gates ever to return.   For this reason, to die, to go to
Hades's house, to pass out of sight, to be lost in the darkness of the lower world, was looked forward to as the dismal
inevitable fate awaiting all men.   Yet there must have been
some consolation in the belief that the life thus claimed by
him had been originally his gift, as were the means of comfort and pleasure in life thus cut off.   In later times, when
the benevolent side of his character came more into view,
assuring hopes arose concerning a future happy life that
robbed death of its terrors.   To impart such hopes was the
purpose of the Eleusinian Mysteries.

It seems to have been to make this union of two such

opposite powers in the person of one god more explicit that
the myth concerning his marriage with **Persephone** originated, she being, as we shall afterward see, a personification
of young blooming life.　The grim god of the dead carries
off by force a young
goddess full of life
But no new life is-
sues from the mar-
riage.　Yet she loved
him, it would seem;
for when her mother,
Demeter (Ceres),
implored her to come
back to earth, her
answer was that she
had accepted from
her husband the half
of a pomegranate, or
apple of love as it
was called, and had
eaten it.　It is ap-
parently in reference
to this that both
Hades and Perseph-
one are represented
in works of art hold-
ing each a fruit.

Hades Throned.

Hades, being a
son of **Rhea** and
Cronus, was enti-
tled, after the dethronement of the latter, to a share along with
his two brothers, **Zeus** and **Poseidon**, in the management of
the world.　They cast lots, and to Hades fell the dominion
over the lower world.　The importance assigned to his dominion may be judged from the fact of its monarch being a

brother of Zeus, and styled, too, sometimes, "Zeus of the lower world."

With regard to the region where the realm of Hades was to be looked for we find the ancient authorities at variance, some representing it as in the under-world proper—that is, under the crust of the earth, others in the remote west, in Oceanus, where were the gloomy groves of Persephone. It was entered from the upper world by any spot of sufficiently sombre or wild natural aspect, particularly chasms with dark waters such as inspire terror. The most celebrated place of this kind was Lake **Avernus**, at Cumae in Italy, of which it was said, as of the dead sea, that no bird tried to fly across it but fell lifeless in its waters. Beyond these entrances was an open gate through which all comers had to pass, and having passed could not, as a rule, retrace a step. Exceptions to the rule were made in favor of heroes such as **Hercules** and **Orpheus**, who were permitted to visit the home of the dead, and return alive. The entrance was guarded by the dog of Hades, the dreaded **Cerberus**, a monster with three heads and a serpent's tail, fawning on those who entered, but showing his horrible teeth to those who tried to pass out. But besides by this gateway, the lower was separated from the upper world by rivers with impetuous torrents, of which the most famous was the **Styx**, a stream of such terrible aspect that even the highest gods invoked it as witness of the truth of their oaths. Across this river the departed were conveyed by an aged ferryman appointed by the gods, and called **Charon**, but not until their bodies had been buried in the earth above with all due ceremony of sacrifice and marks of affection. Till this was done the souls of the departed had to wander listlessly about the farther bank of the Styx, a prospect which was greatly dreaded by the ancients. For the ferry Charon exacted a toll (*naulon*), to pay which a piece of money (*danake*) was placed in the mouth of the dead at burial.

The other rivers of the under-world were named **Acheron**

—that is, the river of " eternal woe;" **Pyriphlegethon**, the stream of "fire;" and **Cocytus**, the river of " weeping and wailing." To these is added by a later myth, **Lethe**, the river of " forgetfulness "—so called because its waters were believed to possess the property of causing the departed who drank of them to forget altogether their former circumstances in the upper world. The purport of this myth was to explain and establish the idea that the dead could not take with them into the realm of everlasting peace the consciousness of the pains and sorrows of their lot on earth. In the waters of Lethe they drank a happy oblivion of all past suffering, wants, and troubles—an idea of the means of forgetting sorrow which later poets have made frequent use of.

In the last book of the Odyssey the souls of the slain suitors, conceived as small winged beings, are described as being conducted to the realm of Hades by Hermes (Mercury) in his capacity of **Psychopompos**. The way is dark and gloomy. They pass the streams of Oceanus, the white rock, the gates of Helios, the people of dreams, and at last reach the Asphodel meadow, where the spirits of the dead inhabit subterraneous caves.

With regard to the condition of the dead under the dominion of Hades, the belief was that they led a shadowy sort of apparent life, in which, as mere reflections of their former selves, they continued as in a dream, at any rate without distinct consciousness, to perform the labors and carry on the occupations to which they had been accustomed on earth. It was only to favored individuals like the Theban seer, **Tiresias**, of whom we have more to say afterward, that the privilege of complete consciousness was granted. Such was the sad condition of the dead; and how they bore it may be guessed from the complaint of **Achilles** to **Odysseus**, in the Odyssey: " I would rather toil as a day-laborer on the earth than reign here a prince of dead multitudes." Occasionally the shades of the dead were permitted to appear to their friends on earth. It was also possible to summon them by a sacrifice, the blood of which, when they had drunk of it, restored consciousness and speech, so as to enable them to communicate with the living.

We must, however, clearly distinguish between this under-world as the abiding place of the great mass of the dead, and two other regions where spirits of the departed were to be found—the one **Elysium** (the Elysian Fields), with the islands of the blest, and the other **Tartarus.** The former region was most commonly placed in the remotest West, and the latter as far below the earth as the heavens are above it. In early times it appears to have been believed that **Elysium**

Tantalus.   Sisyphus.   Ixion.

and the happy islands were reserved less for the virtuous and good than for certain favorites of the gods. There, under the sovereignty of Cronus, they lived again a kind of second golden age of perpetual duration. But in later times there spread more and more the belief in a happy immortality reserved for all the good, and particularly for those who had been initiated into the Eleusinian Mysteries. **Tartarus**, on the other hand, was the region where those were condemned to punishment who had committed any crime against the gods while on earth. What was the misery of their condition we shall be able to judge from the following account of a few of the best known of those condemned to such punishment, as **Tantalus, Ixion, Sisyphus, Tityus,** and the **Danaides.**

Tantalus, once a king of Phrygia, had given offence to the gods by his overbearing and treachery, as well as by the cruelty which he had practised on his own son. For this he was doomed to Tartarus, and there to suffer from an unceasing dread of being crushed by a great rock that hung above his head, he the while standing up to the throat in water, yet possessed of a terrible thirst which he could never quench, and a gnawing hunger which he tried in vain to allay with the tempting fruits that hung over his head but withdrew at every approach he made.

Ixion, once a sovereign of Thessaly, had, like Tantalus, outraged the gods, and was, in consequence, sentenced to Tartarus, there to be lashed with serpents to a wheel which a strong wind drove continually round and round.

Sisyphus, once king of Corinth, had by treachery and hostility incurred the anger of the gods in a high degree, and was punished in Tartarus by having to roll a huge stone up a height, which he had no sooner done, by means of his utmost exertion, than it rolled down again.

The Danaides.

Tityus, a giant who once lived in Euboea, had misused his strength to outrage Leto (the mother of **Apollo** and **Artemis**), and was condemned by Zeus to Tartarus, where two enormous vultures gnawed continually his liver, which always grew again.

The **Danaides,** daughters of **Danaus,** king of Argos, were sentenced to Tartarus for the murder of their husbands. The punishment prescribed for them was to carry water, and continue to pour it into a broken cistern or vase, the labor being all in vain, and going on forever.

Hades (Pluto) and Persephone (Proserpina), however, were not only rulers over the souls of the departed, but were also believed to exercise the function of judges of mankind after death. In this task they were assisted by three heroes who while on earth had been conspicuous for wisdom and justice—Minos, Rhadamanthus, and Aeacus, the last being also, apart from this, the gate-keeper of the lower region, according to a later opinion.

Both among the Greeks and Romans the worship of Pluton-Hades was wide-spread, and the honors paid him great. In Greece, his principal temples were at Pylos, Athens, and Olympia in Elis. The cypress, narcissus, and boxwood were sacred to him. In Rome a great festival was held in his honor in the month of February, at which sacrifices (*februationes*) of black bulls and goats were offered, and the officiating priests wore wreaths of cypress, the whole ceremony extending over twelve nights. The Saecular Games, which were held once in a century, were in his honor, and as a tribute to the dead. Their origin was lost in antiquity even in the time of Augustus. It is said, however, that the first celebration took place in the consulship of Valerius Publicola, to avert a plague; the last was celebrated in the reign of Philippus, A. D. 248.

In works of art Hades is represented as having inherited the same type of face as his brothers Zeus and Poseidon, differing only in a certain grimness of expression. His hair shades his brow in heavy masses. In attitude he is either seated on a throne with Persephone by his side, or standing in a chariot and carrying her off. His attributes are a sceptre like that of Zeus, and a helmet, which, like the cloud cap of Siegfried in German mythology, made its wearer invisible. His attendant is the three-headed dog Cerberus. On the painted vases scenes of torment in Tartarus are not unfrequent—such, for example, as the Danaides pouring water into the broken vase, or Ixion bound to the wheel, or Sisyphus pushing up the stone : Hercules car-

A SATYR.

rying off Cerberus, and Orpheus on his memorable visit to bring back Eurydice, are also represented on the vases.

PERSEPHONE, OR PROSERPINA,

Or Persephoneia, also called Cora by the Greeks, and by the Romans Libera, was a daughter of Zeus and Demeter, and the wife of Aides (Hades), the marriage being childless. Struck with the charms of her virgin beauty, Hades had obtained the sanction of his brother Zeus to carry her off by force; and for this purpose, as the myth relates, he suddenly rose up from a dark hole in the earth near to where she was wandering in a flowery meadow not far from Aetna in Sicily, plucking and gathering the narcissus, seized the lovely flower-gatherer, and made off with her to the under-world in a chariot drawn by four swift horses, Hermes (Mercury) leading the way. Persephone resisted, begged, and implored gods and men to help her; but Zeus approving the transaction let it pass. In vain Demeter (Ceres) searched for her daughter, traversing every land, or, as other myths say, pursuing the escaped Hades with her yoke of winged serpents, till she learned what had taken place from the all-seeing and all-hearing god of the sun. Then she entreated with tears the gods to give her daughter back, and this they promised to do provided she had not as yet tasted of anything in the under-world. But by the time that Hermes, who had been sent by Zeus to ascertain this, reached the under-world, she had eaten the half of a pomegranate which Hades had given her as an expression of love. For this reason the return of Persephone to the upper-world for good became impossible. She must remain the wife of Hades. An arrangement was, however, come to, by which she was to be allowed to stay with her mother half the year on earth and among the gods of Olympus, while the other half of the year was to be spent with her husband below.

In this myth of **Persephone-Cora**, daughter of Zeus, the god of the heavens, which by their warmth and rain pro-

duce fertility, and of Demeter (Ceres), the maternal goddess
of the fertile earth, we see that she was conceived as a divine
personification of the process of vegetation — in summer

Persephone, or Proserpina.

appearing beside her mother in the light of the upper world,
but in the autumn disappearing, and in winter passing her
time, like the seed, under the earth with the god of the lower
world.   The decay observed throughout Nature in autumn,

the suspension of vegetation in winter, impressed the ancients, as it impresses us and strikes modern poets, as a moral of

Pluto and Persephone.

the transitoriness of all earthly life; and hence the carrying off of Persephone appeared to be simply a symbol of death.

But the myth at the same time suggests hope, and proclaims the belief that out of death springs a new life, but apparently

The Abduction of Persephone.

not a productive life, and that men carried off by the god of the under-world will not forever remain in the unsubstantial region of the shades. This at least appears to have been the sense in which the myth of Persephone and her mother was presented to those initiated into the Eleusinian Mysteries, which, as we have remarked before, held out assuring hopes of the imperishableness of human existence, and of an eternal real life to follow after death.

As queen of the shades Persephone had control over the various dreaded beings whose occupation, like that of the Sirens, was to beguile men to their death, or like that of the Erinys, to avenge murder and all base crimes. She shared the honors paid to her husband in Greece, lower Italy, and especially in the island of Sicily. Temples of great beauty were erected for her in the Greek Locri, and at Cyzicus on the Propontis. The principal festivals held in her honor in Greece occurred in the autumn or in spring, the visitors at the former appearing dressed in mourning to commemorate her being carried off by Pluto, while at the spring festival all wore holiday garments to commemorate her return.

There remains, however, the important phase of her character in which she returns to the upper-world and is associated with her mother Demeter. But this it will be more convenient to consider in the next chapter. The attributes of Persephone were ears of corn and poppies. Her attribute as the wife of Hades was a pomegranate; her sacrifice consisted of cows and pigs. In works of art she has a more youthful appearance, but otherwise closely resembles her mother Demeter. The Roman Proserpina, though the name is clearly the same as Persephone, appears to have had no hold on the religious belief of the Roman nation, their goddess of the shades being Libitina.

DEMETER, OR CERES,

A daughter of Cronus and Rhea, was the goddess of the earth in its capacity of bringing forth countless fruits, the all-nourishing mother, and above all the divine being who watched over the growth of grains and the various products of vegetation most important to man. The first and grand thought in her worship was the mysterious evolution of life out of the seed which is cast into the ground and suffered to rot—a process of nature which both St. Paul (1 Corinthians xv. 35) and St. John (xii. 24) compare with the attainment of a new life through Christ. The seed left to rot in the ground was in the keeping of her daughter Persephone, the goddess of the lower world, the new life which sprang from it was the gift of Demeter herself; and from this point of view the two goddesses, mother and daughter, were inseparable. They were regarded as "two in one," and styled "the great deities."

From being conceived as the cause of growth in the grain Demeter next came to be looked on as having first introduced the art of agriculture, and as being the source of the wealth and blessings which attended the diligent practice of that art.

When Hades carried off her young loved daughter, Demeter, with a mother's sorrow, lit her torch, and mounting her car drawn by winged snakes, drove through all lands searching for her, leaving, wherever she rested and was hospitably received, traces of her blessing in the form of instruction in the art of agriculture. But nowhere in Greece did her blessing descend so richly as in the district of Attica; for there Celeus, of Eleusis, a spot not far from Athens, had received her with most cordial hospitality. In return for this she taught him the use of the plough, and before departing presented to his son, Triptolemus, whom she had nursed, the seed of the barley along with her snake-drawn car, in order that he might traverse all lands, teaching by the way mankind how to sow and to utilize the grain, a task which Triptolemus performed faithfully, and so extended the art of agriculture to most distant lands.

In Arcadia, Crete, and Samothrace we find her associated with a mythical hero called Jasion, reputed to have been the first sower of grain, to whom she bore a child, whose name cf **Plutus** shows him to be a personification of the wealth derived from the cultivation of grain. In Thessaly there was

Demeter, or Ceres.

a legend of her hostility to a hero sometimes called **Erysich-thon** "the earth upturner," or "the ploughman," and some-times **Aethon**, a personification of famine. Again we find a reference to her function as goddess of agriculture in the story that once, when Poseidon threatened with his superior strength to mishandle her, Demeter took the form of a horse and fled from him; but the god, taking the same shape, pursued and overtook her, the result being that she afterward bore him Arion, a wonderful black horse of incredible speed, and gifted with intelligence and speech like a man. Pain and shame at the birth of such a creature drove her to hide for a long time in a cave, till at last she was purified by a bath in the river Ladon, and again appeared among the other deities. From the necessities of agriculture originated the custom of living in settled communities. It was Demeter who first inspired mankind with an interest in property and the ownership of land, who created the feeling of patriotism and the maintenance of law and order.

The next phase of her character was that which came into prominence at harvest time, when the bare stubble-fields reminded her worshippers of the loss of her daughter Persephone. At that time two kinds of festivals were held in her honor, the one kind called **Haloa** or **Thalysia,** being apparently mere harvest festivals, the other called **Thesmophoria,** which was significant of the introduction of civilization, of which Demeter always stood as an exponent. As conducted in the village of Halimus in Attica, we know that it was held from the 9th to the 13th of October of each year, that it could only be participated in by married women, that at one stage of the proceedings Demeter was hailed as the mother of the beautiful child, and that this joy afterward gave way to expressions of the deepest grief at her loss of her daughter. At night orgies were held at which mysterious ceremonies were mixed with boisterous amusements of all sorts. The Thesmoi or "institutions" from which she derived the title of Thesmophoros appear to have referred to married life.

We have no means of knowing to what extent the ancient Greeks based their belief in a happy existence hereafter on the mysterious evolution of life from the seed rotting in the ground, which the early Christians adopted as an illustration of the grand change to which they looked forward. But that the myth of the carrying off of Persephone, her gloomy

Triptolemus.

existence under the ground, and her cheerful return, originated in the contemplation of this natural process, is clear from the fact that at Eleusis Demeter and Persephone always retained the character of seed goddesses, side by side with their more conspicuous character as deities in whose story were reflected the various scenes through which those mortals would have to pass who were initiated into the Mysteries of Eleusis. These mysteries had been instituted by Demeter herself, and whatever rites they may have consisted in, we know from the testimony of men like Pindar and Aeschylus. who had been initiated, that they were well calculated to awaken most profound feelings of piety and a cheerful hope of better life in future. It is believed that the ceremony of initiation consisted, not in instruction as to what to believe or how to act to be worthy of her favor, but in elaborate and prolonged representations of the various scenes and acts on earth and under it connected with the myth of the carrying off of Persephone. The ceremony took place at night, and it is probable that advantage was taken of the darkness to make the scenes in the lower world more hideous and impressive. Probably these representations were reserved for the Epoptae or persons in the final stage of initiation. Those in the earlier stages were called **Mystae.** Associated with Demeter and Persephone in the worship at Eleusis was Dionysus in his youthful character and under the name of **Jacchus.** But at what time this first took place, whether it was due to some affinity in the orgiastic nature of his worship, or rather to his local connection with Attica as god of the vine, is not known.

Two festivals of this kind, **Eleusinia,** were held annually —the lesser in spring, when the earliest flowers appeared, and the greater in the month of September. The latter occupied nine days, commencing on the night of the 20th with a torch-light procession. Though similar festivals existed in various parts of Greece and even of Italy, those of Eleusis in Attica continued to retain something like national importance, and from the immense concourse of people who came to take part in them, were among the principal attractions of Athens. The duties of high priest were vested in the family of Eumolpidae, whose ancestor Eumolpus, according to one account, had been installed in the office by Demeter herself. The festival was brought to a close by games, among which was that of bull-baiting.

In Italy a festival founded on the Eleusinian Mysteries and

conducted in the Greek manner was held in honor of Bacchus and Ceres, or Liber and Libera as they were called.

It appears, however, to have never commanded the same respect as the original. For we find Romans who had visited Greece, and like Cicero been initiated at Eleusis, returning with a strong desire to see the Eleusinian ceremonies transplanted to Rome. Altogether it is probable that the Roman Ceres was but a weak counterpart of the Greek Demeter.

Demeter, or Ceres.

The attributes of Demeter, like those of Persephone, were ears of corn and poppies; on her head she wore a modius or corn measure as a symbol of the fertility of the earth. Her sacrifice consisted of cows and pigs.

Statues that can positively be assigned to Demeter are very rare, the best by far being that found at Cnidus and now in the British Museum, which represents her seated, draped, and with a veil falling from the back of her head. On her head is neither the modius nor the crown which she also wears sometimes. On the painted vases, however, figures of her are less rare. On a vase in the British Museum she appears beside Triptolemus, who is seated in the winged car which she gave him. On another vase, also in the national col-

lection, we find the scene at the institution of the Eleusinian Mysteries.   In the centre is Triptolemus seated in the car; before him
Persephone (here called Pherephatta, a more ancient form of her
name), and a figure called Eleusis; behind him Demeter and Eumolpus; on the other side of the vase are Zeus, Dionysus, Poseidon, and
Amphitrite.   A marble relief, found at Eleusis, represents, it is believed, Demeter, Persephone, and the youthful Jacchus.

HECATE,

Though, properly speaking, not one of the supreme order of
deities, is entitled to be placed here on account of a resem-

blance to Persephone in
her mysterious functions
both in the upper and
lower world.   She is a
goddess of Titanic ori-
gin, daughter of Tar-
tarus and Night, or of
Perses   and   Asteria
(Starry-Night), the sis-
ter of Leto, according
to other accounts.   The
stories current among
the ancients concerning
her vary greatly, and
often confuse her with
other deities, especially
those of the night, such
as Selene or Luna, the
goddess of the moon,
while standing to Per-
sephone in the relation
of servant or companion.
She belongs to the class

Hecate.

of torchbearing deities, like Artemis, and was conceived as
carrying a burning torch, to suit the belief that she was the

nocturnal goddess of the moon, and a huntress who knew her way also in the realm of spirits. All the secret powers of nature were at her command, it was thought. She had a control over birth, life, and death, and enjoyed great honor among the gods of Olympus as well as in the under-world. To express her power in the three regions of nature, heaven, earth, and the under-world, she was represented as of triple form, and named **Triformis**. Dogs were sacred to her. Her character being originally that of a mysterious deity, it happened that more prominence was always given in the conception of her to her gloomy and appalling features, her chief function being held to be that of goddess of the nether world, of night and darkness, mistress of all the witchcraft and black arts which were believed in as much in antiquity as in the middle ages. Accordingly her festivals were held at night, worship was paid her by torchlight, and sacrifices of black lambs presented with many strange ceremonies. Her presence was mostly felt at lonely cross-roads, whence she derived the name of **Trivia**. Here her statue was placed so that she could look down all three roads at once, and here she was especially worshipped.

A mysterious festival was held in her honor every year on the island of Aegina, in the Saronic Gulf. Beside the lake of Avernus, in lower Italy, was a dark grove sacred to her.

HESTIA, OR VESTA,

Sister of Demeter, and daughter of Cronus and Rhea, was worshipped both by Greeks and Romans as the goddess of the home-fire, or hearth, the name of which was identical with her own. She was properly, therefore, the guardian of family life; her altars were everywhere, the hearth of every house being her sanctuary, and when the family gathered round it daily it was with feelings of regard for that goddess. Every meal prepared on the fire at home revived a grateful sense of the common enjoyments of family life. In every building of public resort she had a sanctuary in the shape of a fire; and when in Greece a body of colonists were about to emigrate to new and distant homes, one of their chief considerations was to take with them some portion of fire sacred to Hestia, in order to carry with them the favor of the goddess; for the Greeks looked upon the state as a great family, with an altar of Hestia as its central point; and thus, by taking with them to their new homes a portion of the fire from that altar, or state hearth, the colony retained its interest and participation in the public affairs of their parent state. No enterprise was commenced without sacrifice and prayer at her altar; and when the fire of one of those holy places chanced to be extinguished, it could only be rekindled by a light from some other sanctuary, not by ordinary and impure fire.

Hestia, or Vesta.

As the goddess of a pure element, Hestia despised love, and, though pressed to consent both by Poseidon and Apollo, obtained from Zeus the privilege she prayed for, of remaining in a single state. Her spotless purity fitted her peculiarly to be the guardian of virgin modesty.

Though zealously worshipped throughout Greece, there was no temple especially devoted to her. Her proper sanctuary was, as we have said, by the fire of every house where people gathered together. She had a share in all the sacrifices offered at the temple of other gods, and at every burnt-offering her presence was recognized as goddess of the sacred hearth and altar flame, as it was also in the libations of water, wine, oil, and in the prayers addressed to her. At the same time she had her own peculiar sacrifices, consisting of young shoots of grain, the first fruits of the harvest, and young cows. Her priestesses had to remain virgins.

In Rome, however, there was a temple to Vesta that had been built by Numa Pompilius. It was of a round shape, and contained in its centre her symbol of an altar, with a fire that was never allowed to go out. This temple, which stood open by day but was closed by night, contained, besides other very old figures of deities, the Palladium, a small wooden image of Minerva

A Vestal.

(Pallas Athene), which, according to the myth, originally fell from heaven upon the citadel of Troy, and was carried thence to Greece, and afterward to Rome. Upon the preservation of this figure depended, the people believed, the safety and existence of the Roman empire. Her priestesses, six in number, were called vestal virgins, their duty being to feed the sacred flame of her temple, and to present sacrifices and prayers for the welfare of the state. To this office they were chosen by the high priest, who was styled Pontifex maximus. They wore robes of white, with a fillet round the hair, and a veil, additional ornaments being permitted in later times. It was necessary that the girls selected for this service should be between six and ten years of age, and that they should take a vow of chastity, and serve in the temple for thirty years. After that period they were permitted to leave it, and even to marry, though neither proceeding was viewed with pleasure by the public, who feared the goddess to whom they had been devoted might take offence in either case. While engaged in the services of the temple the vestal virgins enjoyed great esteem and important privileges. Their person was inviolable, they were free from paternal control, and had the right of disposing of their own property. In their festal processions through the streets of Rome they were preceded by lictors (or officers of justice), who carried with them the *fasces* —that is, a number of twigs tied together into a bundle, out of which an axe projected as a symbol of sovereign power— an honor which, besides them, only the consuls or highest magistrates of Rome were entitled to. And in the course of the procession, should they meet a criminal on his way to expiate his crime by death, they had the prerogative of ordering him to be set free.

With all this respect and esteem, they were very severely dealt with when guilty of neglect of duty, such as permitting the sacred flame of the altar of Vesta to die out, which could only be rekindled by means of a burning-glass held up to the rays of the sun. A priestess guilty of this was condemned by the high priest of the goddess to a dark chamber, and there flogged. For the crime of forfeiting her chastity she was conveyed to a place called the Campus Sceleratus, or "criminals' field," and there placed in a subterranean chamber provided with a bed, a lighted lamp, and some bread and water. The chamber was then closed upon her, the earth thrown over it and made smooth, and the unfortunate priestess left to die a most agonizing death. Her seducer was publicly scourged to death. The whole city was sor-

PALLAS ATHENE, OR MINERVA

rowful, and sacrifice and long and earnest prayers were offered up to appease the injured goddess. The procession, in which the condemned priestess was carried to her crypt, tied down on a litter, and so closely covered up that even her screams could not be heard, was a spectacle that raised a shudder, and caused that day to be remembered as one of the greatest pain and grief throughout the city.

At first there were only two vestal virgins, this number being afterward increased to four, and again by King Servius to six. They were chosen always from the noblest families of Rome. If the legend concerning the foundation of the city of Rome be true, even Romulus and Remus, the founders of that city, were sons of a vestal priestess named Rhea Silvia and Mars.

The sacred fire on the hearth of the goddess, and the laurel that shaded it, were renewed on March 1 of each year; on June 15 her temple was cleaned and repaired. But previous to this, on June 9, a festival was held in her honor, called the Vestalia, only women being admitted to the temple, and these barefooted, and in the character of pilgrims.

ARES, OR MARS,

A son of Zeus (Jupiter) and Hera (Juno), according to the belief of the Greeks, was originally god of the storm and tempest, and more particularly of the hurricane; but this his natural meaning was lost sight of at an earlier period, and more completely than in the case of most of the other gods, the character in which he appears to us being exclusively that of " god of the turmoil and storms in human affairs," in other words, " god of dreadful war," or more correctly, " of the wild confusion and strife of battle." Of all the upper gods he was the most fierce and terrible, taking pleasure in slaughter and massacre.

In this respect he forms a striking contrast to Pallas Athene, the goddess of well-matched chivalrous fights, whom we often find opposed to him in mythical narratives. When fighting she was invulnerable, and always on the side of the victor; while Ares (Mars) being not only god of battle but

Ares, or Mars.

also a personification of war, with its double issue of victory and defeat, was sometimes wounded, and even taken prisoner. When assisting the Trojans in their war with the Greeks, in the course of which he took under his special protection their leader, Hector, he was wounded by the Greek hero Diomedes, aided by the goddess Athene. He fell—so Homer describes the event in the Iliad (v. 853)—with a thundering crash to the ground, like the noise of ten thousand warriors engaged in battle. Again (Iliad xxi. 400) he was wounded by Athene and fell, his armor clanking, and his body covering with his fall seven acres of ground —an obvious reference to the roar and destruction attending a great storm. He was once captured by Otus and Ephialtes, the giant sons of Aloeus the planter, and kept imprisoned in a great bronze vase (Iliad v. 385) for thirteen months—a space of time which, when we remember that the names of the two heroes are derived from husbandry, seems to indicate a full year of peaceful agriculture. Like himself, his offspring were distinguished for their prowess or delight in strife; as, for example, **Meleager**, the prince of Calydon, who speared the Calydonian boar; **Cycnus**, whom Hercules slew, and for this would have been avenged by Ares had not Zeus stopped the conflict of his two powerful sons by a flash of lightning; then **Parthenopaeus**, one of the seven leaders

in the assault on the town of Thebes; Oenomaeus, and
others. The expression, "a son or offshoot of Ares
(Mars)," frequently applied to other heroes, must not
be understood literally, but merely as indicating physical
strength and valor equal to
that of his actual descendants.

Eris, the personification
of fatal strife, was usually
by his side, Dread and
Alarm (Deimos and Phobos)
attended on his steps. On
the other hand, we find him,
even in the Iliad (v. 355
and xxi. 416), where his
general character is that of
a huge fierce combatant, associated with Aphrodite, the
goddess of love. In the
Odyssey (viii. 266) the story
is told of his secret visit to
her, when he was detected
by Helios (the Sun), who
informed Hephaestus (Vul-
can) of the fact, whereupon
the latter devised a cunning
net, and catching the two

Mars and Venus.

together under it exhibited them to the gods of Olympus,
and called upon Zeus to bring them to trial. This relation
of Ares (Mars) to Aphrodite (Venus), who was even worshipped as his proper wife in Thebes, indicates very probably
the peace and rest that follow the turmoil of war.

It is true that Ares was worshipped in Greece, but not as
a great protecting deity, such as he was deemed by the
Romans. In Athens the Areopagus, or "Mars' Hill,"
on which was held a court of justice for the decision of cases

involving life and death, derived its name from him, the story being that he had once appeared before it in a cause against Poseidon. The warlike people of Tegea, the Spartans, who had a very ancient temple in his honor, the Athenians, for whom Alcamenes the sculptor, a contemporary and rival of Phidias, made a statue of him, and the Eleans, all worshipped him with more or less zeal. But the real home and centre of his worship was Thrace, with its wild warlike population and its stormy tempestuous sky. It was in Rome, however, with its conquests and pride of military power, that he enjoyed under the name of Mars the highest honor, ranking next to Jupiter as guardian of the state. The Romans considered themselves to be actual descendants of Mars, on the ground of his having been, as was believed, the father of Romulus and Remus, styling him Marspiter—that is, Mars Pater, their father Mars. At Reate, in Italy, he had even an oracle. In Rome there was a field consecrated to him, and named the " Field of Mars," where military exercises and manœuvres took place, athletic competitions, called "martial games," were held, and public assemblies were summoned to consider important questions of the state. The race-course and the temples of the god were there; and there every five years, called a lustrum, were held the census and muster of citizens liable to be called into the field in the event of war. On this occasion a sacrifice was presented to him, called the " Suovetaurilia," consisting of a pig, a sheep, and an ox, which were led three times around the assembled multitude, while during the ceremony a prayer was offered up that the immortal gods might still enlarge and ennoble the Roman empire more and more, or, as it was expressed in later times, that they might give stability and endurance to the Roman state. Chariot races were held there twice a year, at the beginning of March and in October; the ceremony of sacrificing to Mars the off-horse of the biga that won the race— the October horse as it was called—being performed at the latter. In the " Field of Mars" was dedicated the booty brought back from campaigns, and no Roman general went to war without first proceeding to the temple of Mars, to swing the sacred shield and spear, adding the words, " Watch over me, O Mars !'' This shield (ancile) was believed to have fallen from heaven at the time when Numa Pompilius was king of Rome, and, like the Palladium in the temple of Vesta, was looked on with veneration. The haruspices of Numa's time having declared that the Roman state would last as long as this shield remained in Rome, eleven other shields exactly like it were made, in order that the sacred one might have small chance of being stolen. These and a sacred spear were preserved in the temple of Mars, under the custody of priests, who were called Salii, and whose duty it was every year to celebrate a festival of thanksgiving for this important present from the gods. In the earliest times the sacrifices offered to Mars consisted of human beings, particularly those who had been taken prisoners in battle; but in later times this custom was abandoned, and horses, rams, dogs, and a portion of the booty captured from enemies, offered instead. Besides these animals, the wolf, cock, and woodpecker were sacred to him.

The attributes of Ares were a spear and a burning torch, such as, according to ancient custom, his priests carried when they advanced to give the sign of battle to opposing armies. The animals chosen as his symbols were the dog and the vulture, the constant visitants of battle-fields.

In works of art Ares is represented generally as of a youthful but very powerful build, armed with helmet, shield, and spear. At other times he is bearded and heavily armed. A favorite subject was his meeting with Venus.

HEPHAESTUS, OR VULCAN,

Was the divine personification of the fire that burns within the earth and bursts forth in volcanic eruptions—fire which

has no connection with the sun or the lightning of heaven;
and such being his character, we can readily understand the
mutual dislike which existed between him and the god of
the light of heaven.   He was indeed the son of Zeus and
Hera, the supreme deities of heaven; but he was born to be
a cause of quarrel between them, and alternately at enmity
with both.   Once, when he took his mother's part, Zeus
seized him by the heels and tossed him out of Olympus
(Iliad i. 560).   Through the air he fell for one whole day;
at evening, as the sun went down, reaching the island of
Lemnos, where he was found by some Sintian people, and
taken under friendly care.   The place where he was found,
and where in after times was the principal centre of his
worship, was the neighborhood of the burning mountain
Mosychlus.

Another version of the myth has it that Hera, ashamed
of the decrepit form which he presented at his birth, threw
him with her own hands from Olympus.   Falling into the
sea, he was picked up by Thetis and Eurynome, was cared
for by them, remained for nine years in the abode of the
sea-gods, none but they knowing his whereabouts, and executed there many wonderfully clever examples of handi-
work.   It may be that this belief originated in observing
the nearness of volcanic mountains to the seashore, and the
fact of whole islands, like the modern Santorin, being suddenly thrown up from the sea by volcanic force.   Among
the works which he fashioned in the palace of the sea-gods
was a cunningly devised throne, which he presented to Hera,
as a punishment for casting him out of heaven, knowing that
when she sat down on it she would be locked within its secret
chains so firmly that no power but his could free her.   This
happened, and Ares went to bring him by force to her assistance, but was compelled to retreat in fear of the firebrand
with which Hephaestus assailed him.   At last Dionysus
(Bacchus), the god of wine, succeeded by his soft conciliatory
speech in restoring friendship between mother and son, and

her bonds were forthwith undone. Perhaps it is from this intimacy with Dionysus that he is said to have once appeared as cup-bearer in Olympus, on which occasion the assembled deities could not contain themselves with laughter at the droll figure limping from couch to couch. It seems to be the unsteady flicker of flame that is represented in the lameness of the fire-god, and it may have been the genial influence of the hearth which was the source of the quaint stories about him.

Hephaestus, or Vulcan.

From being originally the god of fire, Hephaestus naturally developed into god of those arts and industries dependent on fire, especially the arts of pottery and working in metal. He was the artist god who worked in a smoky smithy down in the heart of the burning mountains, and produced clever works of dazzling beauty, which he gave freely away to gods and to favorite heroes. For Zeus he made the dreaded aegis and a sceptre; for Achilles and Memnon their armor; for himself two wonderful handmaidens of gold, who, like living beings, would move about and assist him as he walked; and when Homer has to describe any bronze work of great beauty, his highest praise is always that it was the work of Hephaestus. The throne which he made for Hera, and the net in which he caught Aphrodite and Ares, have already been mentioned.

From being god of the warmth within the earth—of volcanic fire—Hephaestus came also, when the fertility of a
volcanic soil became known by experience, to be looked on
as one who aided the spread of vegetation, this function of
his being recognized most in the spread of the vine, which
thrives and bears its best fruit on volcanic soil.   It was from
knowledge of this fact, no doubt, that the idea arose of the
close friendship between him and the wine-god Dionysus,
which we find exemplified partly in the joint worship of
these two deities, and partly in the story already told, of how
Dionysus led Hephaestus back to Olympus, and smoothed
his differences with the other gods.

His worship was traceable back to the earliest times, Lemnos being always the place most sacred to him.   There, at
the foot of the burning mountain Mosychlus, which is now
extinct, stood a very ancient temple of the god—on the very
spot, it was said, where Prometheus stole the heavenly fire,
and for the theft was taken away among the Caucasus mountains, there nailed alive to a rock by Hephaestus, and compelled to suffer every day an eagle sent by Zeus to gnaw his
liver, which daily grew afresh.   A somewhat gloomy ceremony of expiating this theft of fire took place annually in
the island, all fires being put out, and forbidden to be relit
until the return of the ship that had been despatched to the
sacred island of Delos to fetch new fire.   Then, after being
nine days extinguished, all the fires in dwelling-houses and
in workshops were rekindled by the new flame.

Next to Lemnos, perhaps the most important seat of his
worship was Athens, where the unusually large number of
persons employed in the potteries and in metal-working
recognized him as their patron god, and associating him with
Athene, held annually in October a festival called Chalkeia,
in honor of both.   In the same month occurred the festival
Apaturia, at which, by the side of Zeus and Athene a prominent place was assigned to Hephaestus in his capacity of
god of the hearth, and protector of the domestic life which

gathered around it. On this occasion sacrifices were offered at the hearth, and a public procession took place of men clad in festival garments, carrying lighted torches and singing songs in his praise. Again, the torch race, which formed part of the Panathenaic games, was intended to commemorate the theft of fire by Prometheus. In connection with this community of worship existing between Athene and Hephaestus at Athens, it was said that he once endeavored to obtain the love of the goddess, and that even though this failed she had devoted special care to Erichthonius, the offspring of his intercourse with Gaea, the goddess of the earth.

In Sicily Hephaestus had a temple on Mount Aetna, which was watched by dogs possessed of the faculty of distinguishing the pious from the impious and profane, whose approach they fiercely resisted. His worship had also spread to lower Italy and the Campania.

In Rome it was said that Vulcan had a temple as early as the time of Romulus, who, in fact, caused it to be erected, and instituted the festival called Vulcanalia, which was wont to be held on August 23, the ceremony consisting of a sacrifice for the purpose of averting all the mishaps that arise from the use of fire and lights; for the days were then beginning to be noticeably shorter, and the necessity of light to work by in the evenings to be felt.

The wife of Hephaestus, according to the Iliad, was Charis, but the popular belief of later times assigned that place to Aphrodite. By neither had he any children.

In works of art Hephaestus is represented as an aged bearded man, with serious furrowed face, wearing a short *chiton*, and a pointed cap or *pilos*, the mark of workmen or fishermen (which Odysseus also wears), hammering at an anvil, his attitude showing the lameness of which the myth speaks. On the early coins of Lemnos he appears without a beard. One of the favorite subjects both of the poets and artists was the story of his catching Hera in the throne which he gave her, the ludicrousness of it making it an attractive subject for the ancient comedy. On a painted vase in the British Museum is a scene from a comedy in which Hera appears seated on the throne, while Ares and Hephaestus are engaged in combat before her. Another scene which frequently occurs on the painted vases is that in which Hephaestus appears on his way back to Olympus in a state of intoxication, riding on a mule, or walking, and accompanied by Dionysus, Sileni, and nymphs. At the birth of Athene it was he who split open the head of Zeus to let the goddess come forth, and in the frequent representations of this scene on the vases he appears hammer in hand. At other times we find him fashioning the armor of Achilles, or fastening Prometheus to the rock.

APHRODITE, OR VENUS,

Was the goddess of love in that wide sense of the word which in early times embraced also the love of animals, and the love which was thought to be the cause of productiveness throughout nature. Accordingly we find in her character, side by side with what is beautiful and noble, much that is coarse and unworthy. In the best times of Greece the refined and beautiful features of her worship were kept in prominence, both in poetry and art; but these, when times of luxury succeeded, had to give way to impurities of many kinds.

The feelings awakened by observing the productive power of nature had, it would seem, given rise to a divine personification of love in very remote early times among the nations of the East. The Phoenicians called this personification **Astarte**, and carried her worship with them wherever they established factories or markets in Greece, in the islands of the Mediterranean, and on to Italy. The early Greeks coming in contact with these traders, and obtaining from them a knowledge of coinage, weights, measures, and other necessaries of commerce and trade—including, it is said, a system of writing—appear to have transferred some of the functions of the oriental goddess to their own Aphrodite, as, for instance, the function of protecting commerce. The earliest known Greek coins—those of Aegina—the weights of which correspond accurately with the oriental standard, have the figure of a tortoise, the well-known symbol of Aphrodite.

How much else of the character of their goddess the Greeks may have derived from the Phoenicians it would be impossible to say. But the extraordinary zeal with which she continued to be worshipped in Cyprus, Cythera, Corinth, Carthage, Sicily, and wherever in early times the Phoenicians had made settlements, may signify that others of her functions besides that of protecting commerce had been borrowed from the oriental goddess. The older Aphrodite worshipped in Greece previous to the introduction of Phoenician elements in her character is described as a daughter of Zeus (Iliad v. 312) and Dione, and through her mother was associated with the ancient worship at Dodona.

The younger goddess, on the other hand, is described (Hesiod, Theogony, 188–206) as the offspring of Uranus, born among the foam of the sea, first stepping on land in Cyprus, and styled Anadyomene, or "she who came out of the sea." Under the title of Urania she was regarded as a personification of that power of love which was thought to unite heaven, earth, and sea into one harmonious system, and as such was distinguished from Aphrodite Pandemos, the personification of love among men. As the goddess born of the foam of the sea, she naturally came to be held in veneration by the fishermen and sailors on the coast as the goddess of the smiling sea, and the cause of prosperous voyages. Hence it was the custom in the island of Aegina to follow up the sacrifice and banquet in honor of Poseidon with a festival of great rejoicing and excitement in honor of Aphrodite. In Cnidus she was styled and worshipped as goddess of the peaceful sea; a character which is symbolized by the dolphin frequently given her as an attribute. The island of Cythera (Cerigo) derived its name from one of her titles, Cytherea, the belief being that she had appeared there before landing on Cyprus.

The earlier and pure Greek phase of her character, in

which she is called a daughter of Zeus and Dione, was that of a goddess who presides over human love; she is described as accompanied by her son **Eros** (**Amor**, or **Cupid**), the **Charites** (**Graces**), the **Horae**, **Himeros** (God of the desire of love), **Pothos** (God of the anxieties of love), and **Pitho** (Suadela, or the soft speech of love). But her special favorite was the young rosy shepherd **Adonis**; her grief at his death, which was caused by a wild boar, being so great that she would not allow the lifeless body to be taken from her arms until the gods consoled her by decreeing that her lover might continue to live half the year, during the spring and summer, on the earth, while she might spend the other half with him in the lower world, beside **Persephone** (**Proserpina**); a reference to the change of seasons, which finds its explanation in the fact of Aphrodite being also goddess of gardens and flowers. Her presence in nature was felt in spring, her absence in winter. This change of the seasons was further observed and celebrated by a festival in honor of Adonis, in the course of which a figure of him was produced, and the ceremony of burial, with weeping and songs of wailing, gone through; after which a joyful shout was raised, "Adonis lives, and is risen again!" She was called **Adonai** and **Adonias**, with reference to this love passage. Next to him her chief favorite was **Anchises**, to whom she bore **Aeneas**, who through his son **Ascanius**, or **Julius**, became, as the story goes, the founder of the great Julian family in Rome.

With regard to the story of **Pygmalion**, the Adonis of Cyprus, into whose statue of her she breathed life on the occasion of one of her festivals, perhaps the same meaning is intended to be conveyed as in the alternate life and death of Adonis—that is, the alternate fervor and coldness of love, or the alternate bloom and frost of nature.

The husband of Aphrodite was **Hephaestus** (**Vulcan**), whose manner of punishing her when he found her in company of Ares has already been related. Among her children,

Aphrodite, or Venus.

but not by Hephaestus, were **Eros** (Amor), and **Anteros,** **Hymen,** and **Hermaphroditus.**

But if she had favors for some she had strong antipathies for others, and proved this spirit on **Hippolytus,** whom she slew; on **Polyphonte,** whom she changed into an owl; on **Arsinoe,** whom she turned to stone; and **Myrrha,** whom she transformed into a myrtle tree. Of her strife and competition with Hera and Athene for the prize of beauty, which the Trojan prince, Paris, awarded to her, we shall give an account later on in connection with the narrative of the Trojan war.

As a result of her power to unite by means of love all beings, whether in heaven, or earth, or in blackest Tartarus, she came to be viewed as a goddess presiding over married life and marriage ceremonies. She had a number of temples on the island of Cyprus, but none of them so splendidly decorated as that in the town of Paphus, whither thousands of visitors streamed to take part in the annual festival and rejoicings in her honor. There also she had an oracle, and, as **Urania,** was worshipped jointly with **Ares** (Mars); the latter fact showing that her connection with this god was founded in the religious belief of the people. At times, and particularly in her very ancient sanctuary in the island of Cythera, as also in Sparta, Argos, and on the Acropolis of Corinth, she was represented armed.

The worship of **Venus** did not become general in Rome till later times. A festival, called **Veneralia,** was held in her honor every year, a great part of the ceremony consisting of nocturnal dances and passionate enjoyment in gardens among blooming arbors. She had a temple on the Capitol, and one of the Colline gates was consecrated to her. The month of April was held sacred to her, for then the flowers bud and plants shoot; or, as the Greek myth expresses it, Adonis comes back from the under-world.

The symbols of Aphrodite were the dove, ram, hare, dolphin, swan, and tortoise, with the rose as a flower, the myrtle tree, and other beautiful plants, the apple, and fruits of various kinds.

In Paphus the earliest form or image under which she was worshipped was that of a ball or a pyramid, surrounded with burning torches or candelabra, as is to be seen on the coins of Cyprus; but gradually, as art advanced, she took a finer form, fresh charms being continually added, till all the resources of expressing imperious, overpowering beauty were exhausted. In the best days of art she was always represented draped, in later times nude, and in various attitudes. The scene of her birth from the sea was represented by Phidias, on the base of the statue of Zeus at Olympia, as taking place in presence of the gods of Olympus, she being received first by Eros, who elsewhere is called her son. One of the most famous pictures of Apelles represented her as rising out of the sea. To indicate her connection with Ares she was represented as Venus Victrix, standing with one foot on a helmet and with both arms raising a shield. Of this type are the Venus of Capua and the Venus of Milo. In a temple erected to her as Euploia or goddess of prosperous voyages, in Cnidus, was a statue of her by Praxiteles, which was celebrated above all her other statues in ancient times; and of which the so-called Medicean Venus is believed to be a free copy.

PALLAS ATHENE, OR MINERVA,

Called also Tritogeneia or Tritonia and Athenaea, is usually described, in the myths concerning her birth, as having sprung into life, fully armed, from the head of Zeus, with its thick black locks, all heaven and earth shaking meanwhile, the sea tossing in great billows, and the light of day being extinguished. Zeus, it was said, had previously swallowed his wife Metis (Intelligence), to prevent her giving birth to a son. The operation of laying his head open, that Pallas might come forth, was performed by Hephaestus (Vulcan), or, according to other versions of the story, Prometheus. There is, however, another myth, which ascribes her origin to a connection of Poseidon (Neptune) with the nymph Tritonis, adding that Zeus merely adopted her as his daughter. But this seems to have had no foundation in the general belief of the people, and to have been only an invention of later times,

when her name, Tritogeneia or Tritonia, had become unintelligible.

No being connected with the earth, whether deity or mortal, had part in her birth. She was altogether the issue only
of her father, the god of heaven, who, as the myth very
plainly characterizes it, brought her into being out of the
black tempest-cloud, and amidst the roar and crash of a
storm. Her character must, therefore, be regarded as forming in some way a complement to his. The purpose for
which she was brought into existence must have been that
she might do what he would plan, but as the supreme and
impartial god, could not carry out. She is at once fearful
and powerful as a storm, and in turn, gentle and pure as the
warmth of the sky when a storm has sunk to rest and an
air of new life moves over the freshened fields.

To express both these sides of her character—terrible and
mighty as compared with open, gentle, and pure—she had the
double name of **Pallas Athene**: the former was applied to
her function of goddess of storms—she who carried the aegis
or storm-shield of her father. And further, as Pallas, she
became the goddess of battle—valiant, conquering, frightening with the sight of her aegis whole crowds of heroes when
they vexed her, and even driving **Ares** before her with her
lightning-spear. At the same time the soft, gentle, and
heavenly side of her character took from her functions, as
goddess of battle, that desire of confused slaughter and massacre which distinguished Ares, and formed the contrast we
have already mentioned between the two deities of war.
Pallas presides over battles, but only to lead on to victory,
and through victory, to peace and prosperity.

When the war has been fought out, and that peace established which—whether it be amid the political life of nations
here on earth, or whether it be amid the passions of individual men—is always the result of conflict and war, then it is
that the goddess Athene reigns in all gentleness and purity,
teaching mankind to enjoy peace, and instructing them in all

that gives beauty to human life, in wisdom and art. If we observe and keep clearly before our minds these two sides of her character, the inseparable union of both, and their action and reaction upon each other, we shall see that this goddess, Pallas Athene, is one of the most profound conceptions of a deep religious feeling—a being into whose hands the pious Greek could, with due reverence, commit his keeping.

The mutual relation of these two sides of her character is sufficiently obvious in the various myths relating to the goddess. The principal of these we shall proceed to narrate. But, first, we must call attention to this point, that Athene is represented in the myths as forever remaining a virgin, scorning the affections which are said to have been frequently offered to her. Instead of suggesting her liability, in the smallest degree, to earthly passions and foibles, the myth shows admirably that she was a divine personification of mind, always unfettered in its movements; a personification, at the same time, of the origin of mind from the brain of the supreme Divine Being: a proof that mind is neither of a male nor of a female order, but a single and independent power at work throughout the whole of nature.

In the course of the war with the Giants Pallas rendered most valuable assistance to Zeus, both by advice and deed; being, in fact, the cause of his calling in the aid of Hercules, and thus completing successfully the subjugation of the rebels. Single-handed she overpowered the terrible giant Enceladus; but when Zeus' rule was at last firmly established, she took up the task of assisting and protecting those heroes on earth whom she found engaged in destroying the grim creatures and monsters upon it. In this capacity she was the constant friend of Hercules in all his hardships and adventures, and of Perseus, whom she helped to slay the Gorgon Medusa, whose head she afterward wore upon her aegis, and for this reason obtained the name of Gorgophone, or Gorgon slayer. Along with Hera she protected the Argonauts, while to her assistance was due the success with which Theseus overcame and slew monsters of all kinds. She stood by the Greeks in their war against Troy, which we shall describe afterward, and devised the scheme by which, after ten years' duration, it was brought to a close.

But, in times of peace, her power as goddess in all kinds of skill and handicraft, of clearness like that of the sky, and of mental activity, was uniformly exercised, as has been said, for the general good and prosperity. The arts of spinning and weaving were described as of her invention. She taught how to tend and nurse newly-born infants; and even the healing art was traced back to her among other gods. The flute, too, was her invention. As became the goddess of war, it was her duty to instruct men in the art of taming horses, of bridling and yoking them to the war-chariot—a task which we find her performing in the story of Bellerophon, for whom she bridled the winged horse Pegasus; and in the story of Erichthonius, at Athens, the first mortal who learned from her how to harness horses to chariots. In a word, she was the protectress of all persons employed in art and industry, of those whose business it was on earth to instruct and educate mankind, and, therefore, to help forward the general happiness.

The principal scene of her influence and actions was Attica, that district of Greece which, according to the myth related above, she obtained as her special and peculiar province, after a contest for it with Poseidon, the god of the sea. There her worship and honor surpassed that of all other deities, and from her was named the chief town of the land. The visible proof and testimony of her guardianship of Attica was the olive on the Acropolis of Athens, which she created in the contest with Poseidon, and from which the Athenians believed all the olive trees of Attica to have spread. In the produce of the olives consisted the chief wealth of the land. Ancient writers relate a touching story concerning this olive tree on the Acropolis, which reveals how firmly the belief of their goddess was rooted in the minds of her people. When

Pallas Athene, by Phidias.

the Persians advanced with their overwhelming forces against Greece, it is said that Athene presented herself at the throne of her father, and begged for the preservation of her city. But fate had otherwise decreed : Athens must perish, in order that a better and nobler city might rise from its ruins, and accordingly Zeus was obliged to refuse the prayer of his beloved daughter. The Athenians took to their fleet, abandoning altogether the city, which the Persians then entered, and destroyed utterly with fire and sword, not even sparing the sacred olive of the goddess. But, lo ! as a sign that she had not forsaken her city even in ruins, there sprang suddenly from the root which remained a new shoot, which, with wonderful quickness, grew to a length of three yards, and was looked on as an emblem of the regeneration of the city. With the aid of their goddess the Athenians fought foremost of all the Greeks in the famous sea-fight that ensued at Salamis, in which the Persian fleet, though vastly superior in numbers, was wholly destroyed, while the troops on the mainland were compelled to escape with shame and immense losses from Greece.

Among the great variety of her titles, some derived from her functions as a goddess, and others from the localities where her worship had a special hold on the people, we find Athene at Elis styled " mother," in consequence of her care over the nursing children; in Athens and several other places, Polias, the " protectress of cities;" Soteira, the " saviour;" Glaucopis, "blue-eyed goddess;" Parthenos, " the virgin;" Hippia, " tamer of horses;" Ergane, " mistress of industry;" Nike, the "victorious;" and Mechanitis, "ingenious." Every year a festival lasting several days, and called Panathenaea, was held in her honor at Athens, to commemorate the part she had taken in the war against the Giants : every fourth year—that is, every third year of the current Olympiad—it was celebrated with redoubled splendor. This festival is said to have been instituted by Theseus, or at least to have first derived its importance from him; in any case it was a festival of very great antiquity. Festal processions were formed, athletic games were held, while sacrifices and banquets took place on a large scale—all the Athenians, whether at home or abroad in colonies, having the privilege of taking part. The prizes in the games consisted of large painted earthenware vases filled with pure olive oil, the product of the tree sacred to Athene. Of these vases a small number have been preserved down to our times. On one side is painted a figure of the goddess striding forward in the attitude of hurling her spear, with a column on each side of her, to indicate the race-course. On the reverse side is a view of the contest in which a particular vase was won. But perhaps the chief attraction of the festival was the procession in which a new robe or peplos, woven and embroidered for the goddess by a select number of women and girls in Athens, was carried through the town spread like a sail on a mast, placed on a wagon in the form of a ship. In this procession it appears as if the whole population of Attica took part, the youth of the nobility on horseback or in chariots, the soldiery in arms, and the burgesses with their wives and daughters in holiday attire. The new robe was destined for the very ancient statue of Athene which was preserved in the Erechtheum. This custom of placing actual drapery on statues appears to have been handed down from remote times, when the art of sculpture was unequal to the task of imitating the human figure, and it is not improbable that the statue of Athene, of which we are speaking, dated from that early time. The magistrates of Athens offered sacrifices to her at the commencement of spring. The services of her sanctuary were conducted by two virgins elected for the period of one year.

In Rome the worship of Minerva was conducted with as much zeal as that of Athene at Athens, her character as goddess of wisdom and serious thought being admirably calculated to attract a people like the Romans. She was the protectress of their arts and industries, of the domestic operations of spinning and weaving and embroidering, just as she was among the Greeks. In Rome she had several temples, one of the oldest of them being that on the Capitol.

The Palladium.

A festival, which lasted from March 19th to 23d, was annually held in her honor. But the object connected with her, which the Romans venerated above all things else, was the **Palladium**, or ancient figure of the goddess, the story of which was that it had originally fallen from heaven, and had thereupon become the property of the royal family of Troy, the possession of it being from that time always considered an assurance of the safety of that city. But in the course of the war between the Greeks and Trojans it was secretly carried off by **Diomedes** and **Odysseus**, upon which followed the capture of the town by means of the wooden horse. Another version of the story has it that **Aeneas** took it with him when he fled from the city; and in consequence of this inconsistency in the story it happened in later times that more than one city claimed the possession of the real Palladium—as, for example, Argos, Athens, and Rome. Wherever it was believed to be, there the firm conviction existed that the endurance of the city depended on the possession of the image, and so it happened afterward that the expression Palladium was employed in a wider sense to objects thought to be of similar importance; and when, for instance, we hear of the "Palladium of Freedom being carried off," we understand that the principal provision and security of freedom has been lost. The symbols of Athene were the owl, the cock, the snake, and the olive tree.

In works of art Athene generally appears as a virgin of serious aspect, armed with helmet, shield, and spear, wearing long, full drapery, and on her breast the aegis, with a border of snakes, and the face of Medusa in the centre. She is often accompanied by an owl. Of the many statues of her, the two most famous in antiquity as works of art were those by the sculptor Phidias: the one of gold and ivory stood in her great temple at Athens, the Parthenon.

The other was of bronze, colossal in size, and stood on the Acropolis, towering above the temple just named, the crest of her helmet and point of her spear being visible from the sea as far away as Cape Sunium, the most southern point of Attica. Her attitude was that of preparing to hurl the spear, and the title she bore, that of **Promachos**, or "Van of Battle." A representation of the statue is to be seen on the coins of Athens on which a view of the Acropolis is given.

The last record we have of the statue of gold and ivory is in the year 375 A. D., how and when it perished remaining still a mystery. The attitude of the bronze statue exists, it is believed, in several small statuettes, of which there is one in the British Museum, which was found in Athens. On the painted vases we find many representations of her birth, of her contest with the Giants, of her assisting heroes, such as Perseus and Hercules, in their exploits. The subjects of the sculptures, now in the British Museum, which decorated the pediments of the Parthenon, were, in the front, her birth, and at the back, her contest with Poseidon. In the Erechtheum at Athens was an ancient figure of the goddess, believed to have fallen from heaven; while another ancient figure of her, the Palladium properly so-called, was preserved in the city under the care of a priestly family named Byzigi. It also was believed to have fallen from heaven. In its presence was held a court for the trial of cases of bloodshed.

PHOEBUS APOLLO, HELIOS, OR SOL.

From the sun comes our physical light, but that light is at the same time an emblem of all mental illumination, of knowledge, truth, and right, of all moral purity; and in this respect a distinction was made between it as a mental and a physical pheno-

Helios, or Sol.

menon—a distinction which placed **Phoebus Apollo** on one side and **Helios** on the other. Accordingly Phoebus Apollo is the oracular god who throws light on the dark ways of the future, who slays the **Python**, that monster of darkness which made the oracle at Delphi inaccessible. He is the god of music and song, which are only heard where light and security reign and the possession of herds is free from danger. Helios, on the other hand, is the physical phenomenon of light, the orb of the sun, which, summer and winter, rises and sets in the sky. His power of bringing secrets to light has been already seen in the story of Vulcan and Venus.

The myth of Apollo is, like that of Aphrodite, one of the oldest in the Greek system, but, unlike the latter, which is at least partly traceable to oriental influence, is a pure growth of the Greek mind. No doubt certain oriental nations had deities of the sun and of light similar in some points to Apollo, but this only proves the simple fact that they viewed the movements of the sun and the operations of light in a general way similarly to the Greeks. We have seen in the preceding chapters how the sky, earth, sea, and lower world were personified by divine beings of a high order, while in the same way other forces and powers in nature were imagined as beings. In the myth of Apollo we shall find represented the various operations of the eternal light of the sun.

It is the sun's rays, or the arrows of Apollo, that everywhere, as the fields and gardens teach us, quicken life, and foster it toward ripeness; through them a new life springs all around, and in the warmth of their soft, kindly light the jubilant voice of nature is heard and awakens an echo in the human soul. At the same time these arrows destroy the life of plants and animals; even man falls under them in southern climates, such as Greece. Their light penetrates to dark corners, and is capable of reaching to inmost recesses. All these ideas are represented in the myth of Apollo, who is therefore conceived in various ways corresponding to the genial radiance of the sun, with all its friendly influences : (1) as the personification of youth and beauty; (2) as god of earthly blessings; (3) as god of the herds that graze on the fields which are warmed by him—a character in which he appeared herding the cattle of Laomedon, which multiplied largely under his care, and when alone piping on his flute, till the wild beasts were attracted from their dens; (4) as god of medicine, who provided for the growth of healing plants; (5) as god of music, for everywhere were heard happy, joyful sounds, when his kindly beams spread light and warmth over nature ; (6) as god of oracles which reveal the secrets of the future, as the light of heaven dispels all darkness, and detests nocturnal gloom.

The sun appears ever young and powerful in the heavens, and so also must eternal youth, strength, and endurance be ascribed to Apollo. For this reason he came to be a protector of youth when engaged in athletic contests, as well as in war. But summer heat produces plagues, and so it was necessary to view Apollo as the cause of the same, as the god of death, whose unerring arrows carry destruction with them. In this latter phase of his character we find him styled **Carneius**, and worshipped with particular zeal in Sparta, a festival being held annually in his honor in the month of August, the entire population withdrawing from the town and for several days encamping in tents in the neighborhood, like a besieging army—the object being, by living in tents, to avoid the injurious effects of the intense heat of the dog-days. The name of this festival was **Carneia**. As a religious ceremony, the intention of it was to appease the dreaded god, and accordingly it was attended with great reverence in Sparta, and from thence transplanted to Cyrene, a Greek colony on the north coast of Africa, to the islands of Rhodes and Sicily, and to the Greek cities in lower Italy—such as Tarentum and Sybaris. The finest of the temples in honor of this Apollo was at Amyclae.

Another phase of his character, in which his destroying power is combined with his function as god of youth and blooming vegetation, is represented in the myth from which he derived the title of **Hyacinthus**, and enjoyed a form of worship which was for the most part peculiar to the Peloponnesus, the modern Morea, extending over the whole of the south coast of it, to Sicyon, Messenia, Amyclae, and Sparta. It was accompanied by laments sung from place to place, and by poetic competitions, the idea to be conveyed in the whole ceremony being the transitoriness of nature and the return of life again in course of time. In this spirit the festival of the **Hyacinthia** was celebrated annually at

Sparta in July, and lasted nine days, commencing with sadness and expressions of grief, and concluding with joyous excitement.

The myth to which this festival related tells how Apollo accidentally killed, in throwing his disc, the beautiful **Hyacinthus, whom he dearly loved,** the youngest son of **Amyclas**; or, in another version, how **Zephyrus**, the wind-god, who also loved the boy, hurled back the disc at the head of Hyacinthus, out of jealousy toward Apollo. The sorrow at the beginning of the festival of the Hyacinthia was to commemorate his death, while the belief that he had been transformed into the flower which sprang up where his blood fell, and bears his name, gave occasion afterward to happy feelings of confidence in his return. Clearly the object of the myth, like that of Persephone, was to point to the alternating decay and return of life in nature, which in this

Apollo and Hyacinthus.

instance is conceived under the form of a youth, the disc of Apollo being equally clearly a symbol of the sun, which scorches up vegetation.

A similar idea seems to run through the story which relates how Apollo and Artemis, taking offence at Niobe because, with a mother's pride, she had boasted herself higher than Leto as the mother of beautiful children, shot down her children — Apollo the sons, and Artemis the daughters. When one after another had fallen before the angry deities, all but the youngest daughter, Niobe, with the child clinging to her, implored them in anguish to spare the last of her many children, but could not avert the fatal shaft. When it struck, her mother's heart became like a stone, and she refused to murmur or complain. She was transformed, it was said, into a rugged rock, down which tears trickled silently.

While sometimes bringing a pleasant death with his arrows, Apollo at other times, as during the Trojan war, when he took part against the Greeks, appears to exercise his destroying power with irresistible fury. Whole ranks of fighting men fall dead when he shakes his aegis, and the walls raised by the Greeks tumble like structures of sand made by children at play.

As god of the sun in its friendly influence upon the face of nature, we find Apollo styled **Thargelius**, and a festival, called **Thargelia**, being held in his honor at Athens in the month of May, to celebrate the ripening of the fruits of the field under the warmth of the sun, and at the same time to serve as a festival of expiation in memory of the human sacrifices of ancient days. In August occurred another festival at Athens, called **Metageitnia**, at which Apollo, as god of harvest and plenty, was thought of as entertaining the other gods and encouraging neighborly feelings among his worshippers. In October the first-fruits of the field were presented to him as a sacrifice, and in September was held a festival at which he was invoked as a helper in battle. Under the title of **Nomius** he was regarded by herdsmen as their patron god. But the genial influence of the sun is felt on the sea as well as on land, and for this reason he was styled **Delphinius**, and in this capacity worshipped, among other places, at Athens, where his temple, called the **Delphinian**, was in early times a place of refuge and a court for the trial of capital crimes. An annual festival was held in May, called **Delphinia**, to commemorate the tribute of seven boys and seven girls, whom Athens had been compelled in remote times to send every year to Crete to be offered as sacrifices to the Minotaur.

As a god of the sun in its annual course, Apollo was thought to spend the winter away in a northern region among a mythical people called Hyperboreans, to whom it was always light. As the winter approached poets sang farewell to him. At his birth Zeus had given him a mitra (or cap), a lyre, and a car drawn by swans, in which he was to proceed to Delphi, but the swans carried him off to the bright land of the Hyperboreans. When the summer came the priests of Delphi hailed his return in festal songs. The voice of the nightingale welcomed him back. A peculiar festival, the **Daphnephoria**, was held at Thebes every eighth year in honor of Apollo **Ismenius**, the ceremony consisting of a procession in which was carried a branch of olive hung with wreaths and representations of the sun, moon, stars, and planets, and called the **Copo**. From the statement that the number of wreaths was 365, to indicate the days of the year, it may be gathered that the festival as we know it was not of very high antiquity, symbols so obvious as this being usually of late origin. On the other hand, it may be supposed, from the character of Apollo as sun-god, that the ceremony had existed in a simpler form in early times. The number *seven* was sacred to him. Sacred swans made a circle seven times round the island of Delos at his birth, which occurred on the seventh day of the month. From this he took the title of **Hebdomeius**.

One of the oldest forms of his worship appears to have been that in which he was regarded simply as god of light, and styled **Lycius**, the original centre of this worship being Lycia in the southwest of Asia Minor.

Turning now to that phase of his character in which he represents the light of the sun as the symbol of an all-seeing and all-knowing power, we find Apollo regarded as the great god of oracles, with Delphi as the principal centre of his activity. His oracles were there communicated through a priestess, with the title of **Pythia**, who sat aloft on a sacred tripod of gold which stood above the opening of a chasm in the rock. Out of this chasm rose a continuous stream of cold vapor, which drove the priestess into a state of frenzy when she sat above it. Her method of prophesying was by uttering in her frenzy single words or sounds, which persons educated for the purpose caught up and put into verse, generally in such a cunning way as to have, instead of a clear incontrovertible meaning, a double and easily mistaken import.

To give one example : the oracle, when consulted by the Athenians for advice as to how to meet best the approach of the Persian force, returned as its answer, " Trust to your citadel of wood." This the Athenian sages misunderstood, and proceeded to have the Acropolis protected with wooden bulwarks, which naturally could not for a moment resist the enemy. Themistocles, however, and the younger men of the day, declared that the words referred to the fleet, and succeeded in persuading the people to take to the ships, the result of which was the glorious victory of Salamis. Had the interpretation of the sages been accepted generally, the oracle would have had the answer ready, that it meant the fleet. It was only by such tricks that the oracle of Delphi, clever and far-seeing as the priests were, could have maintained its reputation for unerringness and its vast influence.

Of the same nature, but apparently older, were the oracles of Apollo in Asia Minor; as, for instance, those of Colophon and Didymi near Miletus, the latter of which was in the hands of the priestly family of Branchidae. Sometimes the god exercised the power of communicating the prophetic gift to mortals, as he did to **Cassandra**, and to **Deiphobe**, a daughter of Glaucus. The latter lived in a grotto beside the town of Cumae, in the Campania of Italy, and was known by the name of the **Cumaean Sibyl**. It was from her that Tarquin the Proud, the last king of Rome, acquired the three Sibylline books which contained important prophecies concerning the fate of Rome, and were held in great reverence by the Romans. They were preserved carefully in the

Capitol down to the time of Sulla, when they perished in a fire. In Greece also was a famous seer or prophet, and favorite of Apollo Epimenides, of whom the myth reports that when a herdsman he fell asleep in a grotto, slept for fifty-six years, and on awakening found himself endowed with the prophetic gift in a high degree.

Connected with his gift of prophecy was his power of music. For not only were the oracles expressed in verse, but the strains of music, when spontaneous, were thought to originate in an inspired foresight into the future. As god of music he was leader of the Muses, Musagetes; and himself played on a wonderful lyre which Hermes had made for him.

At Delphi he was styled Apollo Pythius, and enjoyed several annual festivals, such as the Theophania, to celebrate his return from the Hyperboreans, and the Theoxenia, at which, it being harvest time, he was supposed to receive the other gods at his hospitable table. The principal festival, however, was that at which the Pythian Games were held. The games had been instituted to commemorate the victory of Apollo over the dragon Python, which resisted his entrance upon his duties as oracular god at Delphi. They were held at first every seventh, afterward every ninth, and latterly every fifth year.

As being himself possessed of eternal youth, and of the finest conceivable athletic form, Apollo came to be regarded as a patron of the athletic contests of youth, and in this capacity ranked with Hercules and Hermes (Mercury). He was the god also to whom persons polluted either with disease or crime turned for purification, and on this account his high power was brought home frequently and seriously to a great part of the people. He was, therefore, properly viewed as the father of Aesculapius, the god of medicine.

The story of the birth of Apollo is that he, with his twin sister Artemis, was a son of Zeus and Leto (or Latona); that Leto, after wandering long hither and thither pursued by the jealous **Hera**, at last found shelter in the island of Delos, in the Aegean Sea, and there was delivered.   It was said that hitherto that island had been only a waste rock driven about in the sea, but that it became fixed in its present

position on the occasion of the birth of Apollo and Artemis, an event which was celebrated by a blaze of golden light shed over the island, while sacred swans flew around encircling it seven times.   This was in May, and for that reason his festival at Delos, the Delia, was held in that month.   But Leto

Leto, or Latona.

was compelled, through the pursuit of Hera, to abandon her children.   They were entrusted to **Themis**, a name which signifies " justice," and indicates here the indisputable sense of right present with Apollo from his birth.   By her he was fed on ambrosia and nectar, upon which he grew so strong, and that, too, so quickly, that within only a few hours after his birth he was a youth of dazzling appearance, and escaped his divine nurse, proclaiming that his destiny was to be a bowman, a player on the lyre, and to give truthful oracles to mankind.

To accomplish the end of his ambition he set out at once on a pilgrimage to search for a suitable place for an oracle, neither too public nor too retired.   After searching through many districts of Greece he arrived at the quiet rocky valley of **Delphi**, or Pytho, which he recognized as the desired spot, on account of its peaceful position in the heart of Greece.

NIOBE.

Moreover, there had
been an oracle of
Themis there from a
remote early time, and
she was willing to
haud over her duties
to the young god. A
terrible dragon, how-
ever, called Python,
stood in the way, re-
fused entrance, and
tried to repel him; but
in vain, for the young
god, confident in the
unerring aim of his
arrows, attacked the
monster, and slew it
after a short combat.
In this way he ac-
quired his world-
famed oracle, and from
his victory over the
dragon obtained the
title of Pythius.

From that time for-
ward, with one ex-
ception, Apollo re-
mained in undisputed
possession of the sacred
tripod and oracle at
Delphi, and that was
when he had to take up
their defence against
Hercules, who, be-
cause the acting priest-
ess did not prophesy as
he wished, offered her

Marsyas

violence and carried off the tripod. Apollo hastened to the aid of his priestess, and Zeus had to settle the quarrel between his two sons, who thereafter lived in the closest friendship.

Amongst the other incidents of his life, it is related that Apollo once incurred the severe displeasure of Zeus, and was driven for a time out of Olympus, through having shot at some of the Cyclopes in revenge for Zeus having struck Aesculapius, a son of Apollo, with a thunderbolt. During his exile on earth, he acted as a herdsman to his friend **Admetus**, the king of Pherae, in Thessaly, and again in the same capacity to Laomedon, prince of Troy. In vexation at his banishment he joined with Poseidon in an attempt to dethrone Zeus. But the scheme failed, and both deities were in consequence sentenced to assist in building the walls of Troy. **Laomedon** refused to give them the payment agreed on for the service, and Apollo revenged himself by sending a dreadful pestilence which depopulated the town and neighborhood of Troy. During the time of his servitude he had also a quarrel with **Pan**, who insisted that the flute was a better instrument than the lyre. The decision, which was left to **Midas**, a king of Lydia, was given in favor of Pan, for which Apollo punished Midas by causing his ears to grow long like those of an ass. **Marsyas**, too, had boasted that he could surpass Apollo in the art of playing on the flute, and for this had to suffer the cruel punishment of being flayed alive.

In Rome the worship of Apollo was not established till 320 B. C., a temple being raised to him in that year in consequence of a pestilence that had visited the city. Afterward a second temple to him was erected on the Palatine hill. The **Apollinarian Games** were instituted during the second Punic war.

No distinction was made by the Greek poets of later times between Apollo and the sun-god, **Helios.** As little did the Romans distinguish between Apollo and Sol. In both cases

the confusion arose from the fact that the fundamental idea
of both deities was that of sun-gods. The title of Phoebus
plainly designated Apollo as god of pure streaming light,
particularly of the light of heaven, and this phase of his
character was made more conspicuous by the fact of his

Apollo, Pan, and Midas.

mother's name being Leto, " darkness," strictly " goddess
of the dark night." But this, his original signification,
came in time to be lost sight of in the variety of other functions which he assumed. Helios, or Hyperion, on the contrary, remained, properly speaking, only the orb of the sun
which is visible in the heavens by day, and disappears by
night in a regular course. That was the only signification
he had. The number *seven* was sacred to him, as it was to
Apollo, and in the island of Trinacia, supposed to be Sicily,
it was said, he had seven herds of cows and seven herds of
lambs, fifty in each herd, which never increased or dimin-

ished in numbers.   It was one of his pleasures to see them grazing when he rose in the morning and when he descended in the evening.

Of the sons of Helios the most famous is Phaethon, of whom it is said that he once had a dispute about his origin with Epaphus, a son of Zeus and Io, and in consequence begged Helios, if he really was his father, to prove himself such by granting one request; upon which Helios called the river Styx to witness that he would not refuse to grant it.

Phaethon.

The request was, that he, Phaethon, should be permitted for one day to drive the chariot of the sun.   Helios, astonished at the boldness of the request, and alarmed at the danger that threatened his son in such an undertaking, endeavored to move him from his determination.   But Phaethon only clung to the bargain all the more firmly, and Helios, finding himself bound by his oath, instructed his son how to drive and manage the horses, and handed over to him the task for one day.   The youth, however, through being unused to the work, and unacquainted with the right way, soon became confused, and lost his strength and his senses. The spirited horses, named Pyroses, Eous, Aethon, and Phlegon, wheeled out of the right course, and brought the chariot of the sun so near to the earth that in some places the latter took fire, fountains were dried up, rivers began to boil, and part of the human race became black in color. Zeus, alarmed at the unexpected danger in which both heaven and earth were thus placed, slew Phaethon with a stroke of lightning, and cast him from the chariot of the sun down into the river Eridanus. The three sisters of Phaethon, **Heliades,** as they were called—that is, daughters of Helios, **Phaethusa, Aegle,** and **Lampetia,** wept for him for a long time, and finally became transformed into larch trees, that overhang the river's bank, the tears that continually flowed from

Helios, or Sol.

them being changed by the sun into amber (*elektron*). Phaethon's friend **Cycnus** mourned his loss deeply, and was transformed into a swan, while Helios was so grieved at his son's death that only the entreaties of the gods could prevail on him to resume the reins of the chariot of the sun.

The symbols of Helios were horses' heads, a crown of seven rays, a cornucopia, and a ripened fruit. The symbols of Apollo were the wolf, swan, raven, stag, dolphin, laurel, and lyre.

In works of art Apollo is usually represented as having the figure of a youthful athlete—perhaps the finest existing statue of him being the Apollo Belvedere of the Vatican. His hair is long, and usually tied, like that of his sister Artemis, in a large knot above the forehead. In the character of Musagetes he wears long ample drapery girt at the waist, a diadem round his head, and long tresses falling

on his shoulders. Though the general representation of him is that
in which he is engaged in playing on the lyre, or resting from doing
so, we find him also with bow and arrows, as Sauroctonos, killing a
lizard, holding forth his aegis to destroy his enemies, and present at
the flaying of Marsyas.

ARTEMIS, OR DIANA; AND SELENE, OR LUNA.

Originally **Artemis** was the divine personification of the
moon, just as her brother **Apollo** was originally god of the
sun.   But by degrees, as the moon came to be viewed like
the sun, on the one hand as a mere illuminating orb, and on
the other as possessing a real or apparent and generally believed influence upon vegetation, and on human as well as
animal life, there grew up a distinction between moon-
goddesses of two kinds, corresponding to the sun gods of
two kinds.   The one was **Selene**, or **Luna**, whose signification was merely that of goddess of the orb of night, as
Helios, the sun, was of the orb of day.   The other was
Artemis, or **Diana**, who embraced in her character all the
other functions exercised by the moon on earthly life; and
accordingly, like Apollo, became the subject of a largely
developed religious belief; while the myth of Selene, on the
contrary, like that of Helios, was but little and sparingly
improved upon.

Great as was the variety of the real and fancied influences
of the moon upon natural life, proportionately great was the
variety in the myth of Artemis—a locality of worship sometimes, at other times a particular point of view of her character determining the phase of it.   And further, it should be
observed that many peculiar features in the myths of **Artemis** are traceable to the fact of her being twin-sister of
Apollo, whose inner and spiritual qualities she was believed
to share.

It was observed that the vegetation of warm southern
lands spread and flourished most under the quickening influence of the coolness of night and the fall of dew, which

often for whole months was a substitute for the missing rains. It was known by experience that the fall of dew is most copious when the sky is clear and the moon sheds her pure light— and hence to Artemis was ascribed the cause of fer

Artemis, or Diana.

tility in this direction. Hence she was believed to roam by night through woods and groves, over hills and valleys, accompanied by the nymphs of the fountains; beside rivers, fountains, and marshes her presence was felt. But the presence of the moon in the heavens gave security to travellers and to herds, especially from the attacks of wild animals, whose enemy Artemis was, therefore, thought to be. Under the title of **Agrotera** she was the patron goddess of huntsmen, her favorite hunting-ground being Arcadia, with its many heights and glens well-wooded and well-watered. Here she was worshipped under the form of a bear, and called **Calliste**, the Arcadians, or bear-people, boasting their descent from her. On the other hand, the regularly recurring absence of the moon from the heavens, which could only have been regarded as due to a voluntary act on the part of the goddess, showed that though opposed to wild animals, she could also employ them for the purpose of punishing men, and to illustrate this, the story was told of her having sent among the Aetolians the so-called Calydonian boar, which laid waste their fields, till after a great hunt it was slain by **Meleager** and **Atalanta**. As a huntress her favorite animal was the stag, because its swiftness gave the best opportunity for her method of capture, which was by bow and speed of foot. As an instance of how severely she would punish the wanton slaying of the stag, there is a story of how for such a crime on the part of **Agamemnon** she detained the Greek fleet, on its way to Troy, in the harbor of Aulis, and exacted from him the sacrifice of his daughter **Iphigenia**. Actaeon, the huntsman, had seen the goddess bathing, and for this offence to her modesty was transformed into a stag, and devoured by his own hounds—a story which appears to illustrate the destructive influence of the dog-star, **Sirius**. Another hunter whom she slew with her sweet arrows was **Orion**, a personification of the bright constellation, which at the beginning of summer is seen in early morning in the east, where it remains until extinguished by the morning light. To express this in the form of a myth, Orion was said to have been too pressing in his advances toward **Eos**, the morning, and for this the goddess of the moon slew him.

From the coincidence observed between the courses of the moon and the ebb and flow of tides, Artemis came to be viewed as a goddess who protected the occupation of the fishermen, not only on the shore and on arms of the sea, but also on lakes and rivers. In this character she bore the name of Dictynna, or Britomartis, and was worshipped with zeal among other places in the Island of Crete, where, to account for the former of her two names, the story was told of her having, to escape the pursuit of Minos, thrown herself from a rock into the sea, upon which she was caught in a fisherman's net.

From the joyous feelings awakened by calm moonlight, and perhaps partly from her relationship to Apollo, she was described as fond of music and the dance—a view of her character which appears to have presented itself in strong light to the people of Arcadia.

By whatever process the belief was arrived at, whether from some comparison which suggested itself between the life of man and the waxing and waning of the moon, or whether because mankind at birth seemed to come out of night into the light of day, we find Artemis represented as the guardian and helper of childbirth, with the title of Eilithyia, Ilithyia,* or Eleutho. She was throughout looked upon as a goddess of the female productive power in nature, and accordingly the care and nursing of children through their illness were placed under her supervision. A festival, accompanied by the dancing of young girls, was held in her honor as the goddess of youth, in Messenia, Laconia, Elis, and elsewhere in Greece. Similarly from the notion that mankind after death seems to sink into night again, she came to be viewed as goddess of death, particularly of that manner of death which could not be assigned to a known cause—it being said of those who were stricken suddenly, without an ostensible cause, such as an injury or

---

* Both names are also assigned to **Hera**, while **Ilithyia** herself is described as a daughter of **Zeus** and **Hera**.

wound, that Apollo or Artemis had laid them low with a kindly arrow ; and in these cases the death of men was ascribed to Apollo, and of women to Artemis, as a rule.

From the fact that the moon, with its pure serene light, naturally suggested, as it does to us also, the idea of a modest pure virgin, Artemis, as her name implies, the " modest, spotless goddess," came to be looked on as a virgin, and as having under her special care all shy and modest youths, whether boys or girls, from whom she received presents of wreaths of flowers in the springtime. When girls had reached an age at which her care was no longer necessary, it was customary for them to dedicate their girdles to the goddess. Young girls were sometimes called " bears," in allusion to their patron goddess, and her symbol of a bear. She was worshipped in Athens, Corinth, and Thebes as goddess of strict upbringing, of good fame, of upright mind, and of sensibility in the affairs of ordinary life. She chased and fired her arrows at all wild and unchecked creatures and actions.

When only a maiden of tender age she resolved, and obtained Zeus' consent, to remain always in a single state, and, like Athene, continued constant and true to her resolve, punishing with great severity every offence against this principle on the part of the nymphs who accompanied her, as we see in the examples of Daphne, whom she transformed into a laurel tree, and Callisto into a bear.

It may have been from the same motive which assigned the bear as a symbol, that in early times her worship was attended with human sacrifice. Of this kind was the worship of the Tauric Artemis, at first peculiar to the countries on the shores of the Black Sea, the Crimea being the principal centre of it. From the Crimea, it is said, Orestes brought an image of the goddess, and transplanted her worship to Greece, where it took root, among other places, at Sparta. There she was styled Orthia or Orthosia. The sacrifices of human beings were, however, in later times,

commuted for the well-known ceremony of flogging youths
at her altar, said to have been introduced by the Spartan
legislator Lycurgus.

As goddess of marshes she was styled **Limnaea**, and as a
river goddess **Potamia**. In this latter capacity she took
under her protection the nymphs of fountains, as, for example, **Arethusa**, whose beauty had attracted the river-god
Alpheus, and made her the object of his constant pursuit,
till Artemis, to elude him, caused the water of the spring
which she represented to flow under ground. As **Munychia**,
or moon-goddess, she was worshipped at the harbor of Athens, and enjoyed an annual festival, at which cakes of the
shape of a full moon, with lights stuck in them, were presented to her. As **Brauronia**, with the symbol of a bear,
she had a sanctuary on the Acropolis of Athens. In Euboea

she was styled **Ama-
rynthia**, and was wor-
shipped with great
ceremony.

Selene, or Luna, it
has already been said,
stood as goddess of the
moon, in the same re-
lation to Artemis as
did Helios to Phoebus
Apollo, inasmuch as
she merely represented
the orb of the moon,
while Artemis repre-
sented the influence
exercised on nature by
night, the symbol of

Diana and Endymion.

which was the moon, as the sun was symbol of day. Accordingly, as compared with Helios, the rising star of day,
Selene represents evening and night, carrying a torch, and
clad in long, heavy robes, with a veil covering the back of

her head. On her brow she wears a half-moon (less frequently horns), and leans forward, as if moving with speed, in a chariot drawn by two horses; or she rides on a mule. The story of her love for the beautiful young **Endymion**, whom she found asleep on a hillside, and, enamoured of his loveliness, descended to him, is the best known of the myths concerning her, and may be taken as a symbolical representation of the gentle influence of the goddess of night, who watches the slumbers of unconscious creatures. Among the Romans **Luna** had a handsome temple, founded by King Servius Tullius, on the Aventine hill, another on the Capitol, and a third on the **Palatine**.

Temple of Diana at Ephesus.

Compared with the Artemis whom we have up to now been describing, the so-called Ephesian Artemis, or **Diana of Ephesus**, presents so very different and strange an aspect, that at first sight we are completely at a loss to understand how by any possibility the term of a virgin could be applied to her. Her appearance altogether wants the simplicity, humanity, and truth to nature which characterized the Greek deities, and, what is more, bears the most obvious signs of maternity. It would seem that the Greeks, who settled as colonists in very early times on the coast of Asia Minor,

Diana of Ephesus.

found this goddess being worshipped by the native population of that land, and adopted her in the place of Artemis,

who, leaving out the fact of her being a virgin, was probably identical with the Asiatic goddess in respect to her divine power over fertility, childbirth, the moon, and hunting.

The Asiatic Artemis.

The worship of **Diana of Ephesus** extended throughout the part of Asia Minor colonized by Greeks, and thence spread to other places—never, however, obtaining a firm footing in Greece proper. At Ephesus she had a temple, which, for the grandeur of its architecture, its size, splendor, and wealth, was reckoned one of the seven wonders of the ancient world. On the night on which Alexander the Great was born it was set fire to and almost completely destroyed by a man named Herostratus, whose object, being simply to hand down his name in history, was gained. Afterward, when Alexander had acquired renown by his extraordinary conquests in Asia, this coincidence was remarked, and accepted as having been an omen of his future fame. Whether he himself believed so or not, he gladly assisted in the rebuilding of the temple, so that when finished it was more magnificent than before. Diana was still being worshipped zealously when the Apostle Paul went to Ephesus to preach Christianity, and accordingly he was received with hostility, especially by the silversmiths and goldsmiths, whose trade consisted largely in the production of small shrines or representations of the front of the temple of Diana, to be sold among her worshippers and devotees. Feeling that the success of Paul's preaching would ruin their trade, they raised so great an opposition to him and his followers that they were obliged to leave the town. Nevertheless the new religion found converts, who from that time forward formed a Christian community there. This Artemis was also worshipped under the title of Leucophryna in Asia Minor, and as such had a splendid temple at Magnesia on the Maeander.

Among the Romans the worship of Diana appears to have been of native growth, and not, as was the case with that of many of the other deities, imported from Greece. A temple had been erected to her in Rome on the Aventine hill as early as the time of King Servius Tullius. Her sacrifices consisted of oxen and deer; and these, as well as the fruit presented to her, had to be perfectly clean and faultless, as became offerings to a virgin goddess. Stags, dogs, and the first-fruits of the fields were sacred to her.

In works of art Artemis was usually represented as a huntress, either in the act of running with speed in pursuit of her game, or resting, and presenting the picture of a young virgin, fleet of foot, her dress girt high, and unencumbered except by bow and arrows. In type of face she resembles her brother Apollo so closely that, from the face alone, it is sometimes difficult to distinguish them. Her hair, like his, is gathered into a large knot above the forehead. The most celebrated of the statues of her that have come down to us is the so-called Diana of Versailles. In early works of art, and in some of the later—as, for example, a marble statue in the British Museum —her drapery reaches to her feet, but in these cases also she is represented as in active movement, like the moon hastening through the clouds. Of the incidents in which she figured we find that of Actaeon being transformed into a stag and devoured by his hounds, in a sculptured group, on a painted vase, and on the fragment of a cameo in the British Museum. The hunt of the Calydonian boar occurs on painted vases.

The Ephesian Artemis was represented with a mural crown on her

head. Behind the crown is a disc, as symbol of the full moon; on
her breast, like a necklace, a garland of flowers, as a sign of her influence in springtime, while above it are figures of maidens, to indicate her patronage of young girls; lions cling to her arms; as mother
of wild beasts, she has many breasts; her legs are closely bandaged
and ornamented with figures of bulls, stags, lions, and gryphons; at
the sides are flowers and bees. How far this figure may have resembled the original image of the goddess which had fallen from heaven,
it is impossible to say.

Selene or Luna is represented as riding on a mule or a horse; on
the pediment of the Parthenon it is a horse. On a painted vase in
the British Museum there occurs a representation of sunrise; Helios
is seen rising in his chariot, the stars, in the form of youths, dive
headlong into the sea, and the moon (Selene) rides away over the
hilltops on a horse, and as she departs is bayed at by a dog.

DIONYSUS, OR BACCHUS,

Having more titles than any of the other deities, was styled,
to increase their number, "God of the many names," of
these the most familiar being Bromius, Lyaeus, Dithyrambus, and Bacchus. The belief in the existence and
powers of this god appears to have been borrowed by the
Greeks in its primitive form from oriental mythology, to have
been developed by them, and in later times communicated
to the Romans. His original signification was that of a
divine being whose power might be noticed operating in the
sap of vegetation; and, accordingly, spring was a season of
gladness and joy for him, and winter a season of sorrow.
From this sprung his double character of god of the vintage
and its gay accompaniments, and god of the ecstatic and
mystic ceremonies in which his sufferings during winter were
deplored. As time went on he came to be viewed chiefly as
the source of the happiness and mirth which arise from the
enjoyment of the noble fruit of the vine; while afterward,
from the fact that his festivals in spring and summer, with
their gaiety and mirth, gave occasion to the first attempts at
dramatic performances, he added the function of god of the
theatre to that of god of the vine.

DIONYSUS, OR BACCHUS.

He was born, it was commonly believed, at Thebes, and was a son of Zeus and Semele, a daughter of Cadmus, the

Bacchus.

founder of that town, a son of Agenor, and grandson of Poseidon. Of his birth poets relate how Hera, indignant at this rival in her husband's affections, determined to get rid of her; and to this end, assuming a disguise, went to Thebes, and presented herself to Semele; how she succeeded in winning her confidence, and thereupon took occasion to propose that she should ask Zeus to visit her for once in all the plenitude of his majesty as a god of thunder, how Zeus, who, without waiting to listen, had hastily sworn, "by the black waters of the Styx," to grant whatever she should ask, was vexed when he heard the foolish request, from granting which no power could absolve him; how one day he appeared before the luckless Semele with a display of thunder and lightning which caused her death.   So far the desire of vengeance on the part of Hera was satisfied.   But Semele, at the moment of her death, gave birth to a male child, whose life Zeus fortunately restored.   That was the child Bacchus. To prevent its suffering at the hands of Hera, Hermes, the messenger of the gods, was secretly dispatched with the infant to a place called Nysa, where were certain nymphs, to whom, along with Silenus, the charge of bringing up the child was entrusted.   His title of **Dithyrambus**, it is said, means "twice born," and refers to the incident of his life being restored by Zeus.   In after times it was applied to a species of song in honor of the god of wine, of which Arion of Methymna was the reputed originator.

The childhood of **Dionysus** was spent in innocence and happiness among the nymphs, satyrs, sileni, herdsmen, and vine-tenders of Nysa.   But when he arrived at manhood he set out on a journey through all known countries, even into the remotest parts of India, instructing the people, as he proceeded, how to tend the vine, and how to practise many other arts of peace, besides teaching them the value of just and honorable dealings.   He was praised everywhere as the greatest benefactor of mankind.   At the same time, it is said, apparently with reference to the fierce and stubborn mood which in some cases follows copious indulgence in wine, that he met occasionally with great resistance on his journey, but always overcame it and punished those who opposed him most severely. As an instance of this, we will take Lycurgus, the king of Thrace, whom, for his resistance, Dionysus drove mad, and caused to fell his son, mistaking him for a vine-plant, and afterward to kill himself in despair. Or, again, Pentheus, a king of Thebes, whom he caused to be torn to pieces by his own mother and her following of women, because he had dared to look on at their orgiastic rites.

Nowhere was the knowledge of how to utilize the vine appreciated more than in Attica, where the god had communicated it to Icarus, whose first attempt to extend the benefit of it to others brought about his own death, an event which was deeply grieved for afterward. In December a festival, with all manner of rustic enjoyments, was held in honor of Dionysus in the country round Athens. In January a festival called Lenaea was held in his honor in the town, at which one of the principal features was a nocturnal and orgiastic procession of women. Then followed in February the Anthesteria, the first day of which was called " cask-opening day," and the second " pouring day." Lastly came the great festival of the year, the Great Dionysia, which was held in the town of Athens, and lasted from the ninth to the fifteenth of March, the religious part of the ceremony consisting of a procession in which an ancient wooden image of the god was carried through the streets from one sanctuary to another, accompanied by excited songs. The theatre of Dionysus was daily the scene of splendid dramatic performances, and the whole town was astir and gay.

His worship extended to Lemnos, Thasos, and Naxos, where the story was told of his turning the Tyrrhenian pirates into dolphins, and where he found the beautiful Ariadne, when she had been abandoned by Theseus. It spread to Crete, the home of Ariadne, and into Asia Minor. In Phrygia he was worshipped with wild ceremonies, called Sabazia, and in Thrace and Macedonia, called Cotyttia. As the god who had advanced through Asia Minor and on to

India, accompanied by his wild and clamorous following, he was styled the Indian Dionysus, and in this character was represented as advanced in years.

The sufferings which the god was supposed to endure in winter led him to be associated with Demeter in the mysteries of Eleusis, the purpose of which was, as has been said, to celebrate the grief of the goddess in winter, and her prospects of joy in the coming spring.

The vine, ivy, and pomegranate were sacred to this god; his sacrifices consisted of goats and pigs.

In works of art **Dionysus** was represented under a variety of forms; of these, however, two are to be specially noticed. The one called the " Indian Bakchos," represents him as a man of years, with worthy aspect, a long beard, a diadem on his brow, and long drapery sweeping to his feet. In another figure he is represented as a beautiful youth with an almost feminine appearance, beardless, his hair falling in long tresses, and adorned with a wreath of ivy or vine tendrils, sometimes wearing the skin of a stag over his shoulders, or with small horns on his brow, and often in a car drawn by panthers or lions, or riding on one of these beasts.

At other times he appears as a child, and that sometimes when he is being handed over by Hermes to the care of Silenus and the nymphs of Nysa. The youthful Dionysus is frequently represented in the company of Ariadne, while the elder Dionysus is usually accompanied by Sileni and Satyrs, as when he visited Icarus and taught him the use of the vine, a scene which occurs on several ancient reliefs, of which two are in the British Museum. On his journey to India he rides on a camel, and on other occasions he is attended by panthers. His staff is a *thyrsus*—a rod with a pine cone at the top. In his hand is often a drinking-cup. The movement and excitement of the persons who were associated with Dionysus was a great attraction to Praxiteles and the sculptors of his time, and it is probable that the many sculptures of Dionysiac subjects which we now possess come from that school either as originals or direct imitations.

HERMES, OR MERCURY,

A son of **Zeus** and **Maia**, a daughter of **Atlas**, was regarded in the first instance as the special deity to whom was due the prolificness and welfare of the animal kingdom. In conse-

quence, however, of the fact that in early times the chief
source of wealth consisted in herds of cattle, the prolificness
of which was traced to him, it came to pass in time that he
was considered generally to be the first cause of all wealth,
come whence it might. But
as civilization advanced, and
it became known by experience that there was no
means of acquiring wealth so
rapidly as by trade, his province was extended to trade
and the protection of traders.
Again, since the main condition of prosperity in trade
was peace and undisturbed
commerce by land and sea,
he came to be viewed as
guardian of commerce. And,
further, assuming that all
who took part in trade were
qualified to look after their
own interests, shrewd and

Hermes, or Mercury.

prudent, the function of protecting prudence, shrewdness,
and even cunning, was assigned to him. In certain aspects
of trade, if not in the best, it was reckoned a great point to
talk over and cajole purchasers, and from his protection of
this method of doing business, Hermes came to be god of
" persuasive speech" or oratory. Finally, it being only a
short step from this to cunning and roguery, we must not
be surprised to find him described as protector of thieves
and rascals, though no doubt this task was assigned him
more in joke than in earnest.

His office of messenger and herald of the gods, in particular of Zeus, appears to have originated partly in the duty
assigned to him of protecting commerce, the success of which
depends largely on the messengers and envoys employed in

it, and partly in other functions of his which would lead us too far to explain. As messenger and envoy of Zeus, Hermes conducts the intercourse between heaven and earth, announcing the will of the gods to men, and from this office was further derived his character of a god of oracles. In the capacity of messenger or herald he had access even to the under-world, whither, under the title of Psychopompos, he guided the souls of the departed, crossing in Charon's bark, and placing them before the throne of the deities below. From the shadowy world of spirits to that of sleep and dreams is a short step for the imagination, and accordingly we find Hermes described as Oneiropompos, guide of dreams. As the swift messenger of the gods he readily came to be looked on as a model for the youth practising in the palaestra, in which capacity he had the title of Enagonios,

In proportion to the variety of tasks which he had to perform was the variety of mythical stories about his actions and life, some of them taking us back to the very day of his birth. For it was not an uncommon practice in the early myth-making age to ascribe to the infancy of a god some instance of the peculiar qualities by which he was afterward distinguished. So it happened with Hermes.

His birth having taken place on the fourth of the month, that day became sacred to him. Born, as it was believed, during the darkness of night, in an unfrequented, lonesome cave on Mount Cyllene, in Arcadia, and on this account styled Cyllenius, he was only a day old when a remarkable example of his cunning and knavery occurred. Slipping out of the couch in the cave where he was left asleep as was supposed, the night being dark and cloudy, he found a herd of cattle belonging to his brother Apollo (as sun-god), and stole a number of them. When the morning came Apollo searched in vain for the missing cattle; for the infant god had cleverly succeeded in obliterating all traces of them by fastening bunches of broom to their hoofs, and in this condition driving them backward into a cave at Pylos, so as to produce the impression that they had left instead of entered the cave. After this adventure he slunk back to his couch, and feigned to be asleep. He had, however, been observed by a rustic named Battus, who informed against him, whereupon Apollo, angry at such a daring piece of robbery, dragged him out of his couch, and took him off to the throne of Zeus to be punished and made an example of. But Hermes was irrepressible, took up a lyre which he had made the day before out of the shell of a tortoise, and proceeded to play on it, to

Mercury Before Pluto and Proserpina.

the amusement and delight of both Zeus and Apollo, and further ingratiated himself with his brother by giving him the lyre, inventing for his own use a shepherd's pipe. The cattle of the sun-god were the clouds, and Hermes was a god who presided over the fertility of nature. The signification of the story of his stealing some of these cattle on a dark night would, therefore, seem to be simply that of clouds discharging fertilizing showers by night.

The two brothers, having thus made their peace, continued from that time forward on the best of terms, Apollo attesting his good disposition toward Hermes by giving him in return for the lyre a present of a golden divining-rod, and also the power of prophecy. This condition, however, was attached to the gift, that he was not to communicate his revelations of the future by words as did Apollo, but by signs and occurrences. That is to say, that persons revolving some undertaking in their mind were to be guided by certain unexpected sights, accidents, or incidents, and were to recognize in them the favor or displeasure of the gods, with reference to the enterprise in question—a method of proceeding common enough in modern superstition. These signs and incidents were believed to be sent by Hermes, whose counsel in other cases of doubt, as to whether to do or not do a thing, was sought for by recourse to dice, the belief being that a high throw signified his approval, and a low throw the reverse.

The cunning and adroitness, the same good humor and ready answer which he gave proof of in the first days of his infancy, were often afterward and with like success displayed by him—as, for example, when he stole the sceptre of Zeus, Aphrodite's girdle, Poseidon's trident, the sword of Ares, the tongs of Hephaestus, or Apollo's bow and arrows, in each case managing to make up matters, and smooth away the indignation of his victims. But the most celebrated instance in which his brilliant talents were fully displayed, was the affair of Argus with the hundred eyes, whom Hera had appointed to watch over Io, one of the favorites of Zeus, whom the latter, that she might escape the vengeance of the jealous Hera, had transformed into a cow, a trick which the goddess had perceived.

Well, Hermes being commanded by Zeus to release Io from the surveillance of Argus, and in doing so to use no force, found the task no easy matter, seeing that the watchman had a hundred eyes, of which, when in his deepest sleep, only fifty were closed. Hermes succeeded, however, and in this fashion. Presenting himself to Argus, he commenced to amuse him by telling all kinds of tales, and having by these means fairly gained the watchman's confidence, he next

produced a shepherd's pipe, and played on it various tunes
of such sweetness that they gradually lulled Argus into so
deep a sleep that one by one all
his hundred eyes closed. The
moment the last eyelid drooped
Hermes slew him, and at once
released Io, and led her away.
For this service he rose high in
the estimation of Zeus, and from
that time the name of "Argus-
slayer," Argiphontes, was the
proudest title which he bore.
As a memorial of Argus, Hera,
it was said, set his eyes in the
tail of her favorite bird, the

Argus.

peacock. But these and such-like instances of his knavery
and cunning do not by any means express the whole character
of Hermes; for his skill was also directed frequently to pur-
poses of useful invention. It was he, for example, who invented Apollo's lyre, as well as that one by which the
Theban musician, Amphion, did such wonders; and it was
he who taught Palamedes to express words in writing.
And, besides, wherever danger that required skill and dex-
terity as much as courage presented itself, he was always
present to assist. He acted as a guide to heroes in their
dangerous enterprises, and in that capacity frequently, as in
the case of Hercules, was associated with Athene. To
travellers who had lost their way he was a ready guide, and
to exiles a constant and willing helper in strange lands and
among ill-disposed people.

In the primitive form of his worship Hermes was, as has
been said, the god who gives prolificness to flocks and herds.
In this character we find him in what appears to have been
the oldest centre of his worship in Greece—that is, in Samothrace and the neighboring islands of Imbros and Lemnos,
where he bore the title of Cadmilus or Casmilus. His

usual title among herdsmen was either **Nomius** or **Epi-
melius.**

A messenger himself, it became his office to aid human
messengers and travellers, and to this end it was he who
inspired the idea of erecting sign-posts at cross-roads with
directions as to whither each road led. These sign-posts took
the form of statues, if they may be so called, consisting of
a pillar running narrower toward the foot, and surmounted

Io and Zeus.

by a head of Hermes, and called **Hermae.** It was the duty
of travellers on passing one of them to place a stone beside
it, a custom which not only largely helped toward clearing
the fields of stones, but also led to improvement in the roads
themselves, and hence to increased facilities for commerce.
If more than two roads crossed, a corresponding number of
heads were placed on the pillar, one facing each way. Similar figures were also found outside houses in Athens for the
purpose of cheering parting travellers.

The attributes of Hermes were the *caduceus* or *keryceum*— that is, a short staff with a pair of wings and a knotted snake attached to it, and the *petasus* or winged cap. Beside him

Hermes, or Mercury.

sometimes is a cock or a goat. For sacrifice he delighted in the tongues of animals, a suitable sacrifice to the god of oratory.

The Roman Mercurius appears to have possessed in common with Hermes only the character of god of trade and oratory. Roman traders held a festival to him on May 25.

In the earlier works of art Hermes appears bearded and about middle age, frequently carrying a sheep or a kid over his shoulders. His form is athletic. In more recent works we find him of a youthful figure, such as became his office as messenger of the gods. He wears the *petasus*, and sometimes wings at his heels, carries the *caduceus*, and sometimes, as a god of trade, a purse. Among the incidents of his life, one which occurs frequently on the painted vases is that in which he appears presenting the three goddesses to Paris, who had to decide their claims as to which of them was the most beautiful. Sometimes he is represented in sculptures as a mere boy. Many of the Hermae described above have come down to our times.

THEMIS,

A daughter of **Uranus** and **Gaea,** was the personification of that divine law of right which ought to control all human affairs, of that highest and noblest sense of right which is subject to no human influences. In this capacity she came to be viewed also as goddess of the rites of hospitality. She was a personification of divine will as it bore upon the affairs of the world, and accordingly the Delphic oracle had been under her control before it was yielded to Apollo, to whom, as her successor, she communicated the prophetic art. A long time passed before **Zeus** could persuade her to become his wife—his first wife, as some myths have it; his second, according to others, which say that **Metis** was his first. To him she bore the **Horae**, **Moerae** or **Parcae**, and **Astraea**, the goddess of justice, of whom we have already told how she forsook the earth during the Bronze Age. The proper home of Themis was Olympus, and hence she was styled **Urania**. But during the war with the Titans she descended to earth, and there, throughout the Golden Age, taught mankind the exercises of right and moderation. When, afterward, the human race sank into degradation, she returned again to Olympus.

In consequence of the profound wisdom and open truthfulness which formed the essential features of the character of Themis, even the supreme gods consulted and acted on her advice; as, for example, did Zeus, when he declined to marry Thetis, because of the prediction of Themis, that a son would be the issue of the marriage, who would oxool even his father in might. We shall afterward have to relate how Thetis was given in marriage to Peleus, a mortal, in order that her son might not be a source of danger to the gods. The worship of Themis extended to many districts of Greece, where temples, altars, and statues were raised in her honor. The principal centres of it, however, were Athens, Troezen, the island of Aegina, Thebes, and Olympia.

Themis.

Ancient artists represented her as a woman of mature age, with large open eyes; while modern artists— and they alone, it must be observed—figure her as in the illustration.

She is further represented holding a sword and chain in one hand and a balance in the other, to indicate the severity and the accuracy with which justice is to be meted out and administered.

INFERIOR DEITIES.

HITHERTO our descriptions have been confined to those deities of the Greeks and Romans who, because their functions were subordinate to no god but **Zeus**, were styled of the superior order, or Olympian deities, **Hades** and **Persephone** being included, though their realm was the underworld, not Olympus. We proceed now to the inferior order, such as occupied subordinate positions in the system of gods, but were nevertheless worshipped independently, if not so universally as the others.

We begin with the

HORAE,

The goddesses of the "seasons," daughters of **Zeus** and **Themis**. Their number was variously estimated according to the variety of the divisions of year into periods—winter,

One of the Horae.

(142)

however, not being reckoned as one, because it was the season of sleep and death in nature. Thus we find the worship of only two goddesses of seasons in Athens, the one called Thallo, or goddess of "blossoming," and the other Carpo, or goddess of "harvest and fruit." But elsewhere in Greece the usual number was three, and as such they were represented in works of art with the attributes of the seasons: Spring with its flowers, Summer with its grain, and Autumn with its grapes and fruit.

Occasionally we find a fourth season, that of Winter, represented in the act of returning with booty from the chase: but, unlike her sisters, she is nameless. As deities of the kindly seasons which bring about the budding and growth of nature, they were directly under the control of the superior deities, especially of Zeus and Hera. At times they are to be seen along with the Charites (Graces) in the company of

Horae, or Hours.

Aphrodite, and sometimes along with the Muses in the company of Apollo; for it is in the happy seasons of the year that the joyous voice of nature is heard.

In the capacity of goddesses who watched over the blessings of the fields, it became their duty, further, to regulate changes of the weather, now opening and now shutting the gates of heaven, alternately sending rain and sunshine as suited best the increase of vegetation. Tender and gladsome, moving in mazy dances, with crowns of gold and of flowers, they were always good and faithful to mankind, and, though sometimes seeming to be impatient to come late, always bringing with them something sweet and beautiful, never proving untrue or deceitful.

Our first illustration represents a **Hora** dancing, with a wreath of palm-leaves on her head. The dish of fruit in her left hand probably indicates that she is the Hora of Autumn.

Hora, or Flora.

Such were their functions in nature. In consequence, however, of the great and plenteous blessings that were observed to flow from the unchangeable and orderly succession of the seasons, the Horae were also supposed to watch over good order and propriety in human life and morality—a task which seems to have given rise to the belief that they were daughters of **Themis.** Their names, in the cases where the three appear together, have been admirably chosen to suit this metaphorical notion of their character : as, **Eunomia** (wise legislation), **Dike** (justice), and **Eirene** (peace).

Eunomia's services were mostly directed to political life, the results being warmly praised by poets, and her worship never neglected by the State. Dike's sphere of operations was

POSEIDON, OR NEPTUNE.

more among the incidents of the lives of individuals, informing, it was said, her father **Zeus**, of every injustice done on
earth.   Eirene, finally, being the most cheerful of the three
sisters, was said to have been the mother of **Plutus**—that is,
of riches, the gay companion of **Dionysus**, and guardian
goddess of songs and festivities.

The goddess of spring was also especially worshipped as a
Hora under the title of **Chloris**, which corresponds to the
Roman **Flora**.   She was the goddess of buds and flowers,
of whom **Boreas**, the north winter wind, and **Zephyrus**, the
west spring wind, were rival lovers.   She chose the latter,
and became his faithful wife.

POMONA

Was goddess of garden fruits, and was represented wearing
a wreath composed of such, or holding in her hand a horn of
plenty full of them, with a dog by her side.   Her appearance was that of a virgin in rustic garments.   It was said
that she had been orginally a **Hamadryad**, but had yielded
her affections to **Vertumnus**.   Her worship was confined to
the Romans.   She had a priest, styled **flamen pomonalis**,
specially devoted to her service.

VERTUMNUS,

The husband of **Pomona**, was worshipped by the Romans
as a deity of the second order, who watched over the seasons
as well as the garden fruits, and was represented with attributes similar to those of Pomona.   In October an annual
festival, resembling a harvest thanksgiving, was held in his
honor, the offerings brought him on that occasion consisting
of first-fruits from the garden, and wreaths of flowers of all
kinds.   Like Pomona, he, too, had a priest of his own.   At
times he was represented, like **Saturn**, with a pruning-knife
in his hand, and a wreath composed of ears of corn on his

head.   Originally he was worshipped under the form of a rough wooden post, but had afterward a beautiful bronze statue made by a Roman artist.

JANUS

Was a deity unknown to the Greeks, but from the earliest times held in high estimation by the Romans, who placed him on almost an equal footing with Jupiter, even giving his name precedence in their prayers, and invoking the aid of both deities previous to every undertaking.   To him they ascribed the origin of all things, the introduction of the system of years, the change of season, the ups and downs of fortune, and the civilization of the human race by means of agriculture, industry, arts, and religion.   According to the popular belief, Janus was an ancient king who had come in remote early times from Greece to Latium, there instituted the worship of the gods and the erection of temples, and himself deserved high honors like a god, for this reason, that he had conferred the greatest good upon mankind by his instructions in many important ways.   In some of the stories he is confounded with Saturn.   In others it is said that Saturn, driven out of Greece, took refuge with Janus in Latium, and shared the government with him.

It is easy to explain the great honor paid to Janus by a people like the Romans, who, as a rule, had this peculiarity of pondering well the prospects of an undertaking before entering upon it.   The beginning of everything was a matter of great importance to them, and Janus was the god of a " good beginning."   It is in this spirit that the Roman poet, Ovid, makes Janus say, " Everything depends on the beginning."   Even when Jupiter had consented to an enterprise, prosperity in carrying it out was believed to be under the control of Janus, and, accordingly, great stress was laid on the circumstances attending the commencement of any project.   Janus opened and closed all things.   He sat, not only on the confines of the earth, but also at the gates of heaven. Air, sea, and land were in the hollow of his hands. The world moved on its hinges at his command.

In accordance with this belief, he was represented seated, with two heads, one being that of a youth, to indicate "be-ginning," the other that of an old man, to indicate the "end," whence he was styled Bifrons (two-headed). In his left hand is a key, to show that he opens at the beginning, and shuts at the end; the sceptre in his right is a sign that he controls the progress of every undertaking.

Janus.

The first day of January, a month named after him, being the first day of a new year, was the occasion of a celebration in his honor. At the beginning of every month the priests offered sacrifice to him at twelve altars. He was invoked every morning as the beginner of a new day. Even at the sacrifices to other gods he was remembered, and received offerings of wine and cakes, incense, and other things. The husbandman prayed to him at the beginning of seed-time. When war was declared he was invoked.

The public worship of Janus as a god was introduced into Rome as early as the time of Numa Pompilius, a foundation for its establishment having been previously laid during the reign of Romulus. The story runs, that, the Sabines having once made an assault on the newly built town of Rome, a spring of boiling water suddenly appeared, and was the means of destroying these enemies. On this spot a temple was erected in honor of Janus, the gates of which stood open so long as Rome was at war, and were closed with great ceremony and rejoicing only in times of general peace. Rome was, however, so continually engaged in war that, in the course of the first seven hundred years after the foundation of the city, the gates of the temple were closed only three times—in the reign of Numa Pompilius, after the first Punic war, and during the reign of Augustus. Hence the temple of Janus with its gates shut came to be a very emphatic symbol of peace.

TERMINUS

Was the god of boundaries, and had, when represented in art, the figure of a boundary stone or pillar surmounted by a head, as in the case of the figures of Hermes by the wayside in Greece. Such figures of Terminus were occasionally surmounted by the head or bust of another god, as, for example, of Apollo or Athene, and in such cases were styled Hermapollo, Hermathene. Pan and Priapus, both rural deities, were also frequently represented in such form.

Numa Pompilius is said to have erected the first altar to this boundary god, Terminus, and to have instituted his worship among the Romans. To accustom his subjects to respect the boundaries of their neighbors, he ordered them to be marked off with figures of the god, and a festival to be held in his honor annually in February. It was called the Terminalia. Boundary stones were adorned with flowers on the occasion, and a general sacrifice offered, accompanied by lively songs.

PRIAPUS,

Called also Lutinus by the Romans, was a son of Dionysus and Aphrodite. He was a god of the fertility of nature, and, in this capacity, also guardian of vineyards, gardens,

and cultivated fields. The idea of representing the productive power of nature under the form of a god is traceable
back to a very great antiquity, but in later and depraved
times it came to be misused for the purpose of giving expression to coarse sensuality and lust. This accounts for the
diversity of his representations, of which, however, that is
the most correct in which he appears as a man of years holding a pruning-knife in his hand and fruit in his lap. The
principal centre of his worship was Lampsacus, a town in
Asia Minor, on the Hellespont, whence it spread over Greece.
His symbols were, like those of Dionysus, a drinking-cup, a
thyrsus, or a spear. At the festivals in his honor the sacrifices consisted of milk, honey, and asses.

PAN

Was looked upon by the pastoral inhabitants of Greece, particularly in Arcadia, as the god who watched over the
pasture-fields, herdsmen, and herds. Woods and plains,
hunting and fishing, were under his immediate care and
patronage, and on this account he was differently described
as a son now of Zeus, now of Hermes, his mother being in
each case a nymph. As god of green fields he was associated
with the worship of Dionysus (Bacchus), and as mountain
god with that of Cybele. He was fond of sportive dances
and playing on the shepherd's pipe, which afterward took its
name of Pan's pipe from him, the story being that he was
the inventor of it. It seems that a coy nymph named Syrinx,
whom he loved and followed, was transformed into a reed,
that Pan cut it and fashioned it into a pipe (syrinx) with
such sweet notes, when skilfully played, that he once ventured
to challenge Apollo to a competition.

The judge selected was Midas, who awarded the prize to
Pan, and was, in consequence, punished by Apollo, who made
his ears grow like those of an ass.

As a god of herdsmen and country people, he journeyed through woods and across plains, changing from place to place like the nomadic or pastoral people of early times, with no fixed dwelling, resting in shady grottoes, by cool streams, and playing on his pipe. Hills, caves, oaks, and tortoises were sacred to him.

The feeling of solitude and lonesomeness which weighs upon travellers in wild mountain scenes, when the weather is stormy, and no sound of human voice is to be heard, was ascribed to the presence of Pan, as a spirit of the mountains, a sort of Number Nip. And thus anxiety or alarm, arising from no visible or intelligible cause, came to be called "Panic fear," that is, such fear as is produced by the agitating presence of Pan.

His common companions were Nymphs and Oreades, who danced to the strains of his pipe, and were not unfrequently pursued by him with violence. It is said that he rendered important service to the gods during the war with the Titans, by the invention of a kind of trumpet made from a sea-shell, with which he raised such a din that the Titans took fright, and retreated in the belief that some great monster was approaching against them. Another story is, that Dionysus, being once seriously attacked by a hostile and very numerous body of men on his way to India, was freed from them by a sudden terrible shout raised by Pan, which instantly caused them to retreat in great alarm. Both stories appear to have been invented to give a foundation for the expression of " Panic fear," which has been explained above.

Pan, also called Hylaeus or forest god, was usually represented as a bearded man with a large hooked nose, with the ears and horns and legs of a goat, his body covered with hair, with a shepherd's pipe (syrinx) of seven reeds, or a shepherd's crook in his hand.

From Greece his worship was transplanted among the Romans, by whom he was styled Inuus, because he taught them to breed cattle, and Lupercus, because he taught them to employ dogs for the purpose of protecting the herds against wolves. The other forest deities, who were represented like

Pan and Apollo.

Pan with goat's legs, were called **Aegipanes**, and sometimes **Panisci**.

FAUNUS, OR FATUUS,

Was a purely Roman deity, originally resembling the Greek
Pan, as is implied in the name, which is only another form
of the same word.   In process of time, however, his character
passed through many changes, and became different in many respects from that of the Greek god. It was not till late times, when the religion and myths of the Greeks emigrated into Italy, that the comparison of him with the Arcadian Pan was revived and the identity of both asserted. The Roman poets frequently call the Greek Pan by the Roman name of Faunus. But the latter had certain myths peculiar to himself, and is represented by them as a son of Picus, and a grandson of Saturnus, or, according to another version, a son of Mars, and originally an ancient king of Latium,

Faunus, or Fatuus.

who, for the good he did his people, by introducing agriculture and civilization, came to be worshipped after his

death as a prophetic deity of forest and field, under the name
of Fatuus. His oracles were delivered in groves, and communicated by means of dreams, which those desiring them
obtained by sleeping in sacred places on the hides of animals
that had been offered as sacrifices. Fauna also delivered
oracles, but only to women.

As god of the husbandman and patron of agriculture and
cattle-rearing, an annual festival, the Lupercalia, or Faun-
alia, was celebrated in his honor by the Romans on December 5. It was accompanied by sacrifices of goats, offerings
of milk and wine, banquets, and dancing in the open air in
meadows and at cross-roads. In the middle of February
also sacrifice was presented to him. He had two temples in
Rome. Artistic representations of him are rare, and not
easily distinguished from those of Pan. The plural form of
the word, Fauni, is merely a Roman expression for what the
Greeks called Panisci or Panes.

PICUS, PICUMNUS, AND PILUMNUS.

Picus was also a pure Roman deity, a son and a successor
of Saturnus, father of Faunus, and husband of Canens. He
was an ancient prophet and forest god. Another story has it
that he loved and married Pomona. Circe, the witch, was
attracted by his beauty, and finding her affection not returned,
revenged herself by changing him into a woodpecker—a bird
which was held to be a sacred symbol of prophecy by the
Augurs or Roman priests, whose office was to foretell coming
events by observing the flight of birds and by various other
phenomena. In early times his figure consisted of a wooden
pillar with a woodpecker on it, which was afterward exchanged for a figure of a youth with a woodpecker on his
head, the Romans generally considering the appearance of that
bird to be a sign of some special intention of the gods. Picus,
beside being worshipped as a prophet and a god, was also

looked upon as one of the first kings of Italy, and must not be confounded with Picumnus, who, with his brother Pilumnus, formed a pair of Roman deities whose office was to watch over married life. It was the custom to spread a couch for them at the birth of a child. Pilumnus, it was said, would drive away all illness from the childhood of the newly born infant with the club (*pilum*) with which he used to pound the grain; while Picumnus, who had introduced the manuring of land, would give the child growth. Stories were told of the two brothers, of famous deeds in war and peace, such as were ascribed to the Dioscuri (Castor and Pollux).

FAUNA, OR FATUA,

The wife or, according to other myths, the daughter of Faunus, was a Roman goddess, whose origin and signification have been rendered very obscure by the variety of stories about her. She was identified with the goddess Ops, with Cybele, with Semele, the mother of Dionysus (Bacchus), with Maia, the mother of Hermes, with Gaea, Hecate, and other goddesses. In the earliest times she was called simply the " kind goddess," her proper name as well as her origin being given out as a mystery. Her festival took place on the first night of May, and was celebrated with wine, music, merry games, and mysterious ceremonies, at which only women and girls were permitted to be present. Fauna obtained the name of the " kind goddess" because, as some thought, her benevolence extended over the whole creation, in which case it was not strange that she should be identified with other deities. As Fatua she was represented with the appearance sometimes of Juno, sometimes of Cybele, but commonly as an aged woman, with pointed ears, holding a serpent in her hand.

The offspring of Fatua and Fatuus were the Fatui, who were considered to be prophetic deities of the fields, and sometimes evil genii, who were the cause of nightmares and such like. The name and obscure significations of this goddess seem to have given rise to the fantastic creations of modern times, which recall Fays—that is, beings with the power of witchcraft and prophecy, and possessed now with good, now with bad qualities—now useful and helping to men, now mischievous.

THE SATYRS,

Like the Roman **Silvanus**, belong to the order of forest deities, and are often confounded with the Panes and Fauni, though quite distinct from them. They represented the genial luxuriant life in Nature, which, under the protection and with the aid of Dionysus (Bacchus), spreads over fields, woods, and meadows, and were, without doubt, the finest figures in all his company. As such at least they appear in the art of the best times, being never figured, like the Panes or Panisci, as half man, half animal, but at most exhibit only such signs of an animal form as small goat's horns, and a small goat's tail, to show that their nature was only a little inferior in nobility to that within the divine or pure human form.

Satyr.

The Satyrs constitute a large family, and may be distinguished into several classes, the highest of which were those who nearly resembled their god (**Dionysus**) in appearance, and whose occupation was either to play on the flute for his amusement, or to pour out his wine. To another class belonged those older figures, distinguished by the name of **Sileni**; and to a third, the very juvenile so-called Satyrisci.   The figure given in the illustration is that of a satyr of the highest order.   He is represented as a slender youth leaning carelessly on the trunk of a tree, resting from playing on a flute.   His hair is shaggy ; on his brow are very small goat's horns.   His countenance has a touch of animal expression in it.   He wears nothing but a panther's skin thrown over his shoulder.

The life of the Satyrs was spent in woods and on hills, in a constant round of amusements of all kinds : hunting, dancing, music, drinking, gathering and pressing the grapes, or in the company of the god, whirling in wild dances with the Maenades.   Their musical instruments were the syrinx, flute, and cymbals.

We may remark in passing, that the term " satire," commonly applied to poems of abuse, has nothing whatever to do with the Satyrs, and for this reason should not be written " satyre," though derived from *satura*.   The latter is an old Latin word, which signified originally a poetic dialogue or gossip, which from its nature was admirably adapted for conveying criticism and indirect abuse, or satire in our sense of the word.

COMUS

Was worshipped as guardian of festal banquets, of mirthful enjoyments, of lively humor, fun, and social pleasure, with attributes expressing joy in many ways.   On the other hand, he was represented frequently as an illustration of the consequences of nightly orgies, with torch reversed, in drunken sleep, or leaning against something.

SILVANUS,

Like Faunus, was purely a Roman god, whose function also was to watch over the interests of herdsmen, living in woods and fields, and taking care to preserve boundary lines and

banks of rivers. It was said that he erected the first boundary stones to mark off the fields of different possessors from each other, and thus be-
came the founder of a regular system of land-owning. He was distinguished according to the three departments of his activity, house, field, and wood. In works of art Silvanus appears altogether as a purely human figure—a cheerful aged man holding a shepherd's pipe (for he, like the other deities of wood and field, was given to music), and carrying a branch of a tree to mark him specially as god of the forest. This branch, which sometimes is that of a cypress, is explained as referring to his love for the beautiful Cyparissus, whom he is said to have changed into a

Silvanus.

cypress. There was a figure of Silvanus in Rome beside the temple of Saturn, and two sanctuaries dedicated to him. Women were excluded from his worship. The myths are not clear about his origin. Some of them describe him as a son of Saturn.

PALES

Was worshipped originally in Sicily, and afterward by the Romans, as a deity of cattle-rearing, being, according to some, male, according to others, female. A merry festival, called **Palilia**, was held in honor of this deity every year on April 21, the day on which the foundation of the city of Rome was said to have been laid. Offerings of milk and must were presented to her, while pipes were played and cymbals beat round a blazing fire of hay and straw. An ox was driven through this blazing fire, the herdsmen rushing after it, a ceremony intended for a symbol of expiation. This festival, because of its falling on the anniversary of the foundation of the city, served also to commemorate that event. This ancient deity was represented as an aged woman leaning on a leafless branch of a tree, or holding a shepherd's crook in her hand, and was frequently identified with **Fauna,** sometimes with **Cybele,** and even with **Vesta.**

SILENUS, AND THE SILENI.

In some of the myths **Silenus** is represented as a son of **Hermes** (Mercury), in others of **Pan** and a nymph, the latter statement accounting for his being figured with the tail and ears of a goat, while the rest of his form was purely human. He was usually described as the oldest of the Satyrs —of whom, indeed, all those well advanced in years were styled Sileni. Owing to his age, he came to be looked upon as a sort of paternal guardian of the light-headed troops of Satyrs, though with regard to mythological signification he was quite different from them. One myth traces his origin, along with the worship of Dionysus (Bacchus), to Asia Minor, and particularly to the districts of Lydia and Phrygia, the original centre of the worship of Cybele (Rhea). In that quarter he was looked on as a sprite or demon of fertilizing fountains, streams, marshy land, and luxuriant gar-

Silenus.

dens, as well as the inventor of such music as was produced by the syrinx (Pan's pipe) and the double flute which was used in the worship of Rhea and Dionysus.

According to other stories, he was born in and was the first king of Nysa, but which of the many places of that name remains untold. It was most probably Nysa in Thrace; for Silenus, with the help of local nymphs, nursed and tended the infancy of Dionysus, as works of art show, and this, according to the myths, was spent in Thrace.

To the Greek mind he appeared specially as a companion of Dionysus, one who knew how to press the grapes for wine, and so much loved that liquid as readily to indulge in it to excess, in which case the Satyrs kept him steady on his ass, or else he would have fallen. To express this feature of his character, he was figured with a wreath of vine tendrils on his head, with a drinking-cup or wine-skin in his hand, or intoxicated and supported by two Satyrs. He was a short, round-bellied, hairy old man, with a bald head.

The ass or mule he used to ride was described as a most intelligent beast, and said to have distinguished itself at the time of the war with the Giants, in which its master, as companion and body-servant, a sort of Sancho Panza, to Dionysus, took part, by braying so loudly as to alarm the Giants, and help to put them to flight.

OCEANUS, TETHYS, PROTEUS.

Oceanus, son of **Uranus** and **Gaea,** was god of the sea, and, like **Nereus,** was looked upon as the father of a large family of marine deities who went by the general name of Oceanides. He was figured like Nereus, but with the addition of a bull's horn, or two short horns, a sceptre in his hand to indicate his power, riding on a monster of the deep, or sitting with his wife, **Tethys,** by his side in a car drawn by creatures of the sea. He is said to have been the most upright of his brother Titans, and to have had no share in the conspiracy against Uranus. For this reason he retained his office, while the other Titans were consigned to

Tartarus. It was under the care of Oceanus and his wife that Hera grew up, and to them she turned for safety during the war with the Titans. So quickly had his offspring spread among the rivers, streams, and fountains of the earth, that the sons alone were reckoned as three thousand in number. He was also identified with the great stream, Oceanus, which was supposed to flow in a circle around the earth, and to be the source of all rivers and running waters. His daughters, the Oceanides, were, like all marine deities, represented with crowns of sea-weeds, strings of corals, holding shells, and riding on dolphins. Painters rendered them as half human and half fish in shape ; but poets described them as beings of purely human form, giving their number very differently.

Proteus was a son of Oceanus and Tethys, whose proper dwelling-place was the depths of the sea, which he only left for the purpose of taking the sea-calves of Poseidon to graze on the coasts and islands of the Mediterranean. Being an aged man, he was looked on as possessed of prophetic power and the secrets of witchcraft, though he would not be persuaded to exercise the former except by deceit or under threat of violence. Even then he made every effort to evade his questioners, changing himself into a great variety of shapes, such as those of a lion, panther, swine, or serpent, and, as a last resource, into the form of fire or water. This faculty of transformation, which both Proteus and Thetis possessed, corresponds with the great changeability in the appearance of the sea.

NEREUS AND THE NEREIDES,

Or Dorides, as they were sometimes called, are frequently confounded in mythology with Oceanus and his daughters, the Oceanides, all of them being marine deities of a lower order.

Nereus was looked on as an ancient sea-god, a son of Pontus and Gaea, who, when the dominion of the sea fell to

Poseidon, obtained a position under him, and along with it
the power of prophecy.   With Doris, his wife, he had as
offspring fifty, or, according to other accounts, a hundred
daughters, called Nereides or Dorides, of whom **Amphitrite**
and **Thetis**, and next to them **Panope** and **Galatea**, were
the most famous, the first mentioned having become the wife
of Poseidon, while even Zeus desired to marry the second.
But the Fates having announced that from this marriage
would issue a son who would surpass his father in might,

Nereid.

Zeus relinquished his wish, and gave Thetis in marriage to
Peleus, to whom she bore **Achilles**, and thereafter returned
to live among her sisters of the sea.

Nereus is represented in works of art as an old man with
a look of dignity, his daughters as sweet, beautiful maidens.
Poets described them as modest nymphs dwelling in a splendid cave at the bottom of the sea, now riding on dolphins or
other creatures of the deep, now swimming, sporting, splash-
ing about in troops on the sea, sometimes accompanying the
sea-born **Aphrodite**, or playing in the warm sunshine on the

PHOEBUS APOLLO.

shores of bays and at rivers' mouths, drying their wet tresses. In such places they were duly worshipped. To the pious feelings of the Greeks the whole of nature appeared in some way divine, and was accordingly viewed with reverence and sanctity. In this spirit the phenomena of the sea were viewed under the form of divine personifications called Nereides, the peaceful shimmering light upon its gently moving bosom being represented by Galene and Glauce, the play of fantastic waves by Thoe and Halie, the impetuous rush of billows on island shores by Nesaee and Actaea, the fascination of the gaily rising tide by Pasithea, Erato, and Euneice, the swell and impulse of mighty waves by Pherusa and Dynamene, who all followed in the train of Amphitrite.

It may be that these myths gave rise to the modern legends of mermaids.

TRITON AND THE TRITONS.

Triton, sometimes said to be a son of Poseidon and Amphitrite, sometimes of Oceanus and Tethys, was a marine deity of a lower order, and the herald of Neptune, in which capacity he was represented using a long twisted shell as a horn to blow a loud blast from when the sea was to be agitated with storms, and a gentle note when a storm was to be hushed into rest. When Neptune travelled on the waves, it was Triton who announced his approach and summoned the other marine deities. The Tritons were like him in figure, and had similar duties to perform. Occasionally we find him described in stories as a monster who, by his wantonness and voracity, rendered the seashore dangerous, and was, in consequence, attacked by Dionysus and Hercules.

In the war with the Giants he rendered considerable service to Zeus, by raising such a frightful din with his shrill trumpet, that the Giants, fearing the approach of some powerful monster or some fresh danger, retired.

Triton and the Tritons were represented in works of art

as beings of human form down to the hips, covered with small scales, holding a sea-shell in their hands, the lower part of them formed by the body and tail of a dolphin. Triton was also described as driving on the sea in a chariot drawn by horses.

Tritons.

Our illustration represents a family group of **Tritons** with a dolphin in the background.

In the early myths concerning Triton, he appears as the personification of the roaring sea, and, like Neptune and Amphitrite, lived in a golden palace in the depths of the ocean.

LEUCOTHEA

Was regarded by sailors and those who travelled on the sea as their special and friendly goddess, a character which she displayed in her timely assistance of **Odysseus** (Ulysses) in his dangerous voyage. She is said to have been a daughter of **Cadmus**, the great-grandson of Poseidon. Originally the wife of **Athamas**, in which capacity she bore the name of **Ino**, she had incurred the wrath of Hera, because she had suckled the infant Bacchus, a son of her sister Semele and of Zeus, and for this was pursued by her raving husband, and thrown, along with her youngest son, Melicertes, into the sea, from which both mother and child were saved by a dolphin or by Nereides. From that time she took her place as a marine deity, and, under the name of Leucothea, was known as the protector of all travellers by sea, while her son came to be worshipped as god of harbors, under the name of Palaemon. Her worship, especially at Corinth, the oldest maritime town of importance in Greece, and in the islands of Rhodes, Tenedos, and Crete, as well as in the coast towns generally, was traced back to a high antiquity.

THE SIRENS,

According to one version of the myth, were daughters of the river-god Achelous (hence their other name, Acheloides) and a Muse. According to another version, they were daughters of Phorcys. In either case they had been nymphs and playmates of Persephone, and, for not protecting her when she was carried off by Pluto, were transformed by Demeter into beings half woman and half bird at first, and latterly with the lower part of the body in the shape of a fish, so that they had some resemblance to marine deities such as the Tritons.

Siren.

Our illustration represents a Siren, half bird and half woman in form, playing on a double flute.

In the Homeric poems their number is not specified. In later times the names of three of them are commonly given : Parthenope, Ligea, and Leucosia. It is said that once, during the time when the greater part of their body was that of a bird, they challenged the Muses to a competition in singing, but failed, and were punished by having the principal feathers of their wings plucked by the Muses, who decked themselves with them.

The common belief was that the Sirens inhabited the cliffs of the islands lying between Sicily and Italy, and that the sweetness of their voices bewitched passing mariners, compelling them to land only to meet their death. Skeletons lay thickly strewn around their dwelling; for they had obtained the right to exercise this cruel power of theirs on men so long as no crew succeeded in defying their charms. This the Argonauts, of whom more will be said hereafter, were the first to accomplish, by keeping their attention fixed on the unsurpassably sweet music of their companion, Orpheus. The next who passed safely was Odysseus (Ulysses). He had taken the precaution, on approaching, to stop the ears of his crew, so that they might be deaf to the bewitching music, and to have himself firmly bound to the mast, so that, while hearing the music, he would not be able to follow its allurements. In this way the power of the Sirens came to an end, and in despair they cast themselves into the sea, and were changed into cliffs.

This transformation helps to explain the signification of the myth of the Sirens, who were probably personifications of hidden banks and shallows, where the sea is smooth and inviting to the sailor, but proves in the end the destruction of his ship. The alluring music ascribed to them may either refer to the soft, melodious murmur of the waves, or be simply a figurative expression for allurement.

THE RIVER-GODS

Were, as a rule, looked upon as sons of **Oceanus**, exercising

The Nile God.

a dominion over individual rivers. They were represented

The Father of the Tiber.

as bearded men, crowned with sedge, and often with horns
on their heads, reclining and resting one hand on a rudder,

the other on a vase, out of which water flows, to indicate the constant flow of a river.

The names of many of them have been handed down in ancient myths, the most important being Alpheus, Achelous, Peneus, Asopus, Cephissus. Of Alpheus, it is said that he loved Arethusa, one of the myths in the train of Artemis, and so persistently followed her, though his affections were not returned, that Artemis interfered, and changed the nymph, to avoid his pursuit, into a fountain, the waters of which, notwithstanding, were said to join those of Alpheus.

NYMPHS.

The restless and fertile imagination of the ancients peopled with beings of a higher order than themselves every mountain, valley, plain, and forest, every thicket, bush, and tree, every fountain, stream, and lake. These beings, in whose existence both Greeks and Romans firmly believed, were called Nymphs, and resembled in many respects the mermaids and fairies of modern superstition.

Generally speaking, the Nymphs were a kind of middle-beings between the gods and men, communicating with both, loved and respected by both; gifted with the power of making themselves visible or invisible at pleasure; able to do many things only permitted to be done by the gods; living like the gods, on ambrosia; leading a cheerful, happy life of long duration, and retaining strength and youthfulness to the last, but not destined to immortality, like the gods. In extraordinary cases they were summoned, it was believed, to the councils of the Olympian gods, but usually remained in their particular spheres, in secluded grottoes and peaceful valleys, occupied in spinning, weaving, bathing, singing sweet songs, dancing, sporting, or accompanying deities who passed through their territories, hunting with Artemis (Diana), rushing about with Dionysus (Bacchus), making merry with

Apollo or Hermes (Mercury), but always in a hostile attitude toward the wanton and excited Satyrs.

Even the earliest of the ancient myths abound with accounts of the various things done by nymphs, while poetic
fancy in later times delighted to play with such creations.
The Greeks, the great mass of them at any rate, believed
firmly in the existence of a vast number of nymphs, and
attested their belief by erecting frequently very costly altars

Pegasus and the Nymphs.

in places where the presence and influence of these beings
were felt—as by fountains, or in moist meadows, in woods,
and on hills. Grottoes and caves where water dripped or
flowed, and where the bees hummed, were sacred to them.
Sanctuaries, called **Nymphae**, were also erected for their
special honor in well watered valleys, caves, and even in
towns, those in towns being particularly splendid in appearance, and commonly employed for the ceremonies of
marriage. The sacrifices presented to them consisted of
goats, lambs, milk, and oil, wine being forbidden.

As to the origin of the **Nymphs**, the stories are so many and so different that they cannot be all given here. Very many of these beings, it would seem, were the offspring of **Zeus** and **Thetis**. Separating them in the most convenient manner, according to their local habitations or reputed origin, we have the following classes :

1. **Dryades**, or **Hamadryades**, also called **Alseides**, nymphs of woods and trees, inhabiting groves, ravines, and wooded valleys, fond of making merry with **Apollo**, **Hermes** (Mercury), and **Pan**, and very attractive to the **Satyrs**. Sometimes they appeared as rustic huntresses or shepherdesses.

2. **Oreades**, or mountain-nymphs, sometimes also named after the particular mountains which they haunted, as Peliades (from Pelion), Idaean (from Ida), Cithaeronian (from Cithaeron), etc.

3. **Limoniades**, or **Leimoniades**, nymphs of meadows and flowers.

4. **Napaeae**, or **Auloniades**, nymphs of the mountain vales in which herds grazed. The last three families of nymphs were usually found in the company of **Pan**, rushing gaily and merrily over hills and valleys, through woods and meadows. A favorite and lovely nymph of the vales was **Eurydice**, who, being bitten by a snake, and dying in consequence, was mourned by all her sisters, and sung by **Orpheus** in most touching melancholy strains.

5. **Oceanides**, daughters of **Oceanus**, nymphs of fountains and streams, and named according to the characteristics of streams, as **Prymno**, " like a cascade which falls over an abrupt height;" **Hippo**, " like a swift current;" **Plexaure**, " like a dashing brook;" **Galaxaure**, " like the refreshing coolness of a shady stream;" **Calypso**, " like the hidden tide;" **Rhodia**, " flowing among rose-trees;" **Callirrhoe**, " like a beantiful stream;" **Melobosis**, " like a river that waters the meadows;" **Telesto**, " nymph of the cool springs," which the Greeks piously used for cleansing and purification.

6. Nereides, daughters of **Nereus**, sometimes also called Dorides, after their mother (see Nereus).

7. Naiades — generally speaking, nymphs of the liquid element, daughters of **Zeus**. They were styled "fostering" nymphs, and for this reason were commonly found in the company of **Zeus, Poseidon,** and **Dionysus,** as well as of **Demeter, Persephone,** and **Aphrodite,** and besides were looked on as deities of marriage and sacred rites.

8. Potameides, nymphs of the rivers.

9. Limnades, nymphs of lakes, marshes, and swamps, most dangerous beings, who allured and misled travellers by their songs or mimic screams for help.

10. Pleiades, seven daughters of **Atlas** and **Pleione,** sisters of the **Hyades.**

11. Atlantides, offspring of **Atlas,** and belonging to the same order as the last mentioned.

12. Hyades, according to the myth, daughters of **Atlas** and **Aethra** ; sisters, or, according to other versions, daughters of **Hyas.** Languishing of grief at the death of **Hyas,** which was caused by a wild animal, they were changed into stars, being the seven stars which form the head in the constellation of the Bull (Taurus). Their ascension takes place from May 17th to 21st, and usually indicates rain, for which reason they were often called the rainy stars. They were also called **Dodonides,** and described as the nurses of **Zeus** of Dodona. One of them was called **Thyene.**

All the most prominent of the nymphs had names of their own.

They were represented as damsels of wonderful beauty, with attributes suitable to their respective avocations.

Our illustration represents three of them tending **Pegasus** at a fountain. All three have their hair bound with sedge; two of them have vases.

ECHO : NARCISSUS.

Echo was a mountain-nymph, and at the same time a servant of Hera, according to one account, but had to be kept

Echo and Narcissus.

at a distance on account of her talkativeness. In other accounts she is described as a beautiful nymph whom the forest-god Pan loved. Happening to meet the beautiful

Narcissus, a son of the river-god Cephissus, she conceived a very tender passion for him, which he unfortunately
did not return. Echo grieved in consequence, and pined
away day by day till at length her voice was all that was
left of her. She then took to the mountains and woods
which Pan frequented, and occupied herself in mimicking
every vocal sound she heard.

Narcissus was a personification of the consequences of
self-conceit in the matter of personal appearance, his vanity
being such that he used to idle by the brinks of clear fountains, and gaze upon the reflection of his own face, till at last
he languished in his unreturned love for it. Other stories
affirm that he was punished for this conduct by the gods, by
being changed into a flower which still bears his name.

THE HESPERIDES

Were daughters of Atlas, an enormous giant, who, as the
ancients believed, stood upon the western confines of the
earth, and supported the heavens on his shoulders. Their
mother was Hesperis, a personification of the " region of the
West," where the sun continued to shine after he had set on
Greece, and where, as travellers told, was an abundance of
choice delicious fruits, which could only have been produced
by a special divine influence. The Gardens of the Hesperides with the golden apples were believed to exist in some
island in the ocean, or, as it was sometimes thought, in the
islands on the north or west coast of Africa. They were
far-famed in antiquity; for it was there that springs of nectar
flowed by the couch of Zeus, and there that the earth displayed the rarest blessings of the gods : it was another Eden.
As knowledge increased with regard to western lands it became necessary to move this paradise farther and farther out
into the Western Ocean.

As to the origin of these precious golden apples, there is a
myth which says that among the deities who attended the mar-

riage ceremony of Zeus and Hera, bringing various presents with them, was **Titaea**, a goddess of the earth, whose gift

Atlas.

consisted in her causing a tree to spring up with golden apples on it. The care of this tree, which highly pleased the newly wedded pair, was entrusted to the Hesperides. But, as they could not resist the temptation to pluck and eat its fruit, it became necessary to place the serpent Ladon to watch it. Hercules, among his other adventures, slew this serpent and carried off some of the apples, which, however, were afterward returned to the Hesperides, through the kindness of Athene.

The common account speaks of only three Hesperides— Aegle, Erytheis, and Hespera. Arethusa was afterward added, and in time three more, so that they were seven in all.

THE MUSES,

Or Pierides, as they were also styled, were regarded as nymphs of the springs that bickered down the sides of Mount Helicon and Mount Parnassus, called Castalia, Aganippe, and Pimpla or Pimplea, the waters of which were thought to have the property of inspiration. Their origin was traced to Zeus and the Titanic nymph Mnemosyne, the name of Pierides being applied to them from Pieria, on Mount Olympus, the reputed place of their birth, a locality which appears to have been originally the principal centre of their worship, whence it spread first and most conspicuously to Mount Helicon, in Boeotia, and father to Athens, Sparta, Troezen, and elsewhere. It was usual to ascribe this extension of the worship of the Muses to a Thracian named Pierus, of whom it was also said that, having nine daughters, he named them each after one of the Muses,

Mother of the Muses.

and challenged the latter to a competition in music, the upshot of which was that his daughters lost the award, and were, as punishment for their daring, transformed into singing-birds. The worship of the Muses on Mount Helicon was celebrated in a grove, in which were the sacred

fountains of **Aganippe** and **Hippocrene**, with many monuments of art dedicated to the Muses, contests called **Musea** being associated with the ceremonies.

The nine Muses whom we are accustomed to read of in the Greek and Roman mythology, were looked upon

Clio.

Melpomene.

as the patron goddesses of music and song, of poetry, and of the fine arts generally, that tended to promote the civilization of mankind. Their local habitation was on the summits of Mounts Helicon, Parnassus, and Pindus. They would, however, frequently visit Olympus, to gladden the blessed existence of the gods there by the exercise of their arts, especially by music and the recital of songs, the burden of which was probably, as on most other occasions, the glory and omnipotence of Zeus. Sometimes they would lend their presence also to enliven happy incidents in the lives of favorite mortals—such, for example, as the marriage of Cadmus and Harmonia, or that of Peleus and Thetis; and sometimes even at moments of great sorrow, as at the death of Achilles, they would descend to mourn in strains which drew forth tears from gods and men. Their leader was Apollo, who in that capacity bore the title of Musagetes. But though generally associated with Apollo, and probably, therefore, imbued with the form of inspiration peculiar to the god of oracles, they are also found to have been connected with the worship of Dionysus, whose inspiration is known to have been of a wild and excited nature. As nymphs

Thalia.

of the sacred streams on the mountains where they lived, their music and song must, for the sake of harmony, have repeated the rushing movement of water, and it may be to this that their association with Dionysus is due.

In addition to the usual nine we hear of three other Muses—Melete, Mneme, and Aoede, who are described as daughters of **Uranus**, and supposed to have existed from the earliest times. As, however, both Homer and Hesiod appear

Calliope.

to know only the number nine, we may assume that the belief in the existence of the other three must have originated in the speculations of comparatively later times.

Urania.

In works of art of the earlier period the Muses were always represented together in company, all wearing the same kind of dress, and all provided with attributes in the forms of musical instruments—such as the lyre, harp, and flute, or with

Euterpe.

rolls of manuscript. The custom of collecting in such rolls literary works produced under the auspices of the Muses was the first foundation of libraries and museums, such as they exist in modern times, and thus the word "museum" carries us back to the early worship of the Muses, and to the early civilization so far as it was due to their inspiration.

The nine Muses were represented according to their various avocations in the following manner:

1. **Clio**, the muse of History, seated wearing a wreath of laurel, and holding out a half-open inscribed parchment roll;

beside her a cylindrical box, containing more of these manuscripts. In other cases she appears standing, holding a roll of manuscript in one hand, an instrument for writing in the other.

2. **Melpomene**, the muse of Tragedy, a serious, dignified figure, standing with her left foot raised on a rock, holding in her right hand a mask, such as was worn by tragedians, and in her left apparently a small roll of a part in a play; her long robe or tunic is girt under her breast, and falls in wide folds; from her shoulder a mantle or *peplos* falls carelessly. In other cases she wears a diadem or a wreath of cypress, and holds a short sword or a club in her hand.

Polyhymnia.

3. **Thalia**, the muse of Comedy and Burlesque, standing, clad in a robe or tunic, over which is a mantle, with a fringe, thrown over the left shoulder, and wrapped round the legs, leaving the right arm free; in her right hand is a shepherd's crook, in the other a mask, such as was worn by actors in the Satyric plays.

4. **Calliope**, the muse of Heroic Poems, and looked on as the chief of the Muses, on which account she sometimes appears as their representative; seated, holding a writing tablet and a *stylus*. In other cases she is standing, crowned with a wreath, and holding a manuscript roll in her hand, or a pipe (*tuba*) round which a branch of laurel is twined.

5. **Urania**, the muse of Astronomy, seated beside a globe, holding a pair of compasses in one hand, while with the other she points upward toward the heavens. In other cases she wears a crown of stars, and holds a lyre, her eyes turned toward the stars, and pointing out at the same time something on a globe beside her.

6. Euterpe, the muse of the art of Music, the "giver of pleasure," as her name implies, standing, playing on a double flute. In other cases she plays on other instruments.

7. Polyhymnia, or Polymnia, the muse of Song and of Oratory, her name signifying "rich in song," was also described as the inventor of myths, on which account she was represented in the attitude of contemplation, with one finger raised to her lips; on her head a laurel wreath. In other cases she appears in a quiet, attentive, observant mood, leaning forward on a pillar, her arms concealed under her drapery, and wearing at times a veil, to indicate the hidden truths within the myths, while her posture was intended to indicate the process of revolving the meaning of them. For this reason she was also viewed as the goddess of serious and sacred poems and hymns.

Erato.

8. Erato, the muse of Love and Marriage Songs, wearing a wreath, and playing on a large lyre with many strings. In other cases she appears holding a lyre by her side in one hand, and in the other an arrow or a wreath of myrtle and roses.

9. Terpsichore, the muse of Dancing, wearing a wreath, and playing on a lyre. At other times she holds cymbals, has her robe girt up, and appears in the attitude of dancing.

The mother of the Muses was called, as has already been stated, Mnemosyne, that is, "Memory," and especially the memory or recollection of great events, such as the war with the Titans, that was said to have occurred at the commencement of the world's history, and must continue to occur until the universe is brought into perfect harmony. In later times she came to be viewed merely as goddess of memory, and worshipped along with the Muses.

In art she is represented standing in a quiet, thoughtful attitude, both arms under her drapery, to indicate the silent mysterious action of memory.

It was the custom of the Muses to play under the leadership of Apollo, at the banquets and marriage ceremonies among the gods, while the Horae, Charites (Graces), Aphrodite, and other deities given to mirth and gaiety, danced. In this fashion the ancients represented under the form of persons the union of joy, music, poetry, dance, and merriment.

Terpsichore.

IRIS,

Goddess of the rainbow, was a daughter of **Thaumas** and **Electra**, a grand-daughter of **Oceanus** and **Gaea**, and a sister of the **Harpies**. As messenger of Hera and Zeus, she lived among the other deities of Olympus, which she only left for the purpose of conveying the divine commands to mankind, by whom she was looked on as a guide and adviser. She travelled with the speed of wind always, from one end of the world to the other, could penetrate to the bottom of the sea, or to the Styx, and in this respect formed a female counterpart of **Hermes** (Mercury) in his capacity of messenger of the gods, she holding much the same position toward Hera as he did toward Zeus.

It was Iris, the ancients believed, who charged the clouds

with water from lakes and rivers, in order that they might
let it fall again upon the earth in gentle fertilizing showers;

and, accordingly, when her bow
appeared in the clouds the
farmer welcomed it as a sign
of rain to quicken his fields,
and gladly paid honors to the
goddess whose presence he recognized in the rainbow with its
splendid colors.

She was represented as a
beautiful virgin with wings of
varied hue, in robes of bright
colors, and riding on a rainbow; at other times with a
nimbus on her head, in which
the colors of the rainbow were
reflected.

Our figure represents her
standing, clad in a long robe,

Iris.

holding in one hand a herald's staff, such as Hermes also
carries (*caduceus*), and in the other a helmet.

AEOLUS

Was the son of a king named Hippotes, and lived on one of
the abrupt rocky Lipara islands close to Sicily, along with
his offspring, six sons and six daughters, who were married
in pairs, and made life merry with their music. In the
caves of the island were imprisoned the winds, Aeolus letting
them out in gales, or in a soft favoring breeze, at the will of
the higher gods.

The idea of the winds being thus kept in a cavern under
the restraint of a divine person, appears to have suggested
itself to the ancients from the strong draught that is felt on

entering a cave or subterraneous passage; but whether the belief in the existence of such a personage reached back to primitive times, when mankind lived to a great extent in places of that kind, is not certain. The influence of Aeolus was felt both genially and the reverse on land and on sea, but principally on sea, which he could more readily command from the island where he lived.

As an instance of his kindliness to travellers by sea, we may here mention his hospitable reception of Odysseus (Ulysses) on that errant homeward voyage of his. On departing, Aeolus gave him a great bag containing all the contrary winds, putting it on board the ship, so that he might reach Ithaca with a fair wind. Odysseus himself remained steadily and anxiously at the helm for several days, but his native land coming at length in sight, he sank overpowered with sleep. His followers observing this proceeded to indulge their curiosity to see the costly presents which they fancied the bag contained, opened it, and out burst the imprisoned wind with a roar and a force that drove the ship again far out of her course.

But besides this conception of the winds as mere elements in the hands of Aeolus, there was another which represented them as each personified by a separate divine being, living apart, and being directly under the control of Zeus and Poseidon.

THE WIND-GODS,

Of whom the principal were Boreas, the north wind, Eurus, the east wind, Notus, the south wind, and Zephyrus, the west wind, were, as we have previously said, the offspring of Eos and Astraeus, the parentage of fierce, destructive winds being assigned to Typhon. According to another report, neither the origin nor the number of the deities of the winds was known, the prevalence in particular districts of winds blowing from this or that point between the four chief quarters, naturally giving rise to a set of personifications such as northwest wind, southwest wind, and others.

The character and appearance ascribed to each of these deities was, as usual in Greek mythology, such as was suggested by the phenomena of each wind—as, for example, the strength and fury of the north wind, or the genial warmth of the southwest. Some were thought to be male, some female, and all winged. Eurus, who brought warmth and rain from the east, was represented holding a vase inverted,

Boreas Carrying off Orithyia.

as if pouring rain from it. Lips, who from the southeast wafted home the ships as they neared the harbor of Piraeus at Athens, held the ornament from a ship's stern in her hands. Zephyrus, coming from the warm, mild west, was lightly clad, and carried a quantity of flowers in his scarf. Apeliotes, the southeast wind, carried fruits of many kinds, wore boots, and was not so lightly clad as the last mentioned. So they were represented on the "Tower of the Winds" at Athens.

Though the winds were looked on as each under the control of a separate divine being, whose favor it was necessary to retain by sacrifice, no particular story or myth is told of any one of these persons excepting Boreas and Zephyrus, the rival lovers of Chloris (Flora), Zephyrus being the successful suitor. Boreas carried off, it was said, Orithyia, the beautiful daughter of Cecrops, king of Attica; and remembering this, the Athenians in their distress, when the Persians advanced the first time against Greece, called upon him for aid, which he rendered by sending a terrible north wind, which overtook the Persian fleet near the promontory of Athos, scattering and largely destroying it. From that time the Athenians had an altar to him, and offered sacrifice at it for their preservation.

The scene of Boreas carrying off Orithyia is represented on a beautiful bronze relief found at Calymna, and now in the British Museum. The wind-god is powerful in form, bearded, but still young, and wearing thick, high boots, and a mantle thrown across his body.

EOS, OR AURORA: LUCIFER.

Eos was a daughter of the Titan pair, Theia and Hyperion; the latter, to judge from the meaning of his name,

Eos, or Aurora.

having been at one time god of the sun, " who travels high above earth." Helios and Selene, the deities of sun and

moon, were her brother and sister, while she herself was a
personification of the dawn of morning.   A fresh wind was
felt at her approach, the morning star still lingered in the
sky, and ruddy beams " shot the orient through with gold;"
and because these beams appeared like outspread fingers, she
was called " rosy-fingered Morn."   The star and the winds
of the morning, **Zephyrus, Boreas, Notus,** and **Eurus,** were
ner offspring by **Astraeus,** the god of starlight.   The moon
and the other stars vanished gradually as she advanced, but
Helios followed her closely.   To poets she seemed to lift the

Eos and Cephalus.

veil of night with rose-tinted fingers, and to rise in the east
out of the ocean in a car with four white steeds, shedding
light upon the earth.   Others imagined her coming riding
on the winged horse, Pegasus, which Zeus had given her
after **Bellerophon's** failure to ride on it up to Olympus.

   She loved all fresh young life, and showed special favor to
those persons whose active spirit led them abroad in the
morning to hunt or to make war.   When struck with the
beauty of a youth she would carry him off, and obtain immortal life for him, as she did with **Cleitus, Orion, Cepha-**

lus, and Tithonus. So it appeared to the Greeks, who recognized in the brief duration of the freshness and glow of morning a comparison with the early death of promising and beautiful youth, and from the comparison proceeded to construct a myth which should trace both to the same divine cause.

Tithonus became her husband, and she lived with him pleasantly beside the Oceanus so long as his youth and beauty lasted. Unfortunately, in obtaining immortality for him from Zeus, she had omitted to add to her request, "and eternal youth." When white hairs showed themselves on

The Death of Procris.

his head she was not the same to him as before, though still supplying him with ambrosia and fine raiment. But he became quite helpless at last, and, to avoid the sight of his descrepitude, she shut him up in a chamber, where only his voice was heard like the chirp of a grasshopper, into which creature, it was said, he became transformed. By the story of Tithonus we would understand day, in its eternally returning course, fresh and beautiful at dawn, wearied and worn at the close.

Of Cephalus it is said that from love to his wife, Procris, he resolutely withstood the advances of Aura, the goddess of the morning wind, and that the latter in revenge stirred up discord between him and his wife. Another version of the story is, that Aura caused him to kill his wife by mistake when out on the chase. Procris, it would seem, jealous of her husband's meetings with the goddess, had secreted herself in a thicket to watch them; but happening to stir, Cephalus caught the noise, and suspecting it to be caused by some lurking animal, hurled his spear, and slew his wife.

Eos and Tithonus had two sons, Memnon and Emathion, the former widely celebrated for his beauty, and mourned for his early death at the hands of Achilles. His dead body was carried by his weeping mother to Aethiopia; and at Thebes, in Egypt, she erected in his memory, so the story goes, that wonderful monument which, when the first rays of the morning sun touched it, gave forth a sound like the snapping of a harp-string.

In art she was represented as a spirited maiden, with large wings, clad in robes of dazzling white and purple, a star or cap on her head, a torch in her hand, and driving in a chariot with four horses, or riding on Pegasus; at other times she appeared floating in the air, and pouring morning dew from a vessel down to the earth.

In our illustration (p. 185) she is figured driving a *quadriga* with great speed, as is indicated by the flow of her drapery. The bull's head signifies that the moon and stars are still in the sky. Lucifer precedes her with a torch. Flowers and plants, quickened by her dew, wake and raise their heads. In the British Museum is a beautiful example of early gem engraving, representing a head of her.

In other representations we find Hermes advancing before her, a duty which Lucifer, the morning star, and a favorite of Aphrodite and Hera also, most usually performs.

EROS, OR AMOR: PSYCHE.

Amor, or Cupido, as he was also called, was not, it should be noticed, a native Roman deity, but had been introduced from the mythology of the Greeks by poets, his name being

Cupid and Psyche.

a direct translation of the Greek Eros. It should further be observed that this translation presents an instance of the difference in character of these two ancient races; the word for "love" among the Greeks being feminine, while its Roman equivalent was masculine.

We must at the outset distinguish the double character of Eros; first, as we find him described taking part at the creation of the world out of Chaos, and secondly, as a mere god of love, a son of Aphrodite and Zeus, or Ares, as some said, or even of Uranus. In the former phase of his character he is represented as sorting the shapeless mass of the world, with its conflicting elements, into order and harmony, dispelling confusion, uniting hitherto jarring forces, and making productive what was barren before. In the latter phase he is the deity who sways the passions of the heart both of gods and men. In the one case he was conceived as having existed before the other gods, as being the god of that love which operates in nature; and in the other case as the youngest born of them all, the god of that love which holds the hearts of men in tyranny. It seems to have been as a combination of both characters that Phidias* represented him at the birth of Aphrodite, receiving her as she rose out of the sea, in presence of the assembled deities of Olympus.

The chief and oldest centre of his worship was Thespiae, in Boeotia, where a festival called Erotidia was celebrated in his honor, and continued to be a source of attraction down to Roman times. Thence his worship spread to Sparta, Athens, Samos, and Crete, the Spartans and Cretans having a custom of sacrificing to him previous to the commencement of a battle, in the belief that he was also the god of that patriotism or love of country which best unites an army. In Athens there was an altar to him and his counterpart, Anteros.

In early times his worshippers at Thespiae were content with a rude stone as an image. But in later times, and in contrast with this, we find him the most attractive figure among the works of the second Attic school of sculptors, the

---

* On the base of the statue of Zeus at Olympia.

school of Scopas and Praxiteles,* both of whom directed
their splendid talents to adding fresh grace and beauty to

Psyche at the Couch of Cupid.

his form. While artists rivalled each other to this end, poets
were no less zealous in singing his praises. In daily life his

---

* The famous statue of him by Praxiteles was afterward carried off to Rome, and
is known to us through copies of it made by other sculptors.

influence became more generally acknowledged. In the gymnasia where the youth practised athletics his statue was set up between Hermes and Hercules; for he was then represented as lithe of limb and graceful of form—a model of ripening youth. As time went on, however, his figure became more and more that of the chubby boy who plays all manner of tricks with the hearts of men, with which we are most familiar. He was supposed to exercise his influence over the hearts of deities as well; and to show him in this light, he was represented at times now with the symbol of one god, now of another.

To the later age of Hellenistic and Roman poetry and art belongs the touching story of Psyche—a personification, as she appears to have been, of a soul filled with the passion of love, and as such conceived under the form of a small winged maiden, or, at other times, as a butterfly which bore the same name. Psyche, the story runs, was a king's daughter, and most beautiful. The fame of her beauty awoke the jealousy of Aphrodite, who to get rid of her rival charged her son Cupid to visit the princess, and inspire her with love for some common man. Cupid obeyed so far as to pay the visit, but being himself struck with the maiden's beauty, carried her off to a fairy palace in a vale of paradise, where they spent happy hours together, with only this drawback, that she was not permitted to look upon her lover with her mortal eyes. Even this she would not have considered a drawback, had not her envious sisters stirred up her curiosity in the matter. Yielding to their temptation, she took one night a lamp, and stole into the chamber where the god lay asleep. Alarmed at the discovery she had made, she let a drop of hot oil fall upon his shoulder. He awoke, and charging her with disobedience to his express command, left her alone to her despair. She searched for him everywhere in vain, finding her way at last to the palace of Aphrodite, who, after subjecting her to menial service of various kinds, finally ordered her to go down to the lower world, and fetch

APHRODITE, OR VENUS

Psyche in the Lower World.

a box of beauty's ointment from Persephone. This most painful task she accomplished; but, on opening the box, sank overpowered by its odor. Cupid could resist no longer, ran to her help, and brought her back to life. The anger of Aphrodite was appeased, and the marriage of Cupid and Psyche was forthwith celebrated with great rejoicings, in presence of the higher gods, Psyche obtaining immortality.

The purpose of the story is obviously to illustrate the three stages in the existence of a soul — its pre-existence in a blessed state, its existence on earth with its trials and anguish, and its future state of happy immortality.

The engraving represents the two embracing tenderly. Eros has laid aside his bow and quiver, with its dangerous arrows; roses are strewn on the ground before them, and a shoot of a rose-tree grows behind to symbolize the sweetness and beauty of young love.

In works of art he is frequently to be seen in company of his mother Aphrodite, or playing with the Muses and Graces, or struggling with his opposite Anteros, or accompanied by Pothos, whose name, like the Roman Cupido, signifies a "desire of love"—that is, a "desire of union in love," and Himeros, a "soft yearning for love." In later times artists often surrounded Aphrodite, and occasionally also Dionysus, with troops of little winged figures of children, which we call Erotes or Amorettes.

The word *Psyche*, signifying originally the "soul," came afterward to mean also a "butterfly"—a likeness being observed between the manner in which a soul and a butterfly, freed from the body or chrysalis in which they have been confined on earth, rise on wing, and waft themselves in the light. The flame of love which often scorched the soul was compared with the torch which attracts the butterfly to its doom. When this happened, Eros turned away his face and wept.

HYMEN, OR HYMENAEUS,

Was worshipped as the god of marriage both by the Greeks
and the Romans. His origin is variously stated to have
been now from Apollo and Calliope, now from Dionysus and
Aphrodite, while at other times he is said to have been by
birth a mortal, and afterward deified. Properly speaking,
he is a personification of the marriage song. There are various accounts of his life and deification, and among them the
following :

Young, and of a soft delicate beauty, so that he might be
mistaken for a girl, Hymen loved a young Athenian maiden,
whom, however, because of his poverty, he could not hope
to obtain for his wife. To be near her, he once joined a
troop of maidens, among whom she was engaged in celebrat-
ing a festival to Demeter at Eleusis. Suddenly a band of
robbers appeared from a hiding-place, carried the maidens off
to their ship, and set out with the intention of selling them
as slaves in some distant country. But landing on the way
on a dreary island, the robbers indulged so copiously in wine
that they all fell into deep slumber. Hymen, seizing the
opportunity, incited his fellow-captives to take the weapons
from the robbers and slay them all, which they did. Thereupon he set off to Athens in the ship, and finding the people
there in great distress, presented himself to the parents of
the maiden he loved, and undertook to bring her back un-
harmed on condition of their giving her to him as his wife.
This was readily promised. Finding a crew he at once set
sail for the island, and speedily returned with all the maidens
on board. For this he obtained the title of Thalassius, as
well as the wife that had been promised him. So happy was
his wedded life that at marriage ceremonies generally his
name was on the lips of all the company, and he himself in
course of time came to be looked on as a god, and the founder
and protector of marriage rights. At bridal festivities a

sacrifice was offered to him, festal songs were sung, and flowers and wreaths strewn.

Hymen, or Hymenaeus.

As a deity he was placed among the playmates of Eros and in the company of Aphrodite. His home, it was believed, was among the Muses on Mount Helicon in Boeotia. There is a story which says that he lost his voice and his life in singing the marriage song of Dionysus and Ariadne or Althaea. He is always a picture of youthful beauty, and of the charms of love and song.

Hymen was represented as a beautiful youth with a mantle of a golden color—sometimes nude—and carrying a torch.

THE CHARITES, OR GRACES,

Were looked upon by the Greeks as the goddesses of the gracefulness and the charms of beauty, and of cheerful amusement, which were observed both in nature and in the intercourse with men. As such, their worship dated from a very early time in Orchomenus in Boeotia, in Sparta, Athens, and Crete; the games held in their honor in the last-mentioned place being said to have existed even in the time of the prehistoric king Minos. Their oldest sanctuary was said to be that at Orchomenus. It contained images of them in the form of rude stones which were supposed to have fallen from heaven.

The Graces.

The manifold beauty which the works of nature, especially in springtime, display, would seem to have given rise in very early times to a belief in the existence of certain goddesses at first simply as guardians of the vernal sweetness and beauty of nature, and afterward as the friends and protectors of everything graceful and beautiful—an idea which the poets further developed.

Pindar, in one of his most delightful songs of victory, sing-ing of the Graces, associates with them the source of decorum, of purity and happiness in life, of good will, beneficence and gratitude among men.

They were represented as beautiful young modest maidens, winning and charming, always dancing, singing, and run-ning, or bathing in fountains, or decking themselves with early flowers, especially with roses; for the rose was sacred to them, as well as to Aphrodite (Venus), in whose com-pany, and doing her many a service, according to the myth, they were usually to be found. Their home was among the Muses in the neighborhood of Olympus, where they often appeared as companions of Aphrodite, and danced before the other deities.

Their origin is variously stated—now Zeus and Eurynome, an Oceanid, being assigned as their parents, now Dionysus and Aphrodite. There is a difference also in the statements of their names and number. From Orchomenus, it would seem, come Aglaea, Euphrosyne, and Thalia. In Sparta and in Athens there were only two, the pair worshipped in the former town being called Cleta (clang) and Phaenna (glimmer), in the latter town, Auxo and Hegemone. In the Iliad a whole race of them is mentioned, old and young —the youngest being Pasithea. According to another ac-count, the youngest was Aglaea, the wife of Hephaestus (Vulcan), the object in assigning him such a wife being probably to indicate the perfect beauty of the works of art produced by that god. Beauty and sweetness, the best charm of poetry, came from the Graces. Athene (Minerva) called in their aid in the serious business of life over which she presided, because without gracefulness all labor was in vain, the Greeks believed. They assisted Hermes (Mercury) in his capacity as god of oratory. From these instances of their activity it will be seen how highly the Greeks prized this quality of gracefulness.

In Greece there was a number of temples and beautiful

groups of statuary in their honor, sometimes devoted to them alone, sometimes to them in common with other deities; as, for example, Aphrodite, Apollo, and the Muses. Annual festivals, called Charitesia, accompanied with games, music, and dance, were held in their honor. It was the custom also to call upon them in taking an oath, and at banquets the first cup of wine was offered to them.

In early times they were represented in art as draped figures, but in later times as quite nude, or but sparingly clothed, and occupied in a dance. Their attributes were the rose, the myrtle, and dice, as a symbol of cheerful amusement. At other times they hold apples or perfume-vases, or ears of corn, or heads of poppies, or musical instruments—such as the lyre, flute, and syrinx.

PITHO, OR SUADA,

Or Suadela, was the goddess of persuasion, and, like the Graces, formed part of the escort of Aphrodite, whose daughter she was said to be.

Her worship, along with Aphrodite, was introduced into Athens by Theseus, at the time when he succeeded in persuading the various isolated tribes inhabiting Attica to unite into one people, with Athens as their chief town. But she had temples in other places also, and was looked on as a deity to whose influence much was due.

HEBE,

Or Ganymeda, or Dia, as she was called in the vine-growing districts of Phlius, where she was worshipped as the principal deity, was daughter of Zeus and Hera, and was the goddess of youth, herself remaining always young, and warding off age, like the other deities, by means of nectar

and ambrosia. Her name among the Romans was **Juventas.**
In Olympus she held the office of cup-bearer to the gods, for
which it is supposed that she
was peculiarly adapted, first,
because of her association
with the vine-growers of
Phlius, and, secondly, because
she was the youngest daughter of the regal pair of Olympus, and as such, on the
analogy of human arrange-
ments, would be expected
to wait upon the divine

Hebe.

guests, as Briseis did on Achilles,
or Hippodamia on Oenomaus, or
as, in real life, Melissa, the
daughter of Procles, king of
Epidaurus, poured out wine for
her father's men with a grace
which captivated Periander. The
difficulty of explaining how Hebe
and Ganymedes would both hold
the same office was met in various
ways, of which one was to assume
her to have been cup-bearer in

Ganymedes.

general and him cup-bearer to Zeus in particular, while another
supposed that Hebe only held the office while Ganymedes
was absent from Olympus during the Trojan war, so as

to avoid witnessing the misfortunes of his native country.
Among her other duties she had to assist Hera to yoke her

Hebe.

car.   When Apollo and the Muses played she danced with
other deities.   At times she accompanied Aphrodite.   But the

character in which she was best known and most admired was that of the bride and wife of Hercules when he was

Ganymedes.

raised to Olympus in reward for his extraordinary labors on earth. This union of Hebe, the favorite daughter of Hera, with Hercules, whom she had constantly persecuted while on earth, is unknown to the Iliad. The character of the myth, however, appears to point to a very early origin. The singular climax of events which made Hercules the guest of the gods of Olympus and the husband of the most attractive of the goddesses was a subject which was made the most of by the comic poets. Representations of the marriage procession, and of Hercules receiving a cup of wine from Hebe, occur in ancient sculpture. In other cases she appears in the company of her mother Hera, or alone, or in the character of Ganymeda, fondling the eagle of Zeus, or giving it drink from a cup, as occurs not infrequently on engraved gems.

At the town of Phlius, in the district of Argolis, there was, in a fine grove, a celebrated temple in her honor, which served as a place of refuge or asylum, in which slaves who had been set free hung up their chains among the cypresses sacred to the goddess.

In Rome Juventas had two sanctuaries, one on the Capitol, the other beside the great race-course. It was the custom—dating, it was said, as far back as the time of Servius Tullius—to pay into the temple of Juventas a piece of money for every boy who lived to enter the stage of youth. When the young Roman assumed the *toga virilis,* he went up to the Capitol and prayed to Jupiter and Juventas. At the beginning of every year sacrifice was offered to both deities in behalf of the youth of the city.

GANYMEDES

Was a son of the Trojan king Tros and Callirrhoe, and was therefore, great-grandson of Dardanus, the founder of Troy. Zeus finding him on Mount Ida, and admiring his beauty, carried him off to Olympus, where he appears to have succeeded Hebe in the office of cup-bearer to the gods.

He was represented as possessed of eternal youth and extraordinary beauty, wearing a Phrygian cap to indicate his birthplace. The cup in his hand indicates his office of cup-bearer, while the eagle of Zeus by his side shows that that office was performed among the gods of Olympus.

AESCULAPIUS

Was, according to the most common version of the myth, a son of Apollo and Coronis, a daughter of a Thessalian prince —whence his title Coronides. At his birth his mother died, struck by the arrows of Artemis; but the father saved the child, and taking it to Mount Pelion, gave it in keeping to the famous physician, Chiron, who carefully instructed the boy from early youth onward in the mysteries of the healing

art, training him at the same time to expertness in the chase.
In the former the pupil soon excelled the master, curing the
most malignant diseases, and working real miracles with his
art.　There was but one whom his success could injure, and
that was Pluto, the monarch of the lower world, who urged
his complaint before Zeus.　The latter, astonished at the
boldness of a mortal in thus defying the decrees of fate,
felled the great doctor with a thunderbolt, to the indignation
of Apollo, who was only silenced by banishment from Olympus for some time.　After his death Aesculapius was looked
upon as a god in Greece; festivals called Asclepiea were held
in his honor, and temples were erected to him, of which the
most celebrated was that of Epidaurus, in the Peloponnesus.
Thither even the Romans sent ten deputies once, to inquire
the will of the oracle with regard to a pestilence that was
raging in Rome.　The deputies had hardly entered the temple, when from behind the gold-and-ivory statue of the god
a serpent appeared, the symbol of Aesculapius, and followed
them through the streets of the town, on to the harbor, and
into their ship.　They received it joyfully as a happy por-
tent, and set out homeward.　On reaching Italy the serpent
left the ship, and proceeded to a temple of Aesculapius, in
the town of Antium, but afterward returned to the ship, and
did not leave it again until, on going up the Tiber, it stopped
at an island.　Thereupon the pestilence ceased, and the temple
was erected on the island to Aesculapius, to commemorate
the event.　Thither patients were conveyed and cured—a
short statement of the symptoms of each case, and the remedy
employed, being inscribed on tablets, which were hung up in
the temple, and were found to be a great boon to posterity.

Beside the serpent, he frequently has as an attribute a
cock—that animal being also sacred to him.　The serpent,
by its periodic change of skin, indicates rejuvenescence; the
staff marks him as wandering from place to place, to give
help; while the dish, which he sometimes holds, is a symbol
of his healing potions.　It was the custom of invalids to

sacrifice a cock to him, as Socrates did after drinking the cup of poison, as a token that he did not fear death, but rather looked upon it as a cure and a convalescence.

Among the children of Aesculapius, Hygea is specially mentioned. The name of his wife was Epigone—"the soothing." Like many other deities of the lower order, in common with heroes, he was in after times placed as a star in the sky.

In art the god of medicine is represented as a man of years, bearded, gentle, and earnest, draped, and resting on a staff, round which a serpent, as an emblem of rejuvenescence, is coiled. His type of face resembles that of Zeus so much that in the case of the fine marble head in the British Museum absolute

Aesculapius.

agreement has not yet been arrived at as to which of the two gods it was intended to represent. The head in ques-

tion was found in the island of Melos, on the site of what
is supposed to have been a temple to Aesculapius, from the
discovery in the same place of a native tablet, dedicated to
the god and to his daughter Hygea. A person who had
recovered from a local illness would dedicate a sculptured
representation of the part that had been affected. Of such
sculptures there are a number of examples in the British
Museum.

HYGEA.

Hygea was, as we have just said, the daughter of Aesculapius, and the goddess of health. Others said she was the
wife of Aesculapius.

She was represented as a young, active, smiling goddess, in
whom Apollo took a special interest. In art she appears
draped, and holding a serpent—which, as in the case of Aesculapius, is the symbol of health. She feeds it from a plate
or *patera.*

At other times she is figured wearing a wreath of laurel, or
of plants known for their medicinal properties—a *patera* in
her hand, a serpent coiled round her arm or body.

MEDITRINA

Passed in Rome for a sister of Hygea and a goddess of health,
a festival called **Meditrinalia** being annually held in her
honor at the beginning of October, the ceremony consisting
in drinking some old and some new wine together, and ex-
claiming, " I drink the new and the old wine—with new and
old wine I heal infirmities."

The distinction between the two goddesses of health lay in
this, that while Hygea preserved good health, Meditrina
restored it. The Greek goddess **Jaso** appears to have been
identical with Meditrina.

TELESPHORUS

Was looked upon as a *genius* or deity of that secret and mysterious vitality which sustains the convalescent. He was

Hygea, Aesculapius, and Telesphorus.

represented by the side of Aesculapius, or standing between him and Hygea, as a small barefooted boy, wrapped closely in a mantle, with a hood on his head. This careful wrapping up seems to indicate the secret shrouded nature of the vital force which he personifies, and may also have been meant to express the care in wrapping up so essential to convalescence. The principal centre of his worship was on the coast of Asia Minor.

TYCHE, OR FORTUNA.

The idea that a great part of the incidents and circumstances of life was due to chance had taken hold of the mind in very early times, and had come to be personified in the form of a goddess of luck, whom the Greeks called Tyche and the Romans Fortuna. She was the daughter of Zeus. The Parcae, or Fates, were her sisters. It was believed that she guided the career of men, whether prosperously or the reverse; and to show her in this capacity she was figured holding a double rudder in her hands—the one to steer the barque of the lucky, the other that of the unlucky. In later times she was represented with wings, or with her eyes bound, standing on a ball or a wheel, to indicate that luck rolls like a ball, without choice, undoing all the efforts of this one, and overwhelming that one with wealth and prosperity. Sometimes she was represented with a ball on her head, or with a cornucopia in her hands.

Fortuna.

In art she appears draped, her arms bare, a horn of plenty in one hand and a rudder in the other—the ball beside the rudder indicating the rapid turns of fortune.

Tyche was worshipped in many places in Greece, but especially at Athens, where she was popularly believed to reside constantly as a favoring deity. In Italy the worship of Fortuna was widespread, and a general festival held in her

ARES, OR MARS.

honor annually on June 24. Her principal worshippers, however, were newly married women. She had an oracle of considerable fame in the towns of Praeneste and Antium.

NIKE, OR VICTORIA,

The goddess of victory, was a daughter of the giant Pallas and the Oceanid nymph Styx, and was regarded by the Greeks as inseparable from Zeus and Athene. Except in works of art of an early period, she was represented with wings. Her attributes were a palm-branch, a wreath, and a trophy of armor. Sometimes she carried a staff (*caduceus*) like that of Hermes (Mercury), as a sign of her power, and floated in the air with outspread wings, or appeared coming down to earth —now pointing the way to a victor, now reaching a wreath down to his brow, or driving his horses. As goddess of victories by sea, suitable emblems were assigned to her.

In art she appears standing on a globe, draped, winged, holding a wreath and a palm-branch. On coins apparently struck to commemorate victories, or, as it sometimes hap-

Nike, or Victoria.

pened, success in the national games—on engraved gems, sculptures—figures of Nike are of frequent occurrence. She is also draped, and of a youthful appearance : a favorite subject, to judge from the repetition of it on gems, seems to have been that in which she was represented in the act of sacrificing an ox.

EIRENE, OR PAX,

The goddess of peace, was also represented holding a palm-branch. At other times she stood with armor under her feet or was engaged in closing the temple of Janus. In Greece she was reckoned one of the Horae—the most cheerful, indeed, of the three sisters. In Rome she had a temple, and enjoyed the honor of an annual festival on January 30.

FATE,

The Greek name being **Ananke**, the Roman **Fatum**, was a personification of the unalterable necessity that appeared to control the career of mankind and the events of the world. Gods, as well as men, were subject to its unchanging decrees. This deity was the offspring of Night and Erebus. Her sentences were carried out by the Parcae, who, however, were also looked upon as independent deities of fate. She was represented standing on a globe, and holding an urn.

MOERAE, OR PARCAE.

In very early times the management of the world in regard to social matters involving right and reason was supposed to be directly under the control of a goddess called Moera, who, in her own province, acknowledged the superiority of no other deity, not even of Zeus, the ruler of the world, who, as supreme god, could not be thought to insist on any-

Eirene.

thing unreasonable or wrong. In later times, we find, instead

of this single deity, three Moerae (or Parcae), answering
respectively to the three stages of human life—birth, years,
and death.   In this form, however, they no longer retained
the high position of superiority to Zeus, but, like the other
deities, became subject to him, thus showing that he possessed
in its highest form the consciousness of right and reason, and
was entitled to be called **Moeragetes**, or leader of the
Moerae.

They were described as daughters of Night—to indicate
the darkness and obscurity of human fate—or of Zeus and
Themis—that is, "daughters of the just heavens." Another
story has it that it was they who united Themis and Zeus
in marriage, the same ceremony, according to another version
of the myth, having been performed by them to Zeus and
Hera.   It was natural to suppose the goddesses of fate present
and taking part at marriages and births.

The names of the three sisters were **Clotho, Lachesis,**
and **Atropos.**   To express the influence which they were

believed to exercise on
human life from birth
to death, they were
conceived as occupied
in spinning a thread
of gold, silver, or
wool; now tightening,
now slackening, and
at last cutting it off.
This occupation was
so arranged among the
three, that Clotho, the
youngest, put the wool
round the spindle,

The Moerae.

Lachesis spun it, and Atropos, the eldest, cut it off when a
man had to die.   Tyche, or Fortuna, has been taken as a
fourth sister, on account of the similarity of her functions.
It is not, however, so.

They were represented in art as serious maidens, always side by side, and in most cases occupied as we have mentioned, there being instances, however, in which Atropos, the "unalterable," is represented alone.

They were worshipped very seriously both in Greece and Italy: sacrifices of honey and flowers, sometimes of ewes, were offered to them, while in Sparta and in Rome they had temples and altars.

NEMESIS,

Called also **Adrastea** and **Rhamnusia**, from Rhamnus in Attica, the principal centre of her worship, was a personification of the vengeance which appeared to overtake every act of wrong. She was the goddess of punishment, and as such a figure of her was placed beside the bench of the judges. A mysterious power, watching over the propriety of life, she was conceived as shaping the demeanor of men in their times of prosperity, punishing crime, taking luck away from the unworthy, tracking every wrong to its doer, and keeping society in equipoise. She was represented as a thoughtful, beautiful figure of queenly aspect, with a diadem or crown on her head, winged, except in the case of early sculptures, or driving in a car drawn by gryphons. Among her several attributes were a wheel, to indicate the speed of her punishments, a balance, a bridle, a yoke, a rudder, a lash, a sword, and an apple-branch. Special festivals, called **Nemesia**, accompanied by public sacrifices to assure her good will, were held annually in Athens and in Smyrna.

Now Erebus, now Oceanus, is mentioned as her father, while Zeus is said to have been her lover, and Helena their daughter.

To execute her commands she had three attendants—**Dike, Poena**, and **Erinys** (respectively justice, punishment, and vengeance). She was a terror to evil-doers. At the same time her endeavors to preserve an equal balance in the attitude of man to man were recognized as springing from a deep-seated love, and therefore she was placed beside the Graces.   In Smyrna several winged beings of her type were worshipped.

ERIS,

Called by the Romans Discordia, the goddess of strife, was employed by the other gods to stir up fierce disputes and mortal quarrels among men.   It was she who caused the dispute between Hera (Juno), Athene (Minerva), and Aphrodite (Venus) for the possession of the golden apple, the prize of beauty, which she threw among the company assembled at the marriage of Peleus.

Terrible in form and aspect, with attributes like those of the Eumenides, with whom her home was in the realms below, she was looked on as the sister and companion, sometimes as the wife, of Ares, the god of massacre.   Her daughter was

ENYO,

Whom the Romans called Bellona, now believing her to be the wife and now the sister of Mars.   Similarly among the Greeks, Enyo, the murderous goddess of war, delighting in devastation, was associated with Ares, who also bore the title of Enyalios, either driving his chariot or rushing in front of it to battle.   The peculiar fierceness and fury with which she spread terror and alarm in a battle distinguished her from Pallas Athene.   She was represented as of frightful aspect, with flowing hair, rushing wildly hither and thither, with a lash in her hand, and armed with shield and spear. Her most celebrated temple was that at Comana, in Asia Minor.

At the close of the war against the Samnites a temple was erected to her in Rome by Appius Claudius.   There the

Senate used to meet when they had to deliberate with an embassy from a hostile power, or when they had to decide whether the honor of a triumphal entry into the city should be bestowed upon a general. At the entrance to the temple stood a pillar, which, on the occasion of declaring war, was viewed as marking the boundary between Roman and hostile territory. The ceremony of declaring war was to throw a spear over this pillar—that is, into the territory of the enemy. There festivals of din and wild excitement were held in her honor. Her priests were styled Bellonarii.

PHEME, OR FAMA,

The goddess of fame or report, whether good or bad, was said to be a daughter of Gaea, and born at the time of her great indignation at the overthrow of the Giants. Sleepless, always prying, swift of foot, Pheme announced whatever she saw or heard of, at first in a whisper addressed only to a few persons, then by degrees louder and to a larger circle, until finally she had traversed heaven and earth communicating it. She was represented as a tender, gentle figure, winged, and holding a trumpet.

ATE

Was the goddess of infatuation, mischief, and guilt, misleading men to actions that involved them in ruin. For this her father, Zeus, cast her in anger from Olympus, and from that time she wandered about the earth in search of victims to her malignant influence. She was spoken of as powerful in person and swift of foot, running before men to mislead them. Her sisters were the (con't. on next page)

LITAI,

Sweet-natured goddesses, whose special duty was to recompense the persons whom Ate had reduced to distress and ruin. Their name signifies " prayers of the penitent," and the allegory in this case is not far to seek. Prayers atone and make amends for what a man does to the harm of others in thoughtlessness or from infatuation, without wicked thought or design. In the Homeric poems they are described as lame, wrinkled, and squinting—those deformities being caused by the trouble they had in making good the harm done by Ate. Penitent prayers were at best but sorry aid in making good the evil done from infatuation or carelessness.

The Litai were supposed to be daughters of Zeus, and to place before him the prayers of those who invoked his assistance.

THE ERINYS, OR FURIAE,

Called also Dirae, Eumenides, or Semnae—that is, the " revered" goddesses—were daughters of Night, or, according to another myth, of the Earth and Darkness, while a third account calls them offspring of Cronus and Eurynome. They were attendants of Hades and Persephone, and lived at the entrance to the lower world. Their first duty was to see to the punishment of those of the departed who, having been guilty of some crime on earth, had come down to the shades without obtaining atonement from the gods. At the command of the higher gods, sometimes of Nemesis, they appeared on earth pursuing criminals. Nothing escaped their sharp eyes as they followed the evil-doer with speed and fury, permitting him no rest.

A sad instance of this is the story of Orestes, the son of Agamemnon, who slew his mother, Clytaemnestra, to avenge his father's death. The atrocity of the crime committed by Clytaemnestra was held by Zeus and Apollo to be no excuse for the act of Orestes, and accordingly he was subjected to the long and cruel pursuit of the Furies, from which he was at length freed by bringing, on the advice of an oracle of Apollo, an image of Artemis from Taurus to Argos.

In the illustration one of the Erinys is represented as pursuing Orestes; the face reflected on the mirror which she holds is perhaps that of Clytaemnestra.

The number of the Erinyes, varying in early times, was afterward fixed to three : Tisiphone (the avenger of murder), Alecto (the unwearied persecutor), and Megaera (the grim). They were represented as female figures of odious aspect, clad in black, sometimes winged, with hair formed of vipers, and carrying a serpent, a knife, or a torch in their hands. In time this grim conception of them fell away, and they came to be represented as beautiful, serious maidens, clad something like Artemis. As divine beings, whose office it was to punish neglect of duty, breach of faith, and crimes committed against

One of the Erinys.

parents, they came to be looked upon as aiding the preservation of a high morality, and were called Eumenides, or the " well-minded goddesses." When sacrifices were offered to them, the place chosen for the occasion was of a wild character, the time night, and the animals sacrificed, black. In Greece there were several temples and solemn groves dedicated to them—as, for example, at Colonus, close by Athens.

THE HARPIES,

Also were creatures employed, according to the belief of the Greeks and Romans, by the higher gods to carry out the punishment of crime.   They were three in number : **Aello, Ocypete**, and **Celaeno**, or **Podarge**; and were said to be daughters of the giant **Thaumas** and the Oceanid nymph **Electra.**   Their body was that of a bird, their head that of a woman; and it would seem that they were originally goddesses of the storm, which carries everything along with it.

Harpies.

Their manner of punishing those whom they were sent to punish was to carry off all the food set before their victim, and devour it, or failing that, to render it uneatable.   Among others who were punished in this way was **Phineus**, a king of Thrace, his crime having been cruelty toward his own son and contempt of the gods.   For showing the Argonauts the way to Colchis he was, however, freed from their persecution by **Calais** and **Zetes**, the winged sons of Boreas, who, in gratitude, killed them.   At other times, as in the case of the daughters of **Pandareus**, they are described as carrying off their victims bodily from the earth; while, on the so-called Harpy tomb in the British Museum, they appear to be represented as demons of death carrying away the souls of deceased persons.

THE GORGONS,

By name **Stheino, Euryale,** and **Medusa,** were daughters of **Phorcys** and **Ceto.** Two of them were believed to be immortal, while the third, **Medusa,** the youngest and most beautiful of them, was mortal. She loved Poseidon, and having met him once in the temple of Athene, to the desecration of that building, was punished by having her beautiful hair turned into snakes, thus making her appearance more ghastly than that of her sisters. Her face was terrible to behold, turning the spectator into stone. At last **Perseus,** finding her asleep, cut off her head with his curved sword, and presented it to Athene, who had assisted him in the enterprise, to be worn on her *aegis* or shield as a terror to her enemies.

The ancient poets describe the Gorgons generally as horrid, aged women, and frequently place them by the side of the Furies. In early times there was only one Gorgon— Medusa—instead of the three of later times. The winged horse, **Pegasus,** was the offspring of her and Poseidon.

In art Perseus is represented standing with sword in one hand and the head of Medusa in the other, turning his face away to avoid seeing it (see page 247). The subject of Perseus cutting off the head of Medusa occurs in one of the earliest examples of Greek sculpture—one of the *metopes* of the oldest temple at Selinus, in Sicily; and from the conventional manner in which her face is represented, compared with the other parts of the sculpture, it is agreed that the type must have been familiar for some time to Greek art. To possess a representation of a Gorgon's face was to be pro-

vided with a charm against ills, and accordingly it was frequently employed as a personal ornament. Many hundreds

The Dying Medusa.

of such faces worked in thin gold, and intended to be stitched
down on garments, were found in the tomb of a priestess of

Demeter in Certch, and are now in the hermitage of St. Petersburg. A representation of Perseus escaping after cutting off the Gorgon's head, and being pursued by her sisters, occurs on a small vase in the British Museum, where also is to be seen, on a fragment of a terra-cotta relief, Athene holding up the shield, the polished surface of which reflected her face, and thus guided Perseus to the spot without his encountering its deadly stare.

THE GRAEAE,

Daughters of Phorcys and Ceto, were three in number; Deino, Pephredo, and Enyo; their names meaning respectively "alarm," "dread," and "horror." Sisters and at the same time guardians of the Gorgons, they were conceived as misshapen hideous creatures, hoary and withered from their birth, with only one eye and one tooth for the common use of the three, and were supposed to inhabit a dark cavern near the entrance to Tartarus. The belief in their existence seems to have been originally suggested by the gray fog or mist which lies upon the sea and is a frequent source of danger to the mariner. It is said that Perseus obtained from them the necessary information as to the dwelling of the Gorgons by seizing their solitary eye and tooth, and refusing to return them until they showed him the way.

NYX, OR NOX,

Was, it will be remembered, a daughter of Chaos. She became the wife of Erebus (darkness), and bore to him two children, Aether (the pure air) and Hemera (day). In the earliest form of the myth she was one of the seven elements that constituted the world—fire, water, earth, sky, sun, moon, and night.

In time the lively imagination of the ancients associated with this mysterious goddess of night a control over illness, sufferings, dreams, misfortunes, quarrels, war, murder, sleep, and death, everything inexplicable and frightful that befell men being personified and described as her offspring.

She was supposed to inhabit a palace in the lower world jointly with Day. When the latter entered the palace, Night rode out in a chariot drawn by two black steeds, and, accompanied by many stars, traversed the heavens till daybreak, when she returned to the palace.

She was represented as a serious figure clad in long heavy drapery, on her head a black star-spangled veil; with black wings, and carrying two children in her arms (one of them being white to personify Sleep, the other black, to personify Death), or riding in a black chariot, holding an extinguished torch inverted.

HYPNOS, OR SOMNUS,

Was, as we have just said, a son of Night, twin brother of Thanatos (death), with whom he lived in deep subterranean darkness at the entrance to Tartarus. His influence extended to gods as well as men, and by the latter he was viewed as a special benefactor, giving the weary refreshing rest, and sufferers alleviation of their pain.

He was represented in different forms and attitudes, with different attributes—now nude, or lightly or heavily clad, now standing, or striding hastily, or reposing heavily; or as a powerful youth holding a poppy or a horn, from which sleep trickled down on those reposing; or as a child, and sometimes as a bearded, aged man. On his head were the wings of a hawk or a night bird, and beside him frequently a lizard. He was looked on as a favorite of the Muses, apparently because of the dreams he was supposed to communicate to men.

In the British Museum is a very beautiful bronze head of

Hypnos, with the wings of a hawk growing out from the temples. In the Iliad, Hera commands him to take the form of the bird which men call a hawk. How the idea originated of attaching wings to the temple is uncertain.

ONEIROS AND MORPHEUS

Are two different forms of the god of dreams. According to the meaning of their names, the office of the latter would be to fashion dreams, as the gods desired them to be sent to men. In this task he was assisted by Icelus, who fashioned those dreams that had all the appearance of reality, by Phobetor, the author of alarming dreams, and Phantasus, who tricked sleepers with innumerable and strange phenomena. But we find Morpheus also represented in the capacity of a sort of watchman and guardian of dreams, as Aeolus was of the winds.

Oneiros was properly a personification of dreams, whether idle or deceptive or really prophetic. Dreams of the former class were supposed to issue from the ivory gates, those of the latter class from the horn gate, of the palace where they were kept, beside the Western Oceanus. They were called children of Night, sometimes children of Sleep, and were directly under the control of the superior order of gods, who, as they pleased, despatched deceptive or prophetic dreams to men.

MOMUS

Was a deity whose delight and occupation was to jeer bitterly at the actions both of gods and men, sparing no one with his insinuations except Aphrodite, in whom he could find nothing to blame, and vexed himself to death in consequence. As an example of his behavior, it is said that he

complained of the man that Prometheus had made, because
there was not a window in his breast through which his
thoughts might be seen.

THANATOS, OR MORS,

The god of death, was, as we have said, a son of Night and
twin brother of Sleep. He was, however, also described as
a son of Earth and Tartarus, to whom it was his office to
introduce, some time or other, the whole of mankind. The
relentless severity with which he discharged the task caused
him to be frequently regarded with pain, and to be represented as of a powerful figure, with shaggy beard and fierce
countenance, with great wings to his shoulders, and resembling, on the whole, the figure of Boreas, the god of the wild
north wind of winter. This form, in the case of both deities,
was expressive of the violent nature of their functions.

Thanatos was, however, more frequently regarded with
submission, or as coming opportunely, and in such cases was
represented in the form of a quiet, pensive youth, winged,
standing with his legs crossed, often beside an urn with a
wreath on it, and holding an extinguished torch reversed.
Or, as a personification of endless repose, he appeared in the
form of a beautiful youth leaning against the trunk of a tree,
with one arm thrown up over his head—an attitude by which
ancient artists usually expressed repose. It was probably
owing to the spread of the belief that death was a transition
from life to Elysium, that in later times this more attractive
representation of the god of death took the place of the
former repulsive representations, whether as a powerful and
violent god, or as a black child in the arms of his mother,
Night. Among the figures sculptured on the chest of Cypse-
lus, a description of which we have still in Pausanias, was
that of Night carrying twin children in her arms—the one
white, representing Sleep, and the other black, representing

Death. On Roman sarcophagi, Mors, or the genius of death, was represented in the form of a winged boy, resembling Cupid, resting and holding a torch. In the Alcestis of Euripides he is described as armed with a sword.

DAEMONS, OR GENII,

Were an order of invisible beings, one of whom was assigned by Zeus to every man, to attend, protect, and guide him. They were nameless, and, like the multitude of mankind, innumerable. Some of them acted as personal attendants to deities of a higher order, and in that case were represented under particular forms, and enjoyed distinctive names, while others were believed to watch over particular districts, towns, or nations. While the Greeks regarded these Daemons as deities of an inferior order, the Romans believed them to be a sort of intermediate beings linking mankind to the gods. The Daemons assigned to women were supposed to be feminine.

To every man was assigned a Daemon at his birth. Identifying itself with him, it endeavored, throughout his life, to guide him in a wise course, and at his death died with him. To be of a cheerful mood, and to be careful of prolonging life, was to live in obedience to a man's Daemon or Genius. To be sad and vexed, or to shorten life by recklessness, was to wrong the attendant spirit. On birthdays it was usual to offer a sacrifice of wine, milk, flowers, or incense to the Genius, while at most meals some unmixed wine was poured out to the " Good Daemon " (Agathodaemon).

The usual representation of a being of this class was in the form of a youth holding a horn of plenty and a dish in one hand, and some heads of poppies and ears of grain in the other. The presence of a Daemon was also symbolized by the figure of a serpent.

Besides the general family of Genii, the Romans had one

great Genius whom they reckoned among the gods of the second rank, and esteemed highly, believing that he had some control over the others.

LARES AND PENATES

Were beings peculiar to the religion of the Romans. Every household was supposed to be under the protection of one Lar and several Penates, whose presence was symbolized by images in the form of a youth wearing a short tunic, girt at the waist, and holding a horn of plenty in one hand, and a *patera,* or flat circular dish, in the other. Such images of the Lares and Penates were kept in a particular part of the house called the *Lararium,* received constant offerings of incense and libations, and were decked with garlands of violets and rosemary. When a slave obtained his freedom, it was the custom of his former master to hang a chain upon the figures of his Lares. When a youth left the paternal roof he prayed : " Ye Penates of my fathers, and you, Lar, father of our family, I commend to you my parents, that you may protect them. Other Penates and another Lar I must now seek."

Beside these private household deities there were also public Lares, who were recognized as the protecting spirits of whole states and towns. Of these there were originally two in Rome, and later three—the spirit of Julius Cæsar having been added as the third; for the Lares were considered to be the spirits of deceased persons who continued to watch over and influence the living. The other two were, however, regarded sometimes as sons of Mercury and a nymph called Lara. Statues and temples were erected in their honor. Sacrifice and prayers for the safety of the state were offered up at their altars, which in spring and in summer were frequently decked with flowers. They were protectors of highways and travellers, and in this capacity had the honor of a festival called Compitalia, which was annually celebrated at cross-roads, a few days after the Saturnalia, and consisted of a banquet and sacrifice of cakes, the ceremony being conducted by slaves. To the Lares who protected the fields, sacrifices of lambs, calves, and pigs were offered.

It was believed that the Genii of good people became after their death kindly Lares, while the Genii of evil-doers became Lemures or Larvae—that is, evil spirits who wandered about the earth afflicting mankind with illnesses for which there was no remedy but expiatory sacrifices to the gods. Persons who died without expiation for every wrong they had done were pursued by these Larvae in the lower world.

THE MANES,

Generally speaking, were the souls of the departed inhabiting the realm of shadows. Survivors, however, who believed that departed souls sustained a higher and nobler existence, regarded them as divine beings, calling them Dii Manes, offered sacrifice to them at tombs, and thought it possible to call them up from the lower world.

DEMIGODS, OR HEROES.

DEMIGODS, or heroes, were a class of beings peculiar, it would seem, to the mythology of the Greeks. They were regarded partly as of divine origin, were represented as men possessed of godlike form, strength, and courage; were believed to have lived on earth in remote dim ages of the nation's history; to have been occupied in their lifetime with thrilling adventures and extraordinary services in the cause of human civilization, and to have been after death in some cases translated to a life among the gods, and entitled to sacrifice and worship. They were described as having been the first sovereigns and legislators of the nation, and as the founders of all the kingly and noble families. Monsters that devastated particular localities were destroyed, the oppressed were set free, and everywhere order and peaceful institutions were established by them. They were, in short, the adventurous knights the history of whose deeds formed for the mass of the people the first chapter of the national history, and that in a manner worthy both of the civilization to which the nation had attained and of the gods to whose influence the progress was due. The legends of their adventures furnished to poets and artists an inexhaustible treasure of striking figures, wonderful deeds, and strange events, while they formed at the same time a most powerful element in the national education.

It has been suggested that the belief in these beings may have originated in later times, in an impulse to people the blank early pre-historic age with ideal figures of a sublime order of men, to whom the nation might look back with pride, or that it may have originated in a desire to dwell on the memory of distinguished persons who had actually existed, and in time, by so doing, to exaggerate their actions to a degree quite beyond human powers. But it is far more probable that, like the gods, the heroes had originally been divine personifications of certain elements of nature, and the legends of adventures ascribed to them merely a mythical form of describing the phenomena of these elements. The idea, for example, of a long struggle and ultimate victory over grim enemies, which is so characteristic of these adventures, is the same idea that we find pervading the early myths, in which the powers of light are represented as struggling with, and finally overcoming the powers of darkness. But while the gods always maintained their relationship to the elements of nature, of which they were divine personifications—marine deities, for instance, dwelling in the depths of the sea, and celestial deities in the pure ether—the heroes or demigods, on the other hand, had ceased to be identified with any particular element, and though retaining the form, strength, and courage of gods, came in time to be regarded as men of high order that had once inhabited Greece, but had passed away. The legends, which, as we have said, had been intended to be mythical descriptions of certain natural phenomena, were expanded so as to embrace the new variety of adventures which imagination with its wide scope now assigned to the heroes.

There appears to have been a time when the gods generally were in danger of being reduced in this manner to the condition of demigods or heroes—such events, for instance, as the war of Zeus with the Titans and Giants, the contests of Apollo with Tityus and Python, or of Dionysus with his enemies, being calculated, from their adventurous nature, to present their authors more in the light of heroes than of gods, and to form readily subjects for the epic poets, as indeed the contests of Dionysus did. This tendency was, however, arrested by the necessity of defining, for the pur-

poses of worship, the province of the various deities. From
that time the position of the gods was determined, while the
heroes became less and less distinguishable from men, the
legends concerning them assuming gradually more of a historical than of an ideal character. Traditions of early
battles and victories that still lingered among the people
were made to circle round these imaginary heroes, who in
time became the centres of all the earliest national recollec-
tions, the accredited founders of most of the elementary
institutions of social life, and the guides of colonists.

It does not, however, follow that the particular elements
of nature over which the heroes or demigods had originally
presided were left after this separation unrepresented by
divine beings. For in addition to the vast number of gods
in the Greek national religion, whom we have already described as identified with this or that department of the
universe, there must have been in the early ages a large
number of local deities, who, when the tribes to which they
were peculiar coalesced in after times into one Greek nation,
must have appeared in many cases quite identical in character, though probably very often different in regard to the
details of the deeds or adventures ascribed to them. Thus
many who have been dispensed with as gods would be retained, on account of their local adventures, as heroes or
demigods.

Turning to the oldest examples of the Greek epic poetry
which we possess — the Iliad and Odyssey — we find the
heroes represented as hardly distinguishable from men.
More powerful, more beautiful, and more courageous they
certainly were than the ordinary men of their day, and on
this account were looked on as descendants of the gods; still
their ways of life were distinctly the ways of men, not of
gods.

By the time of Hesiod we find this opinion of the heroes
changed. The heroic age is lamented as a thing of the past.
The people of his time, aware of their weakness and wants,

looked back with reverent feelings to the happy age in which the great heroes stood between the gods and feeble mankind. Zeus, it was taught by Hesiod, had translated the heroes to the islands of the blest, far removed from men, where they lived in a perpetual golden age under the sovereignty of Cronus. The people, however, thought otherwise, believing that the ancient tumuli in Greece and in Asia Minor were the graves of the heroes. The imposing tumuli at the entrance to the Hellespont, for instance, were viewed as the tombs of Achilles, Patroclus, and Ajax. Sanctuaries and temples were erected to heroes, their bones were searched for, and when found regarded as a great source of strength to the town that possessed them; all relics of their stay on earth were hallowed, and a form of worship was specially adapted to them.

In later times the heroes came to be identified more or less with the Daemons. The consequence of this was that all individuals who on account of extraordinary strength, courage, beauty, talent, or self-sacrifice, were supposed to be possessed of special Daemons, were reckoned as heroes. And this was not confined to persons remarkable for their good qualities, successful daring entitling a robber to this rank as much as did the bravery of the men who fell at Marathon and Plataea.

In still later times, as the belief gained ground that every soul had something of the nature of a Daemon in it, and was destined to a higher and nobler life, heroic honors were paid to almost all the dead; so that when a man of particular distinction died, the only course left open of paying him signal honors was to regard him as having been, after the manner of Hercules, translated to a life among the gods, and to worship him as a god.

It is, however, only with the heroes and demigods that occur in the mythology and the epic poetry that we have to do. They may be divided into three classes : First, the demigods, associated with the creation of mankind and the earliest

incidents of human history and civilization—the most strik
ing figure among them being that of Prometheus. Secondly,
the earlier heroes properly so called—such as Hercules,
Theseus, Minos, Perseus, or Bellerophon, who were distinguished for their extraordinary adventures, labors, and
expeditions, such, for example, as that of the Argonauts to
Colchis. Thirdly, the more recent heroes, the tales of whose
deeds and expeditions—for instance, those against Troy and
Thebes—read more like historical traditions magnified by the
imagination of the poets, than allegorical narratives such as
those of the two preceding classes.

THE CREATION OF MAN.

PROMETHEUS AND THE FIRST DEMIGODS.

AMONG the various opinions in ancient times concerning the origin of mankind, the most generally accepted one appears to have been that in which it was asserted that man

Deucalion and Pyrrha.

and all other forms of life had, like the gods, originally sprung from the common mother earth. It was not supposed that the whole human race could trace its lineage back to one primeval pair; on the contrary, it was believed that a primeval pair had been created in all the chief districts in

which mankind was afterward found settled. As the natural
features of these districts varied, so varied the opinions with
regard to the exact substance from which the first beings had
sprung.   In wooded and mountainous districts. for instance,
they were held to have sprung from rocks and trees; in valleys, from the moist element of nature.   As to the time at
which this creation took place, and whether it took place
simultaneously throughout the various inhabited regions, we
have no means of knowing the current belief.

From the primitive condition of savages living like animals in the forests and caves, they advanced slowly in the
direction of civilization — sometimes visited with terrible
punishments, and sometimes assisted by the gods; the different classes or tribes becoming in time united into two great
races—the Pelasgic and the Hellenic. The former traced its
origin to the Argive Phoroneus, and appears to have been
resident mainly in the Peloponnesus, while the latter looked
back to Deucalion as its founder, and was resident in Thessaly and around Parnassus.   According to the story a great
flood had swept away the whole human race except one pair,
Deucalion and Pyrrha, who, as the flood abated, landed on
Mount Parnassus, and thence descending, picked up stones,
and cast them round about, as Zeus had commanded. From
these stones sprang a new race—men from those cast by
Deucalion, and women from those cast by his wife.   From
Hellen, the son of Deucalion, the Hellenic race derived its
name, while its four great branches, the Aeolians, Dorians,
Achaeans, and Ionians, traced their descent and names from
four of his sons.

In such a primitive condition of life, perhaps nothing was
regarded as of greater importance, or more mysterious in its
nature, than fire.   Its beam dispelled the dread of darkness,
and its warmth removed the chill of winter. The fire of
the hearth was the centre of domestic life. At the forge,
tools and weapons were fashioned. It was an emblem of the
life of man, with its flash and sudden extinction on the one

hand, and the illumination of its prolonged blaze on the
other. In storms it was seen descending from the sky, and
in volcanic eruptions it was seen issuing from the earth. The
source of it all was readily believed to be in the close keeping of the gods; and how mankind came to obtain the use of
it was explained in the story of Prometheus.

Zeus, foreseeing the arrogance that would arise from the
possession of so great a blessing, had from the first refused
to transmit any portion of his sacred fire to men. Their

Pandora.

deplorable condition, however, owing to the want of it, found
a champion in the person of Prometheus (a son of the Titan
Japetus), who had previously identified himself with the
cause of humanity in a dispute that arose at Mecone (Sicyon)
as to the rightful share of the gods in all sacrifices offered to
them. On that occasion an ox had been slaughtered as a
sacrifice, and Prometheus, having wrapped up all the eatable
parts in the skin of the animal as one portion, and having
cleverly covered the bones and worthless parts with fat as
the other portion, asked Zeus to select what he thought the

better portion for the gods. Zeus, though perfectly aware
of the deceit, chose the worthless parts, and more firmly than
ever determined to withhold his fire from men. Prometheus,
however, resolved to obtain it for them, and succeeded in
snatching some of it from the hearth of Zeus, or, as another
version of the story has it, from the forge of Hephaestus in
Lemnos. As a punishment, he was condemned to be chained
alive to a rock in the remote Caucasus mountains, and to
submit while every day a vulture came to gnaw away his
liver, which daily grew afresh. For a long time he bore this
suffering, and, indeed, would never have been released but
for the secret which he possessed concerning the ultimate fate
of the dominion of Zeus, who, for the purpose of learning
the secret, permitted Hercules to shoot the vulture, to free
Prometheus, and bring him back to Olympus.

Meanwhile the human race enjoyed the many benefits of
fire, and continued to advance in civilization rapidly. But
that their cup of happiness might be mixed with sorrow,
Zeus ordered Hephaestus to fashion a woman of clay, of
divine beauty, but possessed of all the weaknesses as well as
charms of human nature. Athene instructed her in the
industrial occupations of women, Aphrodite gave her grace
of manners, and taught her the arts of a beauty, while
Hermes qualified her for the part of flattering and soothing.
With the help of the Graces and Horae, Athene robed her
with costly, beautiful robes, and decked her with flowers, so
that, when all was done, **Pandora**, as they called her, might
be irresistibly attractive to gods and men. Hermes conducted
her to **Epimetheus**, who, though warned by his brother Prometheus to accept no gift from Zeus, yielded to the besetting
weakness from which he obtained his name—that of being
wise when it was too late. He received Pandora into his
house, and made her his wife. She brought with her a vase,
the lid of which was to remain closed. The curiosity of
her husband, however, tempted him to open it, and suddenly
there escaped from it troubles, weariness, and illnesses, from

which mankind was never afterward free. All that remained was Hope.

We have thus, in contrast with the general belief described above as the spontaneous origin of man from the earth, an instance of a human being directly fashioned by the gods

Pandora and Her Box.

from clay. From this mean substance it was also asserted the first men were made by Prometheus, Athene assisting him by breathing life into his figures. But this was probably only a learned speculation, indulged in to account for the zeal displayed by Prometheus in the cause of human civilization. It is better to account for that zeal by assuming Prometheus to have been originally a god of fire, who, asserting his right to employ that element for the benefit of mankind, provoked the hostility of the other gods, and from that time forward identified himself with the cause of men. There is good ground for assuming this in the fact that Prometheus was intimately associated with Hephaestus in the very ancient worship of that god in Lemnos and in Attica.

While the progress of civilization, as far as it had depended on, or could be symbolized by, fire, was connected with Prometheus, the progress of agriculture in primitive times was reflected in the story of the two giants Otus and Ephialtes, sons of Aloeus (the planter) and Iphimedia. Small and puny at their birth, they grew quickly, living on grain, and soon became the wonder of men for their great size and beauty. Finding that war and agriculture could not go together, they seized Ares, the god of war, bound and confined him in a large brazen vase for thirteen months. He would have perished in it had not Hermes at length heard of his imprisonment, and set him free. Becoming more and more arrogant in the pride of their strength, the two brothers next determined to assail the immortal gods in Olympus itself, and for this purpose they had placed Mount Ossa on the top of Mount Olympus, and upon Ossa had heaped Mount Pelion, when the shafts of Apollo felled them. They perished in youth, ere their beards had grown.

THE EARLIER RACE OF HEROES.

It will be convenient to separate, for the present, the legends of the adventures of Hercules, together with those that relate to combined expeditions of heroes from different districts—such as the expedition of the Argonauts—from the other legends of this earlier race of heroes, and to arrange the latter class according to the localities assigned as the principal scenes of their actions, beginning with

(a) ARGOS.

At the head of the Argive line of heroes stands Inachus, the river-god, a son of Oceanus, like all the other river-gods. With the nymph Melia for his wife, he became the father of Phoroneus and Io, of whom the former, according to Argive legends, was the first man upon the earth. Such services as Prometheus was elsewhere believed to have rendered to early civilization, were there ascribed to Phoroneus. He was reputed to have founded the town of Argos, and to have established there the worship of Hera. With regard to Io, we have already related (in connection with Hermes) how she was loved by Zeus, and, to escape the jealousy of Hera, was transformed by him into a cow—how Hera, discovering the transformation, set a watch over Io, in the person of Argus, a giant with a hundred eyes, and how Hermes slew the watchman and released Io. Another version of the story says that it was Hera who transformed Io into a cow, for the purpose of thwarting the love of Zeus for her. Argus had

tethered her to an olive-tree in a grove sacred to Hera, between the towns of Mycenae and Argos, and was there keeping guard when Hermes arrived and slew him.   Though set
free, Io did not yet regain her human form, but was compelled to wander through distant lands in the form of a white
horned cow, goaded by a vexatious insect sent by Hera.   At
last, on reaching Egypt, she obtained rest, was restored to
her human form, and became the mother of Epaphus.

Io, the white horned cow, appears to have been a personification of the moon, like the Phoenician goddess Astarte,
who was also represented in this form.   Her wanderings
were like the wanderings of the moon.   Hera, who punished
her, was the supreme goddess of the heavens.   Argus, with
his many eyes, reminds us of the stars.   The slaying of
Argus by Hermes was a favorite subject with ancient artists.

Epaphus became king of Egypt, and had a daughter
called Libya (after the district of that name on the shore of
the Mediterranean), who bore to Poseidon, the sea-god, two
sons—Agenor and Belus.   While the former became the
head of a race that spread over Phoenicia, Cilicia, and on to
Thebes in Greece, Belus remained in Egypt, succeeded to the
throne, and marrying Anchinoe, a daughter of the Nile.
had two sons, Aegyptus and Danaus.   The latter was appointed to rule over Arabia, the former over Libya.   Aegyptus had fifty sons, and Danaus the same number of daughters.
A dispute arose between the two families, and Danaus yielding took ship with his daughters and sailed to Argos, pursued
all the way by the sons of Aegyptus.   At Argos, the home
of his race, he was kindly received by the reigning king, and
protected against the pursuers.

At that time the district of Argos was suffering from a
drought which Poseidon had angrily caused.   Danaus sent
out his daughters to search for a spring, and while they were
so engaged it happened that one of them, Amymone, throwing her spear at a stag, missed it, and hit a Satyr who was
asleep in the brake.   Pursued by the Satyr, she called on

the name of Poseidon for help, and the god instantly appeared, drove off the Satyr, and for love of the beautiful Danaid caused a perennial spring to flow at Lerna, where he met her. Amymone bore to Poseidon Nauplius, the wrecker of Nauplia, who by false lights misled many ships to their destruction among the rocks, and enriched himself from their cargoes. By a singular fatality he perished in this way himself at last. He had three sons : Palamedes, celebrated for his inventive faculty, Oiax, the steersman, and Nausimedon, the ship captain.

Meantime the sons of Aegyptus, it is said, having besieged Argos for some time, at length proposed to forget their difference with Danaus, and to marry his daughters. Without relenting in the least, he agreed to give his daughters to them in marriage, but to each daughter he presented a knife, and commanded them all to slay each her own husband on the marriage night. All obeyed his order except Hypermnestra, who, preferring to be regarded as of weak resolution than as a murderess, spared her husband, Lynceus, and became the mother of the Argive line of kings. While Zeus approved the murderous deed of her forty-nine sisters, and sent Athene and Hermes to give them expiation, Hypermnestra was cast into a dungeon by her indignant father, her husband, Lynceus, saving himself by flight. On being brought to trial she was, however, publicly acquitted ; her husband, returning to Argos, succeeded Danaus on the throne, and in after times was widely respected, among other things for having founded the great festival in honor of the Argive Hera. The prize of victory in the games that accompanied that festival was a shield, not a wreath, as was elsewhere usual; the tradition being that on the first occasion of these games Lynceus presented his son Abas with the shield which had belonged to Danaus.

Whether it was to obtain husbands for his daughters who accomplished their own widowhood, or whether it was to decide among a multitude of suitors for their hands, Danaus held a kind of tournament, the victors in which were to be accepted as husbands. On the morning of the contest he ranged his daughters together on the course, and by noon each had been carried off by a victorious athlete, a scion of some noble house.

It was said that after death the Danaides, with the exception of Hypermnestra, were punished in Tartarus by having continually to carry water, and pour it in the vain endeavor of filling a broken cistern. It may be that this form of punishment was selected for them as the most suitable for women, who generally in Greece were the drawers of water. At the same time it was very suggestive of the dry parched soil of Argos, the streams of which were always dried up in summer.

From Abas, the son of Hypermnestra and Lynceus, sprang the brothers Acrisius and Proetus, famous for their hatred of each other from infancy onward. When they had grown up, Proetus, finding himself constantly defeated in the fraternal encounters, fled to Lycia, and was there hospitably received by the king, Iobates, and the queen, Amphianax, whose daughter, Stheneboea, he married. With the assistance of a Lycian army he was reinstated in his rights of sovereingty over Argos and Corinth, fortifying himself in the citadel of Tiryns, while his brother Acrisius held out in that of Larissa. Of both citadels the massive structures now in ruins still bear witness to the fierce assaults which must have been made upon them.

Proetus had three daughters, whose exceeding beauty made them prizes which the noblest youth of the country sought to win. But they were haughty, despised the common usages of the times, scorned to take part in the worship of Dionysus, and made ridicule of the sanctity of Hera's ancient image and shrine. For this they were punished by a form of insanity which drove them ever to wander restlessly among the woods and hills of Argos and Arcadia. It is further said that, being under the hallucination that they were cows, they lowed like kine as they wandered about. The father summoned **Melampus**, the prophet and priest, to work a cure upon his daughters, but on the prophet's stipulating a third of the kingdom as his reward, dismissed him again. The evil grew worse, for the other women of the country began to yield to the infatuation of abandoning their husbands and slaying their children. Melampus was recalled, and this time demanded an additional third of the kingdom for his brother, **Bias**. Proetus agreed, and Melampus, collecting a body of active youths, pursued the three princesses over the mountains, and on to Sicyon, where the eldest of the three died, and the other two, after being purified, were given in marriage to Melampus and Bias respectively.

This legend also would seem to have originated in connection with the very ancient worship of Hera, as queen of the heavens, at Argos; the wanderings of the three daughters of Proetus, under the imaginary form of cows, having reference, like the similar wanderings of Io, to the moon.

Returning to Acrisius, we find him troubled at the prospect of having no heir to his throne. To his question the oracle at Delphi replied that a daughter would be born to him, and that she would bear a son who would slay his grandfather, and rule in his stead. The daughter, **Danae** by name, was born, and to prevent the latter part of the oracle from being fulfilled, she was imprisoned in a subterranean chamber. But a shower of gold, sent by Zeus, penetrated to her, and she became the mother of an infant destined to fulfil the oracle and to become conspicuous among the ancient heroes. He was named Perseus, probably with reference to his being a son of Zeus, the great god of light, and to his having been born in darkness, in which respect, as in several others, he may be compared with Apollo, whose mother was Leto (darkness), while his father was Zeus. The shower of gold would thus signify a beam of golden light.

Acrisius, hearing the voice of the child, summoned his daughter to the altar of Zeus to give a solemn explanation of the circumstance. Disbelieving her story, he placed mother and child in a closed box, and committed them to the waves. After rocking about on the bosom of the sea, the box was at last carried toward the island of Seriphus, and was there caught in a net belonging to a fisherman named Dictys, who took the waifs to his house, and acted kindly by them. It was a very barren island, affording little but shelter to the families of fishermen that inhabited it. The chief or king of it was Polydectes, a brother of Dictys, just mentioned, and as notorious for the gaiety of his habits as was his brother for his simplicity. Struck with the beauty of Danae, and finding that her son Perseus stood in the way of the fulfilment of his desires, Polydectes became anxious to get rid of him, and gladly availed himself of the opportunity that presented itself when Perseus, not to be outdone in professions of loyalty, vowed that he would even fetch the head of the Gorgon Medusa for the king, should he wish it.

Perseus set forth sadly on his mission, but took courage when Hermes and Athene, who often lent their aid in heroic adventures, appeared to him, and led him to where the Graeae lived—three aged women, with only one eye and one tooth in common. Perseus, seizing the indispensable eye and tooth, refused to give them back until they told him where to find the nymphs who had in keeping the helmet of Hades, the winged shoes, and the pouch necessary for his future movements. On arriving at where the nymphs lived, he obtained from them the objects in question, to which Hermes added the knife (harpe) with which he had cut off the head of Argus. Buckling on the winged shoes, he proceeded toward the Gorgons with the speed of a bird, the helmet of Hades making him invisible, but concealing nothing from his sight. It is further said that Athene instructed him how to approach Medusa without being petrified, as was usual, by her stare. To this end she gave him a shield of polished brass, on which, as in a mirror, he could see the reflection of the Gorgon, while he himself, unseen, advanced

and cut off her head. The instant he had done this there
sprang from the trunk of Medusa Pegasus, the winged horse,
and Chrysaor, the father of Geryoneus. Perseus, placing
the head quickly into the pouch which the nymphs had
given him, hastened from the scene, pursued by the two
sisters of Medusa for some distance.

Among his adventures on the way back to Seriphus were
the turning of Atlas into stone because the giant refused to receive him hospitably, and the release of Andromeda, whom
he found, on passing over Aethiopia, bound to a rock on the

Andromeda.

sea-shore as a victim to a great sea-monster. She was a
daughter of Cepheus and Cassiopea, the king and queen of
Aethiopia. The latter, having vaunted herself equal in beauty
to the Nereides, gave offence to them and to Poseidon also,
who thereupon visited the country with a flood, and sent a
dreadful monster from the sea to destroy both men and cattle.
On appealing to the oracle of Ammon in Libya, Cepheus was
told that the evil would not abate until he exposed his beautiful daughter, Andromeda, to the monster. Compelled by

his subjects to yield, the luckless father took her to the shore, and chained her to a rock, in the position in which Perseus found her.   Struck with her beauty, Perseus undertook to save her on condition that she should become his wife. Cepheus agreed to this, and Perseus, after slaying the monster, unchained the maiden.   She had, however, been engaged beforehand to Phineus, her father's brother, who, arriving with a strong body of soldiers, burst in upon the marriage feast.   But the sight of the Gorgon's head turned them all to stone, and Perseus triumphantly carried off his bride.

Arriving at Seriphus, he found that his mother and Dictys were being persecuted by Polydectes, and obliged to seek protection at the altars of the gods.   His course was to announce his arrival to the king, who at once assembled his nobles to witness how the young hero had kept his word. Perseus appeared in the assembly, and, producing the Gorgon's head, turned the king and all his nobles instantly to stone.   Not content with punishing in this manner the principal persecutors of his mother, Perseus is said to have turned the island itself into a great barren rock, and to have spared only the excellent Dictys and the fishing population attached to him.   Even the frogs of the island became dumb, said an ancient proverb.

Having thus fulfilled his promise, and rescued his mother, Perseus handed over the winged shoes, the pouch, and the helmet that made him invisible, to Hermes, to be restored to the nymphs.   The head of Medusa he gave to Athene, who ever after wore it on her shield.   Accompanied by Danae and Andromeda, he set out for Argos to find his grandfather, Acrisius, who, however, in the meantime having left Argos in consequence of an increasing dread lest the oracle should be fulfilled regarding his death, had established himself at Larissa in Thessaly.   Thither Perseus proceeded, and found, on his arrival, the king, Teutamias, occupied with public games in honor of his deceased father.   Perseus took part in the games, and by a fatality which justified the oracle, the disc which he threw fell upon the foot of Acrisius, and caused his death.   After burying his grandfather honorably at Larissa, Perseus returned to Argos to his mother and wife

Perseus.

but instead of establishing himself there, exchanged Argos for Tiryns, which was then held by Megapenthes, a son of

Proetus, and soon after founded the ancient Mycenae, with its massive walls.

Perseus and Andromeda had two sons—Electryon and Alcaeus. Alcmene, the mother of Hercules, was a daughter of the former, and her husband, Amphitryon, a son of the latter. It was also said that before leaving the court of her father, Cepheus, Andromeda had borne a son, whom they called Perses, and left behind with his grandfather. From this Perses the Persian kings traced their lineage. The kings of Pontus and Cappadocia, claiming the same descent, introduced a figure of Perseus on their coins. In Tarsus and in Egypt also were traditions of ancient benefits derived from the Greek hero.

While the wanderings of Io remind us of the wanderings of the moon, and lead us to connect the origin of the legends concerning her with the worship of Hera at Argos, the adventures of Perseus similarly suggest the apparent movement of the sun, and the effect of his light, particularly in slaying the dread monsters with which the imagination peoples darkness. It would seem, therefore, that the origin of the belief in these adventures must have had some connection with the Argive worship of Zeus and Athene.

His adventures, either as an entire story or in parts, formed a most attractive subject to ancient poets, and were frequently represented in works of art, many of which we still possess. One of the earliest examples of Greek sculpture to which an approximate date can be assigned is a group on a temple at Selinus in Sicily, which represents him cutting off the Gorgon's head, and belongs to the seventh century B. C.

In art he is figured holding the head of Medusa in one hand and the curved sword in the other.

(b) CORINTH.

Owing to its convenient situation on the isthmus between two seas, Corinth was from very early times an important seat of commerce; and as such being chiefly dependent for its prosperity on the benignity of the sea-god Poseidon, had at an early period established his worship, and exalted him as its principal god. In the legends concerning the Corinthian heroes we would, therefore, expect to find decided traces of this worship, just as in those of Argos we found traces of the early worship of Hera.

With regard to Sisyphus, the first of these heroes, the legend was that he had chanced to see Zeus carrying off Aegina, the daughter of the river-god Asopus, and having marked the direction of their flight as toward the island of Aegina, determined to make capital of his knowledge, by informing Asopus of what he had seen, on condition that the river-god would create a spring of water on the parched citadel of Corinth—Acrocorinth as it was called. The terms were agreed to, and Sisyphus at once secured the afterward famous fountain of Peirene. But Zeus could not permit the act of treachery to pass unpunished. He sent the god or daemon of death to claim him. Instead of yielding, Sisyphus bound the daemon with strong chains, and retained him, no one dying in the meantime, till Ares arrived and broke the chains. Sisyphus was then handed over to the daemon, but before departing charged his wife, Merope, not to offer the customary sacrifices for the dead, and thus to disappoint Pluto and Persephone. Arrived in Hades, he began to denounce this neglect on the part of his wife, and repeated his complaint so often that he was at last allowed to return to the upper world. Another version of the story has it that Hercules carried him off by force from Hades. In either case he returned to Corinth, lived to an advanced age, and after death was punished as we have already related, by having to roll a huge stone up a height, which when it had gained the summit immediately rolled back.

It may be that the idea of such a punishment was suggested by the backward and forward rolling of stones by the treacherous waves on the shore. At any rate, we find a connection of Sisyphus with the worship of Poseidon in the statement that he, at the command of the Nereides, received the dead body of Melicertes from his mother, and instituted in his honor the Isthmian games, which afterward were held in honor of Poseidon.

More directly connected with the worship of the sea-god is the legend of Glaucus, the son of Sisyphus. The reference in his name to the color of the sea is strengthened by the title of **Pontius**, which he bore, and yet it was not with the sea directly, but with horses, the accredited symbols of the waves, that he is associated. For some reason—from having been fed on human flesh, according to one report— his horses became furious, and tore their master to pieces In after times his name was a terror to equestrians in the hippodromes, the current belief being that Glaucus survived as an evil spirit wandering about and frightening horses.

A figure of far greater importance than Glaucus in the legendary history of Corinth was his son **Bellerophon**. Not that Corinth had been to any extent the scene of his exploits; for, except the incident of the bridling of Pegasus, his memorable adventures were all conducted elsewhere—in Argos at first, and afterward in Lycia. His story was, moreover, strangely blended with that of the Argive Perseus. It may be that the proximity of the two towns, and the political dependence of Corinth on Argos, wrought in time an assimilation in the legends of the two heroes originally quite distinct. Or, on the other hand, it may be that the difference in the pursuits and religious inclinations of the two towns acted on the imagination in such a way as to alter a legend originally common to both, so much that each might in time fairly claim a separate hero of its own. Whichever

way it may have been, the Corinthians were proud of Bellerophon, and in early times had a figure of his horse Pegasus,
on their coins.

Bellerophon.

With regard to that wonderful winged horse, we have
already related how it sprang from the neck of the Gorgon
Medusa, when Perseus cut her head off. The legend proceeds to tell how it flew through the air, and did not set foot
on earth until it reached the citadel of Corinth, where it
halted to quench its thirst at the famous fountain of Peirene.

Bellerophon, after trying in vain to catch it, applied to the seer Polyidus for advice, and was told to lay himself down to sleep at night beside the altar of Athene. This he did, and in the course of his sleep dreamed that the goddess came and gave him a golden bridle, bidding him show it to his father, Poseidon, and at the same time sacrifice a white ox to him. Waking, he found the bridle, sacrificed the ox, and, on the advice of the seer, dedicated an altar to Athene. The horse at once took the bit, and from that time proved of great service to its master.

According to the ancient derivation, the name of Bellerophon signifies the "slayer of Belleros," the story being that he had accidentally caused the death of a person of that name, either his own brother or a Corinthian noble. To obtain the necessary purification, he repaired to Argos, and was there kindly received by Proetus, the reigning king. Unfortunately, however, the wife of Proetus, Stheneboea (or, as Homer calls her, Anteia), resembled Potiphar's wife in the bent of her passions, and finding the young hero firm against her temptations, resolved to accomplish his ruin, to this end charging him before the king with an attempt to violate her. Proetus, on hearing the charge, decided to send the youth to Lycia, to the court of Iobates, the father of Stheneboea, with a letter written in strange characters, in which the Lycian king was instructed to compass the death of the bearer. The parting scene, where Bellerophon receives the letter, and Stheneboea still gazes affectionately on him, is represented on several ancient painted vases.

Arriving at the Lycian court, Bellerophon was entertained hospitably for nine days. On the tenth day the king inquired the business of his guest, and received the letter of Proetus. Acting on the instructions of the letter, Iobates despatched him with orders to slay the Chimaera* (a monster composed

---

* It was represented in art as a lion with a goat's head springing from its back. The statement of its spitting fire may have reference to the volcanic features of Lycia.

of a lion in front, a goat in the middle, and a serpent behind), which infested the mountains, and slaughtered all who
attacked it.   But Pegasus carried his master up in the air
beyond the reach of the monster, and yet not too far for his
spear to have deadly effect.   Bellerophon returned triumphant.   Though his scheme had not succeeded, the king had
at any rate got rid of a terrible enemy to his subjects, and
determined a second time to profit by the prowess of the
young hero, if he should fail in causing his death.   Accordingly he sent him to fight against the Solymi, a hostile neighboring tribe, from which he
again returned victorious.
With like success he fought
against the Amazons, those
warlike women of Asia
Minor, whom the ancient
poets and artists delighted
to represent as fighting
stoutly against the best heroes of Greece, but always
being vanquished.   With
this result they opposed, for
example, Hercules and Theseus, and afterward, in the

Bellerophon, Pegasus, and the Chimaera.

Trojan war, took part against the Greeks.   It would seem
from their connection with the Ephesian Artemis, among
other reasons, that the legends concerning them originated
in the worship of the moon goddess.

In a last effort to secure the death of Bellerophon, the
Lycian king planned an ambush for him of his bravest
knights, all of whom, when the time came, perished at the
hands of the hero, who, it then became clear, could be no
other than the son of a god.   Instead of being put to further
encounters, he received the hand of the king's daughter in
marriage, and with her the half of the kingdom.   The grateful Lycians bestowed on him a large estate, well wooded and

fitted for agriculture. His wife bore him three blooming children : Isander, Hippolochus, and Laodamia. In short, he had reached the pinnacle of happiness. But the gods prepared a catastrophe for him. He became insane, and wandered about sad and alone, avoiding the company of men. His son Isander was slain by Ares, his daughter Laodamia, by Artemis. According to another report, repeated success in hazardous adventures had inflamed him with the desire to mount to Olympus on the back of his wonderful horse. In the attempt he fell to earth, smitten by the thunderbolt of Zeus, and died.

(c) THEBES.

It is a relief to turn from the bloodshed and perilous adventures of the Corinthian and Argive heroes to the comparatively tranquil tone of the Theban legends, with all their variety of character and incident. We would not be understood to say that the tales of Thebes are free from horrors, but only that the general impression left, especially by the earliest of them, concerns the daring and achievements of mind rather than the exploits of physical courage.

First among the heroes of Thebes is Cadmus, the founder of the ancient city—the Cadmeia, as it was called—who, while rendering important services to the population gathered round him there in the management of their public affairs, is said to have conferred on Greece generally an inestimable blessing in the form of an alphabet, or means of communicating thoughts in writing, previously unknown in that land. It is this alphabet, more or less modified, that we still employ. That he found the letters of it in use among the Phoenician traders who visited Greece in remote early times, establishing factories in many places—among others, in the neighborhood of Thebes—is probable; but to believe, as the Greeks did, that Cadmus was a Phoenician by birth, and that the system of civilization which he introduced was, like the alphabet, Phoenician, was only another instance of the readiness with which the Greeks listened to stories that traced the beginnings of their civilization back to the influence of the more ancient nations of the East.

The genealogy of Cadmus, according to the legend, commenced with the sea-god Poseidon and Libya, who had two sons—Belus (Baal) and Agenor; the former becoming king of Egypt, the latter of Phoenicia. By his wife, Telephassa,

Zeus Carrying off Europa.

Agenor had one daughter—Europa—and three sons—Cadmus, Phoenix, and Cilix. The sister having disappeared—carried off, it was said, on the back of a white bull, into which Zeus had transformed himself for love of her—the brothers were sent to search for her in different directions. Phoenix and Cilix, wearied of searching in vain, settled down in the countries named after them, while Cadmus, accompanied by his mother, proceeded through the Greek islands northward to the coast of Thrace. There his mother died and was buried. He proceeded to Delphi, to ask the

oracle concerning his sister. The advice was to search no
longer, but to follow a cow which should come in his way,
and where it lay down to rest there to found a city.   Leaving Delphi, he saw a cow, and followed it through Boeotia,
till it reached the place where Thebes was afterward built,
and there lay down. Intending to sacrifice the cow in honor
of Athene, his protecting goddess, Cadmus sent his attendants to a fountain not far off to fetch water. It happened,
however, that the fountain was watched by a terrible dragon,

Cadmus Slays the Dragon.

which killed his men. With the aid of Athene, Cadmus slew
the monster, and, at the command of the goddess, sowed its
teeth in the ground, from which there instantly sprang a
number of wild armed giants, called Spartae.   By throwing
a stone among them, Cadmus so roused their passions that
they fell upon each other with such fury and effect that only
five of them survived.   From these five the noblest families
of Thebes afterward traced their lineage.

LAOCOON.

To appease Ares, whose dragon he had slain, Cadmus was compelled to devote himself to the service of that god for eight years, or a " long year," as it was called, the usual period prescribed for penance in such cases. His term of service having expired, he was raised by Athene to the throne of Thebes; and to complete his happiness Zeus gave him Harmonia, the beautiful daughter of Ares and Aphrodite, for his wife. The gods of Olympus went to the marriage feast, and made presents to the pair. The Muses sang a marriage song. The gift of Cadmus to his wife consisted of a splendid dress (*peplos*), which Athene had worked for him, and the famous necklace made by Hephaestus. From the marriage sprang four daughters—Semele, Ino, Autonoe, Agave—and one son—Polydorus.

Autonoe married Aristaeus, to whom she bore Actaeon, the young huntsman who, for the misfortune of having once seen Artemis bathing, was transformed into a stag, and devoured by his own hounds. Ino married Athamas, of whom it is said that, being seized of a frenzy, he pursued his wife to do her violence, and that she eluded him by leaping into the sea, after which she was regarded as a marine goddess under the name of Leucothea. Semele became the mother of the wine-god Dionysus, and at the birth of her child was, as has been already related, struck dead by the thunderbolt of Zeus. Agave, marrying Echion, one of the five surviving Spartae, became the mother of Pentheus, who, after the death of Polydorus, succeeded to the sovereignty of Thebes.

Semele being dead, her statement that Zeus himself was the father of her child was disbelieved by her sisters, especially by Agave. But after her son Dionysus had grown up, and returned to Thebes from his triumphant journey eastward to India, Agave and the other women of Thebes changed their minds, and embraced his worship with its extravagant rites. Pentheus, then king of Thebes, opposed the introduction of the new religion, but in the course of his opposition was slain by his mother and her excited compan-

ions. Labdacus, the son of Polydorus, succeeded to the
throne. Meantime Agave, recovering her senses under the
affliction, fled to Illyrium.

Grief at the calamities that fell so thickly on their children at last drove Cadmus and Harmonia from Thebes.
They wandered to Illyrium, and there found peace in the
grave. Their bodies, it was believed, had been transformed
into two snakes that lay beside their tomb, while their spirits
had been placed in Elysiun by Zeus.

After Cadmus, the next figures of importance are the twin-
brothers Amphion and Zethus, who resemble in many respects the " great twin-brethren " Castor and Pollux, being
like them represented riding on white horses, and appearing
with aid in times of distress. Between the two brothers
there was a great difference of character, Amphion being
devoted to music, and excelling in the skill with which he
played the lyre given him by Hermes, while Zethus applied
himself wholly to rough life, such as hunting and herding.
What Zethus did by physical force, Amphion accomplished
by the persuasion of his strains, as was shown in the case
of their building the walls of Thebes, the population of
which had so far outgrown the limits of the old town
founded by Cadmus as to require new barriers against inva-
sion. While Zethus toiled in bringing huge stones for this
purpose, Amphion, like Orpheus, had only to strike his lyre,
and still larger stones followed whither he led the way.
Such was the story, the intention of which seems to have
originally been to point to the combination of actual strength
with harmony in placing the blocks required in good masonry.
The same idea recurs in the legend of the building of the
Trojan walls by Apollo and Poseidon, the former god corresponding to Amphion and the latter to Zethus. The seven
gates of Thebes answered to the seven strings of the lyre.

The mother of the two Theban brothers was Antiope,
who, according to an early report, was a daughter of the
river-god Asopus. In the usual genealogy, however, she

Amphion and Zethus.

was described as a daughter of Thebe and Nycteus (the "dark and stormy"), who held the office of regent in Thebes during the minority of Labdacus. Zeus having approached Antiope in the form of a Satyr, she was driven from her father's house, and forced to seek refuge, which she found with Epopeus, the king of Sicyon. Under his protection she remained some time, the father meanwhile demanding in vain that she should be given up to him. Ultimately she was given up to Lycus ("light") the brother of Nycteus, but, as his name implies, of quite an opposite character. Returning with him, she gave birth to twin boys on the way, in the neighborhood of Eleutherae. The infants were entrusted to a herdsman to be brought up. The mother was carried off to Thebes, where, as a contrast to the gentle treatment she had experienced from Lycus, she was subjected by his wife, Dirce, to relentless cruelty. After enduring continued persecution for some years, Antiope fled from Thebes, and taking the direction of Mount Cithaeron, where her children had been left, at last reached the house of the herdsman who had taken care of them. She did not, however, recognize him, nor was she aware that the two youths, who took kindly to her, were her sons. It happened just then that Dirce, who had come to Mount Cithaeron to take part in some Bacchic ceremony, detected her escaped victim, and ordered the two young herdsmen to fetch a wild bull from their herd, and to bind her to its horns, that she might be dragged to death. They would have obeyed her command, had not the old herdsman at the moment recognized Antiope, and revealed her as their mother. On hearing the story of her former troubles, Amphion and Zethus, in their indignation, seized Dirce, bound her to the bull which they had brought, and looked on while she perished miserably. The legend adds that Dirce was transformed into a fountain, which bore her name.

On the return of Antiope with her sons to Thebes, Lycus abdicated in their favor, and then commenced the building of the walls, of which we have already spoken. Amphion married Niobe, the daughter of the Lydian king Tantalus, and had a family of sons and daughters, whose beauty, in their mother's eyes, might measure with that of Apollo and Artemis. How she was punishsd for her pride has already been related. After the death of Amphion and Zethus, caused, it was said, by the arrows of Apollo, the sovereignty of Thebes finally passed to Labdacus, of whose reign little is said, his fame consisting chiefly in his being the father of Laius and grandfather of Oedipus.

This Laius married Jocasta, a daughter of Menoeceus, and had by her a son, Oedipus. An oracle had said that the child, on growing to manhood, would cause the death of his father. To avert this danger, Laius exposed the newly-born infant on Mount Cithaeron, expecting it to perish. It was, however, found by some herdsmen, conveyed by them to Corinth, and there given over to the king, Polybus, whose wife was childless, and took readily to the castaway. Arriving at years of manhood, Oedipus inquired at an oracle concerning his parentage, and was told in reply to avoid the lands of his ancestors, for otherwise he would cause his father's death, and thereafter marry his own mother. Puzzled by an answer so mysterious, and being uncertain whether Polybus might not have been his father, he left the court at Corinth, and wandered about the country. In the course of his wanderings he met Laius travelling with a retinue. A quarrel arose between Oedipus and some of the royal attendants. Laius took the part of his men, and was slain in the fight by his son, who, unaware of the blackness of the crime he had committed, proceeded on his way to Thebes. There he found great distress prevailing, in consequence of the loss of life caused by a Sphinx—a monster with the body of a lion, and the head, breast, and arms of a woman. This creature had a riddle which she propounded to all who approached her, and on their failing to resolve it, as always happened, threw them from the high rock where she lived.

Not so Oedipus, who read the riddle rightly; upon which the sphinx cast herself from the rock, and perished. The prize offered to the man who should succeed in getting rid of the Sphinx was the hand of Jocasta, the widow of Laius, along with the throne of Thebes. Oedipus married her and fulfilled the oracle.

They had two sons, **Eteocles** and **Polynices**, and two daughters, **Antigone** and **Ismene**, neither being aware of the criminality of their marriage, until, on inquiring at the oracle the cause of certain misfortunes that had befallen the country, they received an answer which revealed the facts in all their horror. Jocasta slew herself, while Oedipus, after putting out his eyes, forsook Thebes, and wandered about accompanied by his faithful daughter Antigone. His two sons succeeded him in the government, quarrelled with each other, however, and ultimately fell, both of them, in a personal encounter, as we shall relate afterward.

The various acts of this terrible tragedy were reproduced on the Athenian stage with all the poetic power of Aeschylus and Sophocles.

(d) THESSALY.

In harmony with the wild, rocky features of the country, the early legends of Thessaly tell of furious wars, in which the combatants fought with trunks of trees, or hurled rocks and even hills at each other. It was there that the war of the gods against the Giants and Titans took place. There the brothers Otus and Ephialtes heaped hill on mountain in their ambition to scale the heavens. There Poseidon (Neptune) cleft the mountain-range asunder with his trident, and formed the pleasant vale of Tempe. Mount Olympus, with its clouded summit, where the gods were once supposed to dwell, was there, and there also was Iolcus, the seat of the ancient race of the Minyae. Gyrton was the hold of the **Lapithae**, and the scene of those combats between them and the Centaurs which formed in after times so attractive a subject to Greek sculptors.

Among the Lapithae the two principal figures are Ixion and his son, Pirithous. Ixion's wife was Dia, a daughter of Deioneus. Previous to the marriage he had promised her father, accord-ing to ancient usage, many valuable pre-sents, which he af-terward refused to give. Deioneus en-deavored to indem-nify himself, but in the course of the attempt perished in a great hole, full of fire, which had been cunningly prepared for him by Ixion. For this—the first murder of a rela-tion, it was be-lieved, that had taken place in the world — Ixion was punished with fren-zy, and wandered about, unable to ob-tain expiation from gods or men, till at last Zeus received him compassion-

Centaur.

ately, and purified him. But the purification was not so complete as to prevent him from conceiving a passion for the goddess Hera, who, knowing his desires, deceived him with a cloud shaped like herself. From this union sprang

the race of Centaurs. Ixion, being blind enough to boast
of his supposed success with Hera, was despatched by Zeus
to Tartarus, and there bound by Hermes to a winged wheel,
which constantly revolved, as an eternal example of the
punishment due to such crime.

The same passion for a goddess descended to his son Pirithous, who tried to carry off Persephone from Hades, for
which he was placed in chains in Tartarus. But the event
on which his fame chiefly turns was his marriage with Deidamia. By his invitation the Centaurs of the neighboring
mountains went to the banquet, and, being unused to the
influence of wine, could not suppress excitement. The wild
Eurytion laid hold of the bride, his fellows rushed toward
her maidens, and a scene of grand confusion took place;
Pirithous and the Lapithae, with the help of his friend
Theseus, from Attica, at last succeeded in driving the
Centaurs away.

Of Caeneus, another of the Lapithae, it is related that, having been originally a beautiful virgin, she was changed into
a man by Poseidon, and made invulnerable, as was proved in
a fight with the Centaurs; for, in spite of the rocks and trunks
of trees which they struck him with, and heaped above him,
he remained unwounded, and sank into the earth alive—a
scene represented in several ancient works of sculpture and
vase-painting still in existence.

With regard to the Centaurs, the usual form in which they
were represented was that of the body and legs of a horse,
with the head, arms, and body of a man down to the waist.
In early works of art, however, they have the legs of a man
in place of the forelegs of the horse.

Chiron seems to have had nothing in common with them
but his form; for he was wise and just, well-meaning and
kindly, a friend of gods and heroes, and skilled in medicine,
music, and various arts. The young Achilles was brought
up under his care and tuition, in the cave where he lived,
on Mount Pelion. So also were Jason and Aesculapius.

He was the friend of Peleus and of Hercules, and his death was an example of the self-sacrifice which had characterized

Chiron.

his life. In trying to make peace between Hercules and the Centaurs he had been accidentally hit by a posioned arrow from the bow of Hercules. The wound baffling all his skill, and causing acute pain, he offered himself to die in the room of Prometheus, and was accepted by the gods.

(*e*) THRACE.

The burden of all the early Thracian legends is the strange divine influence of music and song. Whether the passion for music, which may be supposed to have given rise to the legends, originated among the ungenial northern hills and the valleys of Thrace, or whether, as is supposed, it was transplanted thither by immigrants from the district of Pieria, with its ancient fountain of the Muses, it would be hard to decide. All that is certain is, that the belief concerning **Orpheus**, the principal figure in these legends, was common to both regions.

Orpheus was regarded as a son of the muse Calliope and the god Apollo. From his mother he inherited the fascinating power with which he played the lyre and sang, so that the birds of the air, the fish in the streams, wild beasts, even trees, rocks, and hills, gathered round him to listen. The subject of his song was always the beautiful **Eurydice**, whom he had loved and lost. She had died through the poisoned bite of a snake that lurked in the grass over which she had to run to escape from **Aristaeus**, who also loved her. Her sister nymphs, accompanied by Orpheus, wandered over the hills and valleys, filling the air with plaintive strains to call her back again. Orpheus carried his search for her even down to the gloomy shades of the lower world, the sweetness of his music soothing the monsters and wicked spirits that dwell there, and otherwise would have resisted his progress. Even the hardened hearts of Persephone and the merciless Erinyes were touched by his passionate grief. It was agreed that Eurydice should be permitted to return with him to the upper world—the only condition attached to the agreement

being that he should not turn to look upon her face all the
way back. His patience, however, gave way. The bar-

Orpheus and Eurydice.

gain became null, and Eurydice must instantly retrace her

steps, and be lost to him forever.   For seven months he sat
in doleful mood by the banks of the river Strymon, under
the open sky, refusing food or drink.   Then he withdrew to
the higher wintry regions of the mountains Rhodope and
Haemus, to nurse his sorrow in greater solitude, but was
discovered by a band of Maenades, out upon some wild
Bacchic mission, and torn by them limb from limb.   The
Muses, it was said, gathering the limbs, conveyed them to
Pieria, on Mount Olympus, and buried them there.   His
head and lyre floated down the Hebrus, and were carried by
the sea, the lyre sounding sweetly with the swell and fall of
the waves, to the island of Lesbos, celebrated in after times
for its poets and musicians.   There the head was buried, and
nightingales sang sweeter beside it than elsewhere in Greece.
But in Thrace also a tomb was pointed out as being that of
Orpheus, while a sanctuary was established in his honor.

In later times a religious system with mysterious rites and
ceremonies, said to have been instituted by Orpheus, and
bearing his name, was widely propagated in Greece.   It may
be that his connection with the worship of Dionysus, referred
to in the legends both of Pieria and Thrace, was regarded
as sufficient warrant for associating with his name religious
institutions having much in common with the Dionysiac
mysteries.

It is said that Orpheus accompanied the expedition of the
Argonauts, but at what period of his life we do not know.

To the same region of Thrace belongs the legend of Tha-
myris, a son of the king Philammon and the nymph Argi-
ope, distinguished for his personal beauty as well as his
minstrelsy.   He was, however, inordinately vain, and on the
occasion of a visit to the court of Eurytus, at Oechalia,
boasted himself not inferior to the Muses themselves, the
daughters of Zeus.   But on his way homeward he was met
by them; they put his eyes out, and took away his power of
song and music.

(*f*) ATTICA.

The people of Attica, generally speaking, believed that
their first ancestors had sprung from the earth, and by some

Orpheus, Eurydice, and Hermes.

process been transformed from trees or rocks, or perhaps from
animals, into men and women. The change was not supposed to have been direct and instantaneous, as we may infer
from the form ascribed to **Cecrops**, the first of the race,
which was that of a man with extremities in the shape of

snakes in place of human legs. In later times of learned
speculation this Cecrops was thought to have been an immi-
grant from Egypt. Proofs of an early immigration into
Attica are certainly not wanting, but they do not point to
Egypt as the source of it. They point to Crete, which in
the time of Minos held Attica, as it probably held other
places, as a dependency.

Cecrops, according to the legend, ruled as king over the
primitive race of Attica, established himself on the Acropolis of Athens, and gathered a township around him, which
he called Cecropia. He gave his people laws, and taught
them to worship Zeus and Athene-Polias. It was during
his reign that the celebrated contest took place between Poseidon and Athene for the control of Attica. Cecrops was chosen
to decide, and, arguing that the sea was common to all, while
the olive was peculiarly adapted to the soil of his country,
gave his decision in favor of the goddess. He had three
daughters—Herse, Agraulos, and Pandrosos—all three
names apparently referring to the fertilizing fall of dew.
The last mentioned was the first priestess of Athene. Of
the other two, Herse became the mother of Ceryx, from
whom the priestly family of heralds in Attica derived their
lineage. His father was Hermes, the divine herald. Agraulos bore a daughter to the god Ares. Her name was
Alcippe, and her story, that she loved Halirrhothius, a son
of Poseidon, and was slain by Ares. For that crime a court
called the Areopagus was appointed to try the god, and continued thereafter to sit on cases of murder.

The successor of Cecrops was Erichthonius, who was described as being altogether of the form of a snake. He was
the offspring of Hephaestus and Gaea, was the fondling of
Athene, and when he obtained the throne of Attica, taught
his people to worship the ancient wooden image of the goddess, and instituted in her honor the famous Panathenaic
games. The story of his infancy was that Athene handed
him in a closed box to the three daughters of Cecrops, with

orders not to open it. Two of the sisters, Herse and Agraulos, yielded to curiosity, opened the box, and, on seeing a
snake within, were seized with frantic terror and threw
themselves from the rocks of the Acropolis. Erichthonius
was brought up within the sanctuary of the goddess.

Erichthonius was succeeded by his son Pandion, and he
again by his son Erechtheus, with whom the dynasty of the
line of Cecrops came to an end, passing over to Ion, a reputed
son of Apollo, and the ancestor of the Ionian race. Erechtheus and all his family perished in a battle against Eumolpus, the prince of Eleusis. The result of their death, however, was that the old strife between Attica and Eleusis was
put an end to, and the two kingdoms united in one.

Besides his son Erechtheus, Pandion had two daughters,
Procne and Philomela, of whom a touching story is told.
It would seem that in the course of a war with Labdacus of
Thebes, Pandion had obtained important assistance from
Tereus, a king of Thrace, and for this offered him the hand
of his daughter Procne. Afterward the Thracian desired
her sister also, and, pretending that Procne was dead,
obtained Philomela as his wife. To prevent the former
from revealing the truth, he tore out her tongue, and placed
her in a cage in a wood. But his end was not thus gained;
for Procne contrived to send her sister a piece of drapery on
which she had embroidered a representation of the facts,
which her sister readily understood. The two sisters then
combined to execute a terrible revenge on Tereus, placing
the flesh of his son Itys, whom they killed, before him as a
dish. Tereus drew his sword, and pursued the sisters till
all three were changed into birds—he into a lapwing, Procne
into a swallow, and Philomela into a nightingale. The
Latin poets reversed the story of the two sisters, saying that
it was Philomela whose tongue was cut out, their object
being, since her name is the same as that of the nightingale,
to account for the silence of that bird except in the spring-
time.

The Attic legend of Boreas, the wind-god, who carried off Orithyia, has already been given, as has also that of Cephalus and Procris. We shall, therefore, pass on to Ion, who, when the male line of Cecrops had become extinct, succeeded to the throne of Attica.

Ion was a son of Apollo and Creusa, a daughter of Erechtheus, and at his birth was taken away from his mother, who afterward married Xuthus, and remained childless. Going to Delphi to consult the oracle about their prospects of posterity, Xuthus and Creusa were told by the god to adopt as their son the first youth they should meet. This happened to be Ion, who had been brought up in the temple of Delphi, and who, agreeably to the command of the god, was adopted by the childless pair.

According to another legend, Pandion was driven from Attica by the sons of Metion, and took refuge with Pylus, the king of Megara, where he found and adopted Aegeus, who, after Pandion's death, advanced upon Attica, and, with the assistance of his brothers, Pallas, Nisos, and Lycus, recovered the kingdom of his adopted father, reigned in Athens, and became the father of the renowned hero Theseus, whose exploits we shall relate hereafter.

(g) CRETE.

The position of the island of Crete, its extent and fertility, appear to have attracted the early Phoenician traders to its shores. They founded the towns of Gnossus and Gortyn, and so developed the resources of the island as to give it a powerful ascendency over the other islands of the Archipelago, and extending to various districts of the mainland of Greece, including Attica, as has just been said. They introduced the worship of Astarte and Moloch; and when, generations afterward, the island had become completely Hellenized, through the successive immigrations of Achaeans

HERMES, OR MERCURY.

and Dorians, there were still found current among the people
legends that could only be explained in connection with the
religion of the Phoenicians.   Of this kind were the legends

Theseus and the Minotaurus.

of Talos, Itanus, and the river Jardanus.   The Greek
immigrants settled in the towns that had been planted by
the Phoenicians, adapting themselves to existing arrange-

ments, it appears, and accepting the ancient traditions of the
island as a basis for legends of a purely Greek construc-
tion.

These legends commence with Europa, whom Zeus saw
and loved while she was gathering spring buds near Sidon,
where her father, Agenor (or Phoenix, as some said), was
king. The god, transforming himself into a white bull,
carried her off on his back over the sea toward the south
coast of Crete, and landed with her in the district of Gortyn
and Phaestus, where Asterion was then the reigning king.
Europa gave birth there to three sons—Minos, Rhadamanthus, and Sarpedon—who grew up under the care of Asterion, to whom Zeus had commended their mother. How
familiar the people of the island must have been with the
various phases of this legend may be seen from the ancient
coins of Gortyn and Phaestus, with their representations,
now of a bull alone, now of Europa riding on him, and at
other times of Europa seated among the branches of a plane-
tree.

The oldest traditions describe Minos as ruling the island
with exemplary justice, extending its maritime power and
its supremacy over the neighboring islands and countries.
He established among his people a wise system of laws,
which formed, it was believed, in after times, the basis of the
legislation of Lycurgus. These laws, he said, were communicated to him by his father, Zeus, with whom he went every
ninth year to hold communion in a sacred cave in the island.
So high was his reputation for justice that when he died, so
people thought, he was appointed a judge in the lower world.

The wife of Minos was Pasiphae, a daughter of the sun-
god Helios and Perseis. It is necessary to bear her parentage in mind for the sake of obtaining a right clue to the
explanation of the legend concerning her. For, as a daughter
of Helios and Perseis, she may well have been originally a
goddess of the moon, and as such represented under the form
of a white cow. Her name, Pasiphae, would be appropriate

for such an office. She bore to Minos two daughters—

Daedalus and Icarus.

Ariadne and Phaedra—of whom more will be told hereafter.

Minos, it was said, on being chosen king of the island, proceeded to the sea-shore to offer, in presence of his people, a sacrifice to his father, Zeus, calling on the sea-god Poseidon to send up a victim for that purpose from the sea. Poseidon heard, and sent a shimmering white bull. In this act of compliance on the part of the sea-god, Minos perceived that his supremacy at sea was secured. Instead, however, of sacrificing the white bull, he placed it among his own herd which browsed near Gortyn—a herd which is elsewhere said to have belonged to the sun-god. Poseidon, taking offence at the deceit, caused the bull to become wild, and at the same time inflamed the queen, Pasiphae, with an unnatural desire toward it. The bull broke from his stall, and was pursued by Pasiphae over hills and through woods, till finally the great artist **Daedalus** succeeded in holding him to the meadow and in satisfying the desires of the queen, who afterward gave birth to **Minotaurus,** a creature with the body and limbs of a man and the head of a bull. Daedalus had now to employ his skill in making a vast labyrinth, with intricate winding passages, from which no one who entered could find his way out. Within it Minotaurus was placed, and received as victims the persons sent to Minos periodically by tributary states. Such tribute, consisting of seven boys and seven girls of noble families, Minos had levied on Athens as a satisfaction for the murder of his son **Androgeos** by Aegeus, the king of Attica. Every eight years the grievous levy was despatched to Crete, till **Theseus,** the son of Aegeus, put an end to it in a manner which we shall afterward have occasion to relate.

Minos met his death at Agrigentum, in Sicily, whither he had pursued Daedalus, who had escaped from the labyrinth, into which he and his son **Icarus** had been thrown for making a figure of a cow for Pasiphae so lifelike as to be mistaken by the herd. He had escaped by means of wings which he had made for himself and his son. The latter fell into the sea, and was drowned, while his father, reaching Sicily in safety, was received under the protection of King Cocalus, whose daughter killed Minos by pouring boiling water on his head while he was in a bath. Minos was buried there, and had a tomb erected in his memory.

On the coins of the town of Phaestus is the figure of a youth, winged and nude, rushing with great strides, and holding what appears to be a stone in each hand. This figure has been identified with the legends of **Talos**, who is described as having been made of bronze, a remnant of the

Daedalus and Icarus.

Bronze age, or, as others said, a living work of art produced by Hephaestus. He had been placed in Crete by Zeus, to watch over Europa, his duty being to run round the island three times a day, and see who landed on the coast. When

the Argonauts arrived, he opposed their landing, but unsuc-
cessfully; for it happened that they were aware of the fact
that, though apparently altogether made of bronze, he still
had a vein reaching from neck to heel, and containing his
life-blood.   This vein Poeas, the father of Philoctetes, man-
aged to hit with an arrow from the famous bow of Hercules.
Talos fell and died.   Others said that Medea, who accompanied the Argonauts, overcame him by witchcraft.   It had
been the practice of Talos, when he caught any one landing
on the coast, to seize his victim in his arms, to leap with him
into a fire, and press him to his burning bosom, the while
laughing at the pain.   This was the origin of the phrase
"Sardonic laughter."

Though the appointment of **Rhadamanthus** as a judge in
the lower world was said to have been due to the sense of
justice which he had displayed on earth, the region or country
that benefited by his decisions is not given.   It may be right
to assume that he acted with his brother Minos in Crete.
Sarpedon, the third of the brothers, passed over to Lycia,
and there became the founder of an illustrious line of heroes.

(*h*) ELIS AND ARGOS.

With **Pelops** commences a lineage of heroes famous in
Elis and Argos for their deeds of violence and for the retribution that awaited them.   How Niobe, the sister of Pelops,
was punished for her pride, we have already seen.   What
his father, Tantalus, had to endure in Tartarus has also been
described.   Tantalus had ruled his kingdom of Phrygia, in
Asia Minor, well, and on that account gained the esteem of
the gods, who invited him to a banquet.   But he betrayed
their secrets, and, to crown all, invited them to a feast, at
which, to test their power of knowing all things that happened, he set before them the flesh of his own son Pelops.
The gods, perceiving the outrageous attempt, restored the
child to life, giving him in place of the shoulder that had

been eaten, whether by Demeter or Thetis, a shoulder of ivory. His father was despatched to Tartarus.

When Pelops had grown to manhood under the care of the gods—especially of Poseidon, from whom he learned his skill in managing horses—he resolved to win Hippodameia, the daughter of the king of Elis, Oenomaus, a son of Ares, and the owner of horses swift as the wind. The story was that Oenomaus had been informed by an oracle that his death would be caused by the husband of his daughter. Trusting to the extraordinary speed of his horses, he freely offered his daughter's hand to any suitor who should outstrip him in a chariot race. Those who failed, it was stipulated in the challenge, should perish at his hands. This fate had befallen many an ardent suitor previous to the arrival of Pelops, who, with a golden chariot and winged horses, given him by Poseidon, won the race. It is said, however, that his success was rather due to Hippodamia, who had conceived a great love for the youth, and gave practical effect to her passion by bribing her father's charioteer, Myrtilus, to take a spoke out of his master's wheel.

With the hand of Hippodamia, Pelops obtained the throne of Elis, and had, among other children, two sons, named Atreus and Thyestes. He established, or at least greatly promoted, the Olympian games. His grave, the house of Oenomaus, and other monuments of his excellent rule, were afterward gratefully pointed to at Olympia.

Atreus and Thyestes, having slain the beautiful young Chrysippus, a son of Pelops and a nymph, were compelled to leave Elis. They found refuge in Mycenae, establishing themselves in the old fort of Midea, until the death of Eurystheus, when Atreus obtained the government of Mycenae, the ruins of which still attest the power of its ancient kings. Atreus married a daughter of Minos—Aerope—who allowed herself to listen to proposals from Thyestes, and assisted him to carry off the ram with the golden fleece, the possession of which was supposed to secure the government of the country.   But Zeus interfered in the cause of Atreus, the elder of the brothers, and, as a sign of his will, caused the sun to rise in the west.   Thyestes returned to his brother's house, asking to be forgiven, and was received with an appearance of good-will.   Instead of being forgiven, however, he was presented, on sitting down to eat, with the flesh of his own son.   Thyestes fled in horror, and thereupon famine stalked over the land.   On consulting an oracle with regard to the famine, Atreus was told to find Thyestes, and take him back.   He did so, and moreover placed him in confinement in Argos, at the same time trying to persuade Aegisthus, the son of Thyestes, to kill his father.   But events took a different course, Thyestes preferring to make a victim of Atreus.   On the death of Atreus, Agamemnon succeeded to the throne of Argos, and his brother Menelaus to that of Sparta.   Of these two brothers more shall be said in connection with the war against Troy.

HERCULES.

Though regarded sometimes as a god, and honored in the way appointed for immortals, it was chiefly as the hero of a long series of arduous labors, difficulties apparently insurmountable, and sufferings, that Hercules obtained the numerous honors paid to his memory throughout Greece.   In the gymnasia, where the youth of every town were instructed in athletic exercises, the statue of Hercules was pointed to as a model of what a perfect athlete should be ; while the tales of his wrestling with this or that giant were repeated as examples of fearlessness and extraordinary strength.   Soldiers going to battle thought of his fatigues and ultimate triumphs. Laborers oppressed by toil relieved their sorrows by recalling the laborious incidents of his life.   Even the Athenians valued the rugged, stubborn endurance of Hercules higher than the litheness and more perfect form of their own Theseus.   So far,

Hercules was looked upon merely as an example of extraordinary physical strength and patient toiling to the end; but in later times he came also to be held up as an ideal of virtue

Hercules.

and duty, in which capacity a story invented by the sophist Prodicus concerning him, found great applause. That story was entitled "The Choice of Hercules," and represented him

as being met at a crossway, while yet a youth, by two figures
—Pleasure and Duty—the one promising him all possible
enjoyments, the other a life of labor and trouble, if he
would follow her.   He chose to follow Duty.

According to the genealogy, Hercules was a son of Zeus
and Alcmene, the wife of Amphitryon, a descendant of
Perseus, and resident in Thebes.   On the day on which he
was to have been born, Hera, to whose persecution all the
labors and sufferings of Hercules in after life were due,
obtained from Zeus, in presence of the assembled gods, a vow
that the boy to be born on that day should have power and
dominion over all that dwelt about him.   Hastening to
Argos, she lent a helping hand to the wife of Sthenelus, and
enabled her to give birth to Eurystheus, a weakly seven-
months' child.   Meantime she had delayed the birth of Hercules, who, in consequence, became the subject of Eurystheus.
With all this hostility on the part of Hera, it is curious to
compare a scene which not unfrequently occurs on ancient
painted vases, representing Hera suckling the infant Hercules.
The story was that Hermes (Mercury), at the command of
Zeus, had carried the newly born child to Olympus, and put
it to Hera's breast, without her knowing whose child it was.
From this divine milk Hercules drew his godlike strength,
the first promise of which was given soon after his birth, by
his strangling the serpent sent by Hera to kill him.

His youth was spent under the instruction of the most
celebrated heroes of the day, the wise Rhadamanthus teaching him to be wise and virtuous, and Linus the practice of
music.   Unluckily, Linus had to punish him for some neglect,
and in doing so enraged the boy so much that he turned and
slew his master.   For this Amphitryon carried his son away
to the hills, and left him under the care of herdsmen, with
whom, like Romulus, or Amphion and Zethus, he enjoyed a
wild life of hunting and exposure to climate, his limbs growing to enormous size, and his eyes sparkling with unusual
fire.   At the age of eighteen he slew an enormous lion that

infested Mount Cithaeron, destroying the flocks of his father, Amphitryon, and of Thespius, the king of Thespiae. Returning to Thebes from the lion-hunt, and wearing its skin hanging from his shoulders as a sign of his success, he met the heralds of the king of the Minyae, coming from Orchomenos to claim the annual tribute of a hundred cattle levied on Thebes. Hercules cut off the ears and noses of the heralds, bound their hands, and sent them home. A war followed, in which Amphitryon and his two sons, Hercules and Iphicles, did wonders on the part of Thebes, and were duly honored for the same.

But the part taken by Hercules in that war was the last act of his own free will; for Hera, annoyed at the fast-rising fame of the young hero, persuaded Eurystheus to exercise the authority given him at his birth by Zeus, and to call on Hercules to enter his service. Hercules inquired at the Delphic oracle whether it was possible to escape the summons, but was told in reply that he must carry out successfully twelve tasks to be imposed on him by Eurystheus, and that, having done so, he would be reckoned among the number of immortals. With this answer in his mind, he presented himself to Eurystheus at Mycenae, and commenced the serious labor of life.

The Twelve Labors of Hercules.

It may be, as has been often suggested, that the legend of the labors of Hercules, like those of Perseus in the service of Polydectes, or of Bellerophon in that of the Lycian king, or of Siegfried in that of the king of Burgundy, was intended to convey an illustration of the course and operations of the sun. His first labors are performed near home, the distance from which increases with each new labor that is imposed, till at last, after carrying off the golden apples of the Hesperides in the remote west, he descends to the lower world, and brings back with him the hated dog Cerberus. In later times the

twelve labors were openly brought into connection with the
twelve signs of the zodiac. It is, however, more likely that,
originally, this number had no more signification than in the
case of the twelve higher deities of Olympus, that it was
adopted by the poets, such as Pisander and Stesichorus, who
first made these labors their theme, and that through their
influence it became stereotyped both in poetry and art. In
Homer, though the labors are known, there is no mention of
their number. In the *Iliad* (v. 395) Hercules is the hero
whose unerring arrows wounded Hera and Hades. In the
Odyssey (viii. 224) Hercules and Eurytus are described as
the most celebrated marksmen of bygone times, and in early
works of art it is his character as a bowman that is principally represented. But after the time of Pisander and
Stesichorus, a change is introduced. The club becomes his
favorite weapon; and instead of a linen garment wrapped
round his loins, he now appears either carrying the skin of
the Nemean lion over his arm, or wearing it hanging down
his back—the skin of its head fitting to his crown like a
cap, and the forelegs knotted under his chin.

1. *The Nemean lion*, the offspring of Typhon and Echidna,
had been sent by Hera to devastate the neighborhood of
Nemea, and had succeeded, to the horror of the natives.
What made the matter worse was that the plain of Nemea
was sacred to Zeus. The lion was known to be invulnerable
—proof even against the arrows of Hercules. It was, therefore, necessary to adopt novel means for its destruction.
Hercules entered the cave where its lair was, closed the
entrance behind him, and at once grappling the monster in
his arms strangled it. The skin he tore off with his fingers,
and, knowing it to be impenetrable, resolved to wear it
henceforth in his own defence. To the legend as it thus
stands was added, by the Alexandrian and Roman poets, the
story of Molorchus, a native of the district, on whom Hercules called on his way to the cave, and who, when about to
kill his only goat to make a feast for his guest, was told by

the hero to desist and to wait his return. It was arranged that should he not return within thirty days Molorchus was to sacrifice to him as to a dead person. The thirty days had just elapsed when Hercules returned and found his friend in the act of preparing the sacrifice. It is possible that the thirty days may refer to the period of greatest heat in summer, when the lion and the dog are ascendant.

Hercules and the Nemean Lion.

2. *The Lernean hydra*, also the offspring of Typhon and Echidna, and sent by Hera. Hercules killed it with his sword, being assisted in the enterprise by Iolaus and Athene. The legend is given more fully by Apollodorus, whose ver-

sion, though late, is proved to have been founded on an earlier form of it by the remains of poetry and art of high antiquity. The *hydra* was a monster with nine heads, of which eight were mortal and the ninth invulnerable. It lived in the marshy ground beside the fountain of Amymone, and even the smell which spread from its poison was fatal to any one who passed near it. Hercules arrived at the spot in a chariot, attended by Iolaus, and succeeded in driving the hydra from its hole by firing his arrows in upon it. The fight began, and Hercules found that for every head of it which he cut two fresh heads started up, and to increase the difficulty a huge crab came and seized him by the heel. It was necessary to try another form of attack. Hercules ordered Iolaus to set the neighboring wood on fire and to fetch him a brand from it; with the brand so obtained he proceeded, the moment he had cut off a head, to burn it up, and in this way destroying them one by one, he at last came to the invulnerable head, cut it off also, and buried it under a huge rock. He dipped his arrows in the poison of the hydra. When his success was reported to Eurystheus, the latter refused to reckon it as one of the labors, on the ground that Iolaus had rendered assistance. The interpretation of the legend is that the hydra or water-snake is a symbol of the horrors of a marshy district, and that its poison, with its fatal smell, represents the miasma which arises from such districts.

3. *The Erymanthian boar*, like the Ceryneian stag and the Stymphalian birds, carries us to a mountainous and wild rustic scene. Its haunt was on Mount Erymanthus, in the north of Arcadia. But the name of Erymanthus was also applied to a stream which flowed down the mountain side; and it is not improbable that the wild boar was only a legendary illustration of the ravages produced in winter and early spring by the descent of this river with swollen torrents. The orders of Eurystheus were that the boar should be brought back alive to Mycenae; but at the sight of Hercules returning

with it alive on his shoulders, fear took possession of the
king, and he hid himself in a large bronze vessel, into which
Hercules, as frequently represented on ancient vases, proceeded to put the boar, as the safest possible place. The
consternation of Eurystheus may be imagined. In connection with the capture of the boar is told the story of a visit
which Hercules paid on his way to the Centaur, Pholus, who
lived in a cave on Mount Pholoe. The hero was hungry,
and Pholus gave him to eat. He was also thirsty, and

Hercules and the Lernean Hydra.

required some wine Now Pholus had at hand a large vase
full of choice wine, but it was the common property of the
Centaurs who lived in other parts of the mountain. On the
other hand, the wine had been a present from Dionysus, and
had been accompanied with the command that it should not
be opened till his good friend Hercules arrived. Pholus
accordingly had no hesitation in tapping the vase, and both
drank freely from it. The strong aroma of the wine, however, reached the nostrils of the other Centaurs, who now
flocked toward the cave of Pholus in wild confusion, armed
with pine branches, rocks, axes, and torches, and fell upon
Hercules. A violent fight ensued, in which Hercules, besides
with superior numbers, had also to contend with the disad-
vantages of a flood of water sent by the clouds, who were

the mothers of the Centaurs. Ultimately he succeeded in wounding many and dispersing the others into the woods—the only melancholy part of the issue being that his friend Pholus lost his life under circumstances which remind us of the death of that other kindly Centaur, Chiron, who lived on Mount Pelion, and brought up Achilles. Pholus was stooping over a Centaur who had fallen by an arrow from Hercules, and after drawing out the arrow, was wondering how so small a thing could produce such an effect, when it fell from his hands, and striking severely on his foot, its poison entered his body, and he died. The legend appears to have been popular both with poets and vase painters.

4. *The Ceryneian stag*, an animal of wonderful fleetness, with antlers of gold and hoofs of brass, was sacred to Artemis, to whom it had been dedicated by Taygete, one of the Pleiades. It took its name from the hill and hunting district of Ceryneia, on the borders of Arcadia and Achaia; at other times it was called the Maenalian stag. The task imposed on Hercules was to capture and bring it back alive. The chase lasted for a whole year, Hercules pursuing it over hills and plains, ravines and meadows, on to the Hyperborean region, and thence back to where it had started among the Arcadian hills. It sought shelter in the sanctuary of Artemis, but being dislodged was overtaken by Hercules at the banks of the river Ladon. He would have slain it had not Apollo and Artemis appeared on the scene. The stag running a whole year on to the regions of the Hyperboreans, and thence returning to where it had set out, appears to be a mythical illustration of the course of the moon, and may be compared with the much simpler story of the huntress Arge—the "shimmering being" who pursued a stag, crying out, "I will catch you should your speed equal that of Helios;" for which boast the angry god transformed her into a deer.

5. *The Stymphalian birds*. The vale of Stymphalus, lying among the mountains in such a way as to be constantly exposed to the floods and storms of winter, was described in

a mythical form as being subject to the ravages of a number-
less flock of birds, which, with their iron talons and feathers
sharp as arrows, delighted in human flesh. From the description of the figures of some of them, which were preserved in
the sanctuary of Artemis, it appears that they resembled in
form the Harpies, and like them, too, they were, there is every
reason to believe, symbols of the cold, destructive storms of
winter. To get rid of them Hercules first raised an alarm
by ringing a large bell; and when the birds came out from
the thick wood where their nests were, many were shot down
by his arrows, and the rest flew away in fright. They flew,
as it appears from the story of the Argonauts, to an island,
sacred to Ares, in the inhospitable Black Sea, where the
Argonauts suffered severely from the heavy falls of their
sharp biting feathers, and only obtained relief by again
frightening them by raising a great din. As the birds flew
over the sea their feathers fell like a thick snow-storm, the
flakes of which, it should be remembered, are frequently in
the legends of other peoples compared with feathers. Hercules, as a hero representing the influence of the sun, was
very properly called in by the myth-makers to destroy beings
of this kind, more especially as in the neighboring district of
Pheneus he had long been regarded as a beneficent hero.
The statement of his having alarmed the birds by ringing a
bell may have been suggested by a common practice of raising birds from their nests. At the same time it may also
refer to a custom which is known at any rate in more recent
times—that of ringing bells during severe storms, from a
belief that such a proceeding availed against all evil spirits
of the air.

6. *The Augean stables.* Augeas, the rich prince of Elis,
and his daughter Agamede, the sorceress who knew the
potency of all the herbs in the world, were known to the
author of the *Iliad* (xi. 701, 739). His seat was at Ephyra,
a name which occurs in connection with the worship of the
heavenly powers, while Augeas itself means "a being of

streaming light.'' Light streamed from his eyes, and it was said expressly that he was a son of Helios. His daughter Agamede is obviously identical in character with Dirce, Medea, and Megamede, all of whom represented by their witchcraft the occult powers of the moon. Another feature of the story, which confirms the opinion that Augeas in some way was intended to illustrate the phenomena of the sun's light, is his possession of herds of lambs and cattle, fabulous in numbers as are the fleecy clouds, and including twelve bulls, white as swans, and sacred to Helios—one of them being called Phaethon, and described as glittering like a star. The court of Augeas was by the banks of the river Peneus, and the task assigned to Hercules was to clear out his endless line of stalls alone and in one day. To accomplish this, the hero made an opening through the wall at a part where the river approached it. The stream, rushing in at the opening, swept with it, as it flowed along the stables, their accumulated dung. Augeas had promised to reward Hercules with a tenth of his herds; but declined to fulfil his agreement on hearing that the task had been imposed by Eurystheus. This refusal afterward led to a war between Hercules and Elis.

7. *The Cretan bull* had been presented by Poseidon to Minos, and by him placed among the herd of cattle sacred to the sun. How it became wild, and how Pasiphae, the wife of Minos, conceiving a passion for it, followed it over the island, has been told in connection with the legends of Crete. The task imposed on Hercules was to bring this bull to Mycenae. The first difficulty was to capture and subdue it, an act in which he is frequently represented on the painted vases. The second was to bring it over the sea to Mycenae, which he did by sitting on its back while it swam, as did Europa with Zeus, in the shape of a bull. As to the fate of the bull, it is said, that Eurystheus sacrificed it to Hera, and, again, that it escaped, roved wildly over the Peloponnesus, and was finally captured at Marathon by Theseus.

8. *The horses of Diomedes,* a king of Thrace, and reputed to have been a son of Ares, the god of war and the personification of storm. Like the people whom he ruled, Diomedes was fierce in war. His seat was in the neighborhood of Abdera, where in later times the remains of his citadel was pointed out. He was the owner of certain horses which fed on human flesh, and by that means became furious and so powerful that they had to be fastened with iron chains. The human flesh on which they fed was generally that of persons who had been wrecked on that inhospitable coast. Hercules was ordered to bring these horses to Mycenae. To Abdera he went by sea; and on arriving overpowered the guards, and led the horses away to the shore, when he was

The Girdle of Hippolyte.

overtaken by a crowd of the subjects of Diomedes. A terrible fight ensued, in which the king fell at the hands of Hercules, and was himself given as food for his horses. In the course of the combat, Abderus, a beautiful youth, of whom Hercules was very fond, fell: and in his honor the hero raised a mound, and instituted games in his honor,

which the people of Abdera afterward continued annually.
After the horses had been conveyed to Mycenae and presented to Eurystheus, it is said that they escaped among the
hills of Arcadia, and were there ultimately devoured by wild
beasts—probably by the wolves of Zeus Lycaeus. Their
allegorical signification is clearly that of storms and billows,
and hence the legend was located in Thrace, a country with
which we are familiar in connection with other personifications of storm—such as Ares, Lycurgus, and Boreas.

9. *The girdle of Hippolyte*, the queen of the Amazons, had
been a gift from Ares, and was a symbol of the power of a
rushing headlong storm. The task imposed on Hercules was
to fetch this girdle for Admete, the daughter of Eurystheus,
of whom we learn elsewhere that she was a priestess of the
Argive Hera. Hercules slew the Amazon, and returned with
the girdle. From this adventure appears to have arisen the
legend of a war conducted by Hercules against the Amazons.

10. *The cattle of Geryon* or Geryoneus, who was a son of
Chrysaor and the Oceanid nymph Callirrhoe. In one person he had three bodies, three heads, three pairs of legs, and
six arms. He was gigantic in size, heavily armed, powerful,
and provided with wings. The great point in his character
was that he was the lord of immense herds of cattle. Considering that the possession of herds of cattle was also a
prominent feature in the character of Apollo and Helios, in
whose case the cattle represented the days of the year, and
considering further that the local habitation of Geryon,
though assigned to various localities, is always assigned to a
place in some way connected with the worship of Helios, it
may be inferred that Geryon also was an illustration of some
of the phenomena of the sky; and of these phenomena none
but those of wintry storms correspond with his personal
appearance and vehemence. Geryon keeps his cattle at
night in a dark cave in the remote west, into which Hercules
penetrates, and drives them away eastward toward the region
of morning light. The expedition had three stages: first,

the journey to Erytheia, where Geryon lived, and which, judged by the meaning of its name, seems to be connected with the red glow of sunset; secondly, the contest with Geryon; and, thirdly, the return to Mycenae with the cattle. Erytheia was an island somewhere in the remote west, beyond the pillars of Hercules; and to reach it the hero employed a vessel, obtained, some said, from Nereus, while others believed that he had compelled Helios to lend him for the occasion the cup or vessel in which he was accustomed to sail every night round the world from west to east. On the passage Hercules was alarmed, or at any rate disturbed, by a storm, which was only appeased by his drawing his bow on Oceanus. Reaching the island he placed himself on Mount Abas, but was observed by the two-headed dog of Geryon, and attacked by it. He slew the dog, and was next attacked by the herdsman Eurytion, who also fell at his hands. Then Menoetius, who was there watching the cattle of Helios, pointed out to him the cattle of Geryon, grazing in a meadow by the river's side. He was in the act of driving them away, when Geryon himself, in all his strength and fierceness, appeared on the scene. The combat was ended by a fatal shaft from Hercules. Shipping the cattle into the vessel of the sun, and landing them safely, Hercules commenced his homeward journey on foot, through Iberia, Gaul, over the Alps, and down through Italy, with many adventures, in all of which he was successful. At Rome occurred the incident with the robber Cacus, which the Romans incorporated among their national legends, though the elements of it were obviously of a Greek origin. At the Phlegraean fields, near Cumae, he fought the Giants. On the mountains between Rhegium and Locri his rest was disturbed by the noise of the grasshoppers, and at his prayer the gods removed these creatures from the district forever. From the south of Italy one of his bulls escaped across the sea to Sicily, and as it was necessary to follow it, Hercules, holding on by the horns of another bull, crossed with his herd to that island.

through the length and breadth of which he appears to have wandered, encountering giants like Eryx, experiencing kindness from the nymphs of Himera and Egesta, at whose warm springs he was refreshed, and everywhere leaving reminiscences of his visit. Thence he passed up the shores of the Adriatic, round by Illyria and Epirus to Ambracia, where a gadfly, sent by Hera, caused his cattle to run away in great numbers to the mountains. With the remainder he reached the Hellespont, and thence proceeded to Mycenae, where Eurystheus sacrificed them to the goddess Hera.

11. *The apples of the Hesperides.* According to later story, the last labor imposed on Hercules was to procure three of the golden apples which grew in the garden of the Hesperides; and hence in works of art which represent him as *invictus*, the invincible, he appears holding the apples in his hand. As in the case of the cattle of Geryon, here also the chief interest of the legend resides in the adventures on the way. As regards the locality where this wonderful garden was to be found, there was a difference of opinion; some, apparently under the influence of Phoenician traditions, believing it to have been in the remote west, while Aeschylus and others conceived that Atlas and the Hesperides lived in the northern region of the Hyperboreans. From the combination of both beliefs in later times, a very wide scope was given to the adventures of the hero on his way there and back. Hercules himself, not knowing what direction to take, is said to have first passed through Macedonia and on to the Rhone, where he met certain nymphs who advised him that Nereus, the sea-god, knew the secret, and could be made to give it up. In spite of the many transformations of Nereus, Hercules compelled him to tell him the way. He then proceeded to Libya, where he found Antaeus, a giant of enormous strength, whose habit was to kill all travellers who crossed the waste where he lived. He was a son of Poseidon and the Earth, deriving from his mother a strength which rendered him invincible to those who could not lift him from

the ground, which Hercules did. The wrestling scene between the two was a favorite subject in ancient art, and commended itself largely to the Greek youths as they practised in the palaestra. When he had conquered Antaeus, Hercules lay down to rest, and in a little while found himself covered with a host of creatures called Pygmies, who sprang up from the waste. He wrapped them in his lion's skin and killed them. From Libya he went into Egypt, where he was seized by the orders of Busiris and conveyed, as were all strangers, to be sacrificed He burst his bonds, and offered up instead Busiris, his son, and retinue. From Egypt he went to India, and thence returned in a northerly direction toward the Caucasus mountains, where he set free Prometheus, and in return for that kindly act was told the way on through Scythia to the region of the Hyperboreans, where lived Atlas and the Hesperides. Part of the arrangement was that Atlas should pluck the three apples for him; and to relieve him for that purpose it was necessary that Hercules should take the burden of the world on his shoulders. Atlas returned with the apples, and naively proposed that he himself should convey them to Eurystheus. Hercules appeared to appreciate the proposal, and only wished first to find a pad to save his head from the weight. Atlas did not see the joke, and willingly took the world on his shoulders again. Hercules, of course, did not return. Another report has it that Hercules himself entered the garden, slew the dragon which watched the tree, and carried off the apples and returned with them to Eurystheus.

12. *Cerberus*, the three-headed dog of Hades, which guarded the entrance to the lower world, was a symbol of the eternal darkness of Hades. The task of bringing it to the upper world was regarded in the earlier epic poetry as the most difficult of the labors of Hercules. It was supposed that he entered from the upper world through a chasm near Taenarum, returning by the same way. The shades of the dead fled in terror when they beheld him. Near the

gates he found his friends Theseus and Peirithous seated on a rock, to which they were attached as if they had grown from it, and in great trouble. He freed Theseus, but the earth shook when he tried to do the same for Peirithous. To impart life to the shades of his friends whom he freed, he obtained blood from one of the cows of Hades, which he killed after a severe fight with Menoetius, the herdsman. At last he reached Pluto, who agreed that he might take Cerberus, provided he could do so without the assistance of arms of any kind. This he succeeded in doing, and leading the hated dog to Eurystheus, completed his twelve labors.

The labors of Hercules were a favorite subject with the ancient vase-painters and sculptors, and of the latter especially those of later times who worked for Roman patrons, in whose estimation the Greek hero stood high. The manner in which each of the labors was represented seldom varied; and from this it may be assumed that the type of each had originally been established by Greek artists of celebrity, from whose models it would have been presumption to depart.

As an instance of how these labors were represented collectively, we would cite a marble sarcophagus in the British Museum, dating probably from the third century A.D. Without caring to follow the chronological order usually accepted, the sculptor has chosen to dispose his groups according to his ideas of artistic effect, or perhaps according to his ideas of their importance. On the extreme left of the front we find Hercules dragging Cerberus out of Hades, the mouth of which is represented as the rocky entrance to a cave. Among the rocks is hiding a nude diminutive figure, which may be taken to be one of the shades of the dead, who, as it was said, fled in terror when they beheld the hero. Next to this is a group of Hercules removing the girdle of the Amazon Hippolyte, who lies dead at his feet. Then we have the scene in the garden of the Hesperides, then the taming of the horses of Diomedes, and lastly the strangling of the Nemean lion. On one end of the sarcophagus he appears slaying the Lernean hydra, and on the other capturing the Ceryneian stag. In these last three groups he is figured represented as beardless and of a youthful figure, while in the others his form has become colossal, and his features marked with toil. On the lid are sculptured, on a smaller scale, the five remaining labors, of which the first, beginning from the left hand, is the bringing of the Erymanthian boar; next to that we find Hercules hard at work with a pickaxe,

Hercules and Cerberus.

making an opening, as it seems, into the wall of the Augean stables; the third scene represents him shooting the Stymphalian birds; in the fourth he is engaged in subduing the Cretan bull; and in the fifth he fights with the triple-bodied giant, Geryon. These five labors are shut in on the left by the scene where Hercules, as an infant, strangles the snake sent by Hera, and on the right by a group representing him seated after his labors, and receiving a cup of wine from the goddess Victory, while Athene stands by.

HERCULES AS A NATIONAL HERO.

In addition to the twelve labors imposed by Eurystheus, and apparently after the expiry of his servitude to that monarch, Hercules performed many other wonderful feats, which caused his name to be surrounded with glory. Of these it has already been mentioned that he wrestled with and vanquished the Giant Antaeus, who lived in Cyrene, on the north coast of Africa, and slew all who came in his way, and that in Egypt he slew Busiris, whose practice had been to sacrifice all strangers that entered his dominions. Next we find him among the Caucasus mountains, where, having shot the bird that gnawed the liver of Prometheus, he set the Titan free. He saved Alcestis, the wife of Admetus, king of Pherae, under the following circumstances : Admetus, being sick, had caused an inquiry to be made of an oracle as to the issue of his illness, and was told in reply that he would die unless some one could be found to volunteer to lay down his life for him. For this his wife, Alcestis, offered herself, and would have been carried off to the shades, but for Hercules, who seized the god of death in his strong arms, and held him till he promised to allow her to remain with her husband.

He accompanied the expedition of the Argonauts in search of the golden fleece, and took part in the first war against Troy, along with Telamon, the father of Ajax, Peleus, the father of Achilles, and Oicles, the father of Amphiaraus. The cause of this war was a breach of faith on the part of Laomedon, the king of Troy, who, in consideration of Hercules having rescued his daughter Hesione from the jaws of a sea-monster, had promised her hand to Hercules. Laomedon was besieged in his citadel, finally was taken prisoner, and slain along with his sons—all except Podarces, whose life was spared on the entreaty of Hesione. Telamon was rewarded with the hand of Hesione. Podarces assumed the name of Priamus, and, after the withdrawal of Hercules and his expedition, established a new dynasty in Troy. On the way home Hercules and his companions were compelled to take shelter from a storm at Cos, but were refused hospitality by the inhabitants. For this they destroyed the town.

Hercules at the Feet of Omphale.

In an expedition against Pylos, Hercules succeeded, with the assistance of Athene, in overcoming Periclymenus, a strange being, who had the power of assuming any form he pleased.   He next proceeded to Lacedaemon, to assist his friend Tyndareus, the rightful ruler of that state, against the family of Hippocoontides, by whom he had been expelled—this undertaking being also crowned with success, though it entailed the loss, among others of his companions, of the sons of Cepheus, king of Tegea.   Tyndareus was reinstated.

Whether it was on the conclusion of the labors imposed on him by Eurystheus, or at some other period of his life, Hercules is said to have once returned to Thebes, exhausted by toil, and to have fallen into violent illness, followed by raving, in the course of which he committed many unfortunate acts, among others attempting to carry off the sacred tripod from the sanctuary of Apollo at Delphi.   Being afterward informed by the oracle of Apollo that the crimes he had committed through his insanity could be expiated by a period of three years' servitude, he offered his services to Omphale, queen of Lydia, and there, as elsewhere, distinguished himself chiefly for the assistance he rendered to the oppressed, and for the valor of his deeds.

The Death and Deification of Hercules.

Hercules, it would seem, had wooed Iole, a daughter of Eurytus, king of Oechalia, but had been ultimately refused her hand, in spite of his having fulfilled all the conditions laid down by her father.   Turning elsewhere, he became a suitor of Deianeira, a daughter of Oeneus, king of Calydon, who offered his daughter in marriage to the man who should vanquish the river-god Achelous in wrestling.   Having proved himself more than a match for the river-god, Hercules obtained Deianeira in marriage, and next proceeded to punish the father of Iole for his deceit.   Having taken the stronghold of Oechalia, he put the king and his children to death, with the exception of Iole, whom he carried off; but

Instead of returning home directly, proceeded with her to a

The Marriage of Hercules and Hebe.

promontory in Euboea, intending to offer a sacrifice to Zeus. Deianeira, hearing of this, and being jealous of a revival of her husband's former love for Iole, took the white robe in which he had been accustomed to offer sacrifices, steeped it in some preparation given her by the Centaur Nessus, as a charm to bring back her husband's love, and sent it by her son Lichas to Hercules. She was not aware that the preparation contained the deadliest poison. Hercules had hardly put on the robe, when he was seized with violent pain—the poison entering into his frame. Death appeared to be inevitable. He caused a pyre of wood to be erected on Mount Oeta, set fire to it, and after handing over his unerring bow and arrows to his friend Philoctetes, mounted the fire and was consumed in its flames. His spirit, it was said, passed away in a cloud, and was conducted by Iris and Hermes to Olympus, where, after being reconciled to Hera, he was married to the goddess Hebe, and enjoyed immortality and the esteem of all the gods. Deianeira, meantime having heard of the calamity she had caused, put herself to death.

While ancient poets familiarized the people with the exploits of Hercules, artists found in them an endless variety of subjects, as the collections of sculptures and painted vases still testify. In the schools he was held up as an embodiment of heroic virtue, and everywhere honor was done to him.

THESEUS.

The friend, and in many respects the counterpart of Hercules, was Theseus, a son of Aegeus, king of Attica, and Aethra, a daughter of Pittheus, king of Troezen. While his mother was a descendant of Pelops, his father was of the line of Erechtheus. Theseus, brought up under the care of his grandfather, Pittheus, whose wisdom and virtue were well known, soon gave promise of great strength and skill in athletic exercises, such as were then prescribed for youths, and, moreover, became a proficient in playing the lyre. His father, Aegeus, on taking leave of his mother, Aethra, at

Troezen, had secreted his sword and sandals under a great
rock, and told her that when the boy was able to move the
rock, he might come to him at Athens, bringing the sword
and sandals as a token. When only in his sixteenth year,
Theseus accomplished this task, and at once set out for
Athens, where **Medea**, who was then living with Aegeus,
tried to compass his death, but her plan having failed, fled.

Theseus.

On his way to Athens Theseus was the hero of several
exploits resembling more or less the feats which Hercules
performed in his youth. He slew **Periphates**, whose practice had been to crush with a blow of his iron club all travellers across the pathless district between Troezen and
Epidaurus. On the Isthmus of Corinth Theseus met and
overcame **Sinis**, the robber, who was the terror of the neighborhood. It was to commemorate this feat, it was said, that
Theseus established the Isthmian games. At Crommyon he
slew the wild boar that was laying waste the country round.
He threw **Sciron** from a high cliff into the sea—a death to
which that robber had doomed many unlucky travellers.
At Eleusis he slew the powerful **Cercyon**, and afterward
Damastes (usually called **Procrustes**), whose manner of
killing his victims was to place them on a bed which was
always either too long or too short: if too short, he would

cut off part of the victim to suit the bed; if too long, he would stretch his victim to the required length.

Arriving at Athens, Theseus was purified from all this bloodshed by the grateful inhabitants. It happened that, because of the long Ionian dress which he wore, and his long hair, which gave him the appearance of a girl, some scoffed at him for going about alone in public. To show that he was far from being so effeminate as he seemed, he unyoked a laden wagon that was standing by, and threw it up in the air, to the astonishment of all.

His next exploit was against the family of giants, fifty in number, called Pallantides, sons of his uncle Pallas, who were endeavoring to get rid of Theseus, in the hope of succeeding to the government of Athens at the death of their uncle Aegeus. His extraordinary strength enabled him to overpower them. He then proceeded to Marathon, where, as we have already said, in connection with the labors of Hercules, a furious bull was destroying the plains. He captured and led it off to Athens, where he sacrificed it to the goddess Athene, who had lent him her aid in the enterprise.

But the adventure in which he gained the greatest glory was his slaying the Minotaurus, a monster of which we have given a description in connection with the legends of Crete, where we have also explained why Athens was compelled to send a tribute of young men and maidens as victims to the Minotaurus. Theseus offered himself as a victim, and in time arrived with the others in Crete. Before the sacrifice took place, however, he had won the favor of Ariadne, the daughter of Minos, and had obtained from her a clue of thread, by holding on to which he might find his way back out of the labyrinth in which the Minotaur lived. The intricacies of its passages would have otherwise been a source of danger against which his great strength would not have served him. On a very ancient vase in the British Museum there is a picture in which Ariadne is represented as holding the one end of the clue, while Theseus in the interior of the

APOLLO BELVEDERE,

labyrinth is slaying the monster. Having by this act freed
Athens forever from the cruel tribute, Theseus and his companions set out on the homeward voyage, accompanied also
by Ariadne. But at the island of Naxos he abandoned her,
fearing to take a stranger home as his wife. Her grief on
awaking and seeing the ship far away that conveyed her lover
was intense, and has been commemorated frequently both by
poets and artists. She was found sorrowing by the young
wine-god Dionysus, by whose influence her joy returned.

Meanwhile the arrival of the ship was being anxiously

Ariadne Abandoned.

looked for at Athens. That the good news might be known
more quickly, Theseus himself had promised, when he set
out, to hoist a white flag when he sighted Attica, if successful. In his joy, however, he had forgotten the promise, and
sailed toward the port with the black colors with which he
had started. On seeing this, his father, Aegeus, gave way
to grief at the supposed loss of his son, and put an end to
his life.

Among the other adventures in which Theseus took part

were the expedition of the Argonauts and that of Hercules against the Amazons. In the latter expedition he had, as it was said, carried off Hippolyte, whose girdle Hercules had been commanded by Eurystheus to obtain. For the carrying off of their queen, a great body of the Amazons invaded Attica, but were repulsed by Theseus.

His warm friendship for the Thessalian prince Pirithous gave Theseus two opportunities of displaying his heroic qualities. The first was at the marriage of his friend—at which, as has been previously related, the Centaurs present at the banquet, becoming fired with wine, raised a tumult, and would have carried off the bride but for the resistance of Theseus. The second occasion was when Pirithous, having conceived a passion for Persephone, audaciously resovled to carry her away from the lower world, and was aided by Theseus. The attempt failed, however, and both were kept in chains in the lower world till Hercules released them.

After the death of his father Theseus succeeded to the government of Athens, lived in splendor, ruled with prudence, and introduced institutions of a most liberal kind among his people. He united the various independent and previously hostile villages of Attica into one state, with Athens as its head. He enriched and gave a new impulse to the great festival of the Panathenaea, that had been established by Erechtheus. In the island of Delos he founded an annual festival accompanied by games, at which the prize was a wreath of the sacred palm-tree. In Athens the festival of Pyanepsia, in honor of Apollo, and Oschophoria, in honor of Dionysus, were both said to have been established by him. He met his death, it was said, at the hands of Lycomedes, to whose court he had retired on the occasion of a tumult in Athens. His wife was Phaedra, a daughter of Minos, of Crete; according to another report, Antiope.

The memory of his deeds was preserved by a beautiful temple in Athens, erected for that purpose, and called the Theseum.

THE HUNT OF THE CALYDONIAN BOAR.

At the head of this expedition was **Meleager**, a son of

Meleager.

Oeneus, the king of Calydon, and his wife **Althaea**; Deïa-

neira, the wife of Hercules, being a daughter of the same
pair.   At the birth of Meleager the Parcae appeared to
Althaea, it would seem, Atropos telling her that her infant
would live as long as a brand which she pointed to on the
fire remained unconsumed.   Althaea snatched it that moment
from the flames, and hid it away carefully, and thus secured
the invulnerability of her son.   On growing to manhood he
took part in the Argonautic expedition, and is said to have
signalized himself by many acts of bravery; but the enterprise with which his fame was most associated was the successful hunt of the ferocious boar that was laying waste the
country round Calydon, defying the spears and hounds of
ordinary huntsmen.

Meleager sent messengers round Greece to invite all its
bravest heroes to Calydon to join him in the hunt.   There
came Idas and Lynceus from Messene, Castor and Polydeuces (Pollux) from Lacedaemon, Theseus from Athens,
Admetus from Pherae, Ancaeus and the beautiful Atalanta from Arcadia, Jason from Iolcus, Peleus from Thessaly, and many other well-proved heroes.   After enjoying
for nine days, as was usual, the hospitality of Meleager, they
prepared on the tenth for the chase, which, with a few accidents, resulted in the death of the boar by the spear of Meleager, to whom accordingly fell the trophy of the monster's
head and skin.

In art he is represented standing beside an altar shaded
by a laurel-tree, holding two spears in his hand.   His dog
looks up to him.   The head of the boar lies on the altar.

As, however, Atalanta had been the first to wound the
boar, Meleager made that a pretext for presenting her with
its skin.   But on her way homeward to Arcadia she was
met and forcibly robbed of it by the brothers of Althaea,
the mother of Meleager, who considered that they had a
superior claim to that part of the booty.   A quarrel arose
on that account between Meleager and his uncles; they
fought, and the end of it was that the uncles were slain.

To avenge their death, Althaea cast the brand, which up till then she had carefully preserved, into the fire, and thereupon her brave son was seized with dreadful pain, and died. Grief at the rashness of her act caused the mother to kill herself.

THE EXPEDITION OF THE ARGONAUTS.

To understand the object of this expedition, it will be necessary to go back a little into the genealogy of the person at whose instance it was conducted. That person was Jason,

Building the Argo.

a son of **Aeson,** the rightful king of Iolcus in Thessaly, and his wife Alcimede. The father of Aeson was Aeolus (a son of Hellen and a grandson of Deucalion), at whose death he succeeded to the throne, but was driven from it by **Pelias,** his step-brother, at whose hands he and all his relatives suffered cruel persecution. The boy Jason was saved from harm by some of his father's friends, and placed under the care and instruction of the Centaur Chiron. At the age of twenty he was told by an oracle to present himself to

Pelias, and claim his father's kingdom. Pelias also had learned from the oracle that a descendant of Aeolus would dethrone him, and, moreover, that the descendant in question would appear to him for the first time with only one sandal to his feet. Pelias, the usurper, was, therefore, anxiously looking out for the approach of a person in this plight. It happened that the river Enipeus was swollen when Jason reached it, on his way to put forth his claim against Pelias. But Hera, the patron goddess of Iolcus, taking the form of an old woman, conveyed him across, with no loss except that of one sandal. On his arrival at Iolcus, Pelias recognized him as the rightful heir referred to by the oracle, but, at the same time, was unwilling to abdicate in his favor. He would prefer that Jason should first do something in the way of heroic enterprise, and, as a suitable adventure of that kind, proposed that he should fetch the golden fleece from Colchis. Jason agreed to this, and set about building the **Argo**, the largest ship that had as yet sailed from Greece. The goddess Athene aided him with her skill and advice in the work, as did also Hera. When the ship was ready, Jason sent messengers to invite the foremost heroes of Greece to join him in his enterprise. Among the many who accepted his invitation were Hercules, Castor and Pollux, Meleager, Orpheus, Peleus, Neleus, Admetus, Theseus, his friend Pirithous, and the two sons of Boreas, Calais and Zetes.

Turning now to the story of the golden fleece, the finding of which was the object of so powerful an expedition, we must go back to Aeolus, whom we have mentioned above as grandfather of Jason and son of Hellen. This Aeolus had, besides Aeson, another son, **Athamas**, who married **Nephele**, and had two children, **Phrixus** and **Helle**. On the death of his wife, Athamas married a second time Ino, a daughter of Cadmus, by whom he had two sons, **Learchus** and **Melicertes**. The second wife, disliking her two step-children, made several attempts on their lives. To save them from further danger, the shade of their mother, it was said, appeared

to Phrixus, bringing at the same time a large ram with a
golden fleece, on which she proposed Phrixus and Helle
should escape over the sea.　They started according to her
advice, and Phrixus reached safely the opposite shore, but
Helle fell from the ram's back into the sea and was drowned.
The name of Hellespont was in consequence given to the

Phrixus and Helle.

strait which they had to cross.　Phrixus, having reached the
other side, proceeded to Colchis, on the farthest shore of the
Black Sea, and there sacrificed the ram to Zeus, in honor of
his safety.　He hung the golden fleece up in the temple of
Ares.

Previous to starting from Iolcus, Jason offered a sacrifice
to Zeus, calling upon the god for a sign of his favor, or displeasure if it should be so.　Zeus answered with thunder
and lightning, which was taken as a favorable omen.　The

expedition proceeded first to Lemnos, where the heroes were
kindly received, remained a long time, and became the fathers
of a new race of heroes. The women of the island had, it
would seem, at the instigation of Aphrodite, slain their husbands. One of the Lemnian women, Hypsipyle, bore a son
to Jason, and called him Euneus. Leaving Lemnos and its
festive life, the Argonauts continued their journey as far as
Cyzicus, where they landed for a short time, and were in the
act of leaving when Hercules, having broken his oar, left
the ship, accompanied by Hylas, to cut a new oar in the
wood. But some nymphs, admiring the beauty of young
Hylas, carried him off; and as Hercules would not leave the
country without him, the expedition was compelled to proceed without the assistance and companionship of the great
hero. Their next landing was in the neighborhood of the
modern Scutari, where the reigning king, Amycus, was
famed as a boxer and for his cruelty to all strangers who
entered his territories. Seeing the Argonauts land for the
purpose of obtaining fresh water, he sent them, as was his
custom, a challenge to match him with a boxer, which Pollux
accepted, and proved the skill by which he earned his fame
upon the boastful Amycus. Proceeding on their journey,
they passed through the perilous entrance to the Black Sea
in safety, owing their escape from its dangers to the advice
of Phineus, the blind and aged king of the district, whom
they had found suffering great distress on account of his food
being always carried off or polluted by the Harpies just as
he sat down to eat it. This punishment, as well as his blind-
ness, had been sent upon him by the gods in consequence of
his cruelty to his wife (a daughter of Boreas) and children.
The Harpies were driven away effectually by the two sons of
Boreas, who accompanied the Argonauts; and it was in return
for this kindness that Phineus communicated his plan for a
safe passage through the Symplegades, two great cliffs that
moved upon their bases, and crushed everything that ventured to pass between. His plan was first to fly a pigeon

through between them, and then the moment that the cliffs, having closed upon the pigeon, began to retire to each side to row the Argo swiftly through the passage. It was done, and before the cliffs could close upon her, the ship, all but her rudder, had got clear of danger. From that time the Symplegades were united into one rock.

After many other adventures the expedition at last reached Colchis, where they found Aeetes, a reputed son of Helios and Perseis, reigning as king. He refused to give up the

Medea, Jason, and the Golden Fleece.

golden fleece, except to the man who should acquit himself to his satisfaction in certain enterprises which he proposed. The first was to yoke to a plough his unmanageable bulls, that snorted fire and had hoofs of brass, and to plough the field of Ares with them. That done, the field was to be sown with a dragon's teeth, from which armed men were to spring in the furrows. The hero who succeeded so far was then to be permitted to fetch, if he could, the golden fleece, which hung on an oak in a grove sacred to Ares, and was watched continually by a monstrous dragon. Medea, the daughter of Aeetes, having conceived a passion for Jason, prepared him for these dangerous tasks by means of a witch's mixture which made him proof against fire and sword. The goddess Athene also helped him, and his success was complete.

The Argonauts now commenced their homeward voyage, Jason taking with him Medea. On missing his daughter, Aeetes gave pursuit. Seeing that he was overtaking them, Medea, to divert his course, dismembered her young brother, Absyrtus, whom she had taken with her, and cast the limbs about in the sea. The delay caused to Aeetes in collecting the pieces of his child, enabled Medea and Jason to escape. According to another report, Absyrtus had by that time grown to manhood, and met his death in an encounter with Jason, in pursuit of whom he had been sent by his father.

After passing through many other dangers, Jason at last reached Iolcus, and, presenting the golden fleece to Pelias, claimed the throne as agreed upon. But Pelias still refused to abdicate. Jason therefore slew him, and assumed the government of Iolcus, together with that of Corinth, where Aeetes, the father of Medea, had, it is said, ruled before he went to Colchis.

Ten years of peace followed the accession of Jason to the throne. The origin of the troubles that fell upon the royal house thereafter was an attachment formed by Jason for the beautiful Creusa (or Glauce, as others called her), whom he made his wife in Corinth. Medea, stung with jealousy, turned to the arts of witchcraft she had learned in Colchis, and having steeped a dress and a costly wreath in poison, sent them to her rival, and by that means caused her death. Not content with that, she set fire to the palace of Creon, the father of Creusa; and further, finding Jason enraged at what she had done, she put to death the children she herself had borne to him, and fled to Athens, where, as we have seen, she lived for a time with Aegeus. Thence also she had to escape in consequence of an attempt on the life of Theseus. She went back to Colchis, some believed, in a chariot drawn by winged dragons.

Medea.

Jason, it is said, depressed by his troubles, repaired to the sanctuary on the Isthmus of Corinth, where the Argo had been consecrated in the grove of Poseidon. On approaching the ship, part of the stern gave way, fell upon him, and caused his death. Another version of the story says that he took his own life.

THE YOUNGER RACE OF HEROES, AND THE WARS AGAINST THEBES AND TROY.

THE heroes of the succeeding age were regarded as sons or grandsons of those whom we have just described, the great events of the period in which they lived being the two wars against Thebes and Troy. It has already been observed that the accounts of these wars, though apparently having some foundation in historical facts, are altogether mythical in their form and interwoven with incidents of a wholly mythical character.

These two events, more than any of the other adventures of heroes, formed the favorite subject of the national poetry of Greece, the incidents of each having been, as a whole or in part, worked up into a long series of epic poems and tragedies, of which, with two exceptions, only fragments remain to our times. These exceptions are the *Iliad* and *Odyssey*—the oldest, it is believed, and at the same time the most celebrated, of the epic poems upon the subject of the war against Troy, the reputed author of them being Homer. The principal epic on the expedition of the seven heroes against Thebes was entitled Thebais, its author being unknown. We shall relate both these great events in the connection in which they have come down to us.

THE SEVEN HEROES WHO WENT AGAINST THEBES.

THEIR DESCENDANTS, THE EPIGONI.

We have already alluded to the series of grim events by which Oedipus, after killing his father, Laius, came to the throne of Thebes, and married his own mother, Jocasta. It will be rememberd that from this union sprang four children, two of them being sons, Eteocles and Polynices, and two daughters, Antigone and Ismene; and that, when the criminality of the marriage came to light, Jocasta killed herself, while Oedipus, after putting out his eyes, went into voluntary exile, accompanied only by his high-souled daughter Antigone, who resolved to share all his adversity.

The sons, remaining in Thebes, soon fell into a warm dispute concerning the succession to the throne, but at last agreed to reign year about, Eteocles, the elder of the two, having the first period of office. His year, however, having expired, he not only declined to retire in behalf of his brother, but went so far as to expel him from the city.

Polynices, brooding revenge, betook himself to Adrastus, king of Sicyon, and was there hospitably received, meeting also under the same roof another pretender to a throne, Tydeus of Argos. The two youths became friends, and bound themselves to stand by each other in the recovery of their sovereignty. Adrastus gave them his two daughters in marriage, and having thus allied himself to their cause, prepared a powerful army to reinstate, first, Polynices in Thebes, and next, Tydeus in Argos.

Meantime both the young men visited many parts of Greece, with the view of obtaining companions in arms, and many a stout hero answered to their summons—such, for example, as Capaneus, a son of Hipponous, of Argos, Eteoclus, son of Iphis, and Parthenopaeus, a son of Atalanta and Melanion (or of Ares), from Arcadia. These

three, together with Polynices, Tydeus, and Adrastus, and
lastly the princely seer Amphiaraus, the son of Oicles (or
of Apollo), constituted the so-called seven heroes against
Thebes. It was, however, with extreme reluctance that
Amphiaraus took part in the expedition; for he was a man
of profound piety, and a prophet, who knew that the other
leaders of the affair had all more or less been guilty of criminal acts. He foresaw that the undertaking, altogether god-
less as it was—since Polynices, though he had suffered
injustice, had no right to invade his native town with a
foreign army—would have a disastrous issue for all of them.
His warnings, however, were unheeded, and he himself, since
much was thought to depend on his presence, was forced to
take part in the adventure through the following plot :

Amphiaraus and Adrastus, finding themselves greatly at
variance in opinion concerning the projected expedition, at
last agreed to intrust the decision of the matter to Eriphyle
(the wife of Amphiaraus, who was prevailed on by the costly
presents given her secretly by Polynices to decide against
her husband, though she had been informed by him that
Adrastus alone, of all the seven, would ever return from
the expedition. On stepping into his chariot to depart for
battle, Amphiaraus turned round, and called down upon his
wife a curse, which his son, Alcmaeon, afterward fulfilled
by slaying his mother to avenge his father's death.

The army was now ready to march under its seven leaders.
We must, however, before tracing its further adventures,
return for a moment to Oedipus. After wandering about
sad and miserable here and there in Greece, he at last, under
the guidance of his faithful daughter, Antigone, arrived in
Attica, where, it had been predicted, he was to find a peaceful end to all his woes. Neither of the sons had troubled
himself about the ill-fated old man, until an oracle announced
that victory in the approaching battle would be on the side
of him who brought back Oedipus to Thebes and had him
in his camp. Thereupon both sought him, Polynices going

in person to beg for his blessing on the assault upon their
native town.   Oedipus cursed the unholy enterprise.   Eteo-

Oedipus and Antigone.

cles, as the reigning king, despatched his uncle, Creon, a
brother of his mother, to Attica. with commands to bring

back Oedipus by force if necessary. But when Creon attempted to do so, Theseus interfered and expelled him and his followers from the land. Oedipus, after calling down upon his undutiful sons a curse, that they might perish each by the hand of the other, died in the sacred grove of the Eumenides at Colonus, near Athens, and was buried by Theseus with pomp and ceremony. Antigone returned in great grief to Thebes.

About the same time the expedition of the seven set out. On reaching Nemea they found all the springs dry—a judgment sent upon them by Dionysus, it was said, the guardian deity of Thebes. Suffering severely from thirst, and looking about for water, the heroes encountered Hypsipyle (see Argonauts), who, because of Jason's love for her, had been sent by the other women of Lemnos to Nemea, and there sold into slavery to the king, Lycurgus, her duty being to tend his young child, Opheltes. They begged her to take them to a well, which she did; but before going off with them, had, contrary to the oracle, laid down the child on the ground in the wood. Returning from the well, they found the child dead within the coils of a snake. Tydeus and Capaneus would have slain the reptile at once, had not Amphiaraus announced it to be a miraculous creature sent by Zeus as an evil omen. On this account he renamed the child Archemorus, which means the "dawn of mystery." The heroes appeased the angry parents by performing splendid obsequies to the child, the athletic contests and ceremonies of that occasion being afterward looked on as the first celebration of the Nemean games. Hypsipyle was taken back to her home by her son, Euneus, who had gone in search of her.

In spite of this evil omen, the army of the seven advanced upon Thebes, and after several less important adventures arrived before its walls. There they pitched a camp, and as a preliminary attempt to settle the matter amicably, sent Tydeus into Thebes with orders to require that the govern-

ARTEMIS, OR DIANA.

ment be ceded to Polynices according to the original terms
of agreement between the brothers.

Tydeus was, however, received with hostility, and would
have perished in the ambush laid for him by Eteocles, con-

Death of Archemorus.

trary to the universal usages of war, had it not been for his
extraordinary strength. Of the fifty men who surrounded

him he spared only one to take back to Eteocles the tidings of the affair.

The dispute must now be decided by force of arms. Thebes was closely surrounded, each of the seven heroes taking up his position before one of its seven gates.   In a similar manner Eteocles distributed his forces under seven generals within each of the gates, reserving for himself the defence of the gate which his brother was to attack.   When the battle commenced deeds of extraordinary valor were done on both sides; but the gods were against the assailants, the Thebans having gained the divine good-will in a special degree by the sacrifice which Creon's son, Menoeceus, voluntarily made of himself with a view to save his native town, as the oracle announced by the seer Tiresias recommended.   When the last and fatal day of the siege arrived, Amphiaraus warned his companions in arms of what awaited them and the death of all their leaders except Adrastus. Intrusting to him tokens of remembrance for their friends, they rushed into battle with all the courage of despair.

Matters soon began to look grave outside the walls of Thebes.   The fierce Capaneus, who had boasted that he would take the town in spite of Zeus and all the divine portents, had reached the parapet of the walls on his storming ladder, when a lightning bolt from Zeus struck and hurled him to the ground.   A general onset of the Thebans followed this event, the Argive army falling before them everywhere, and their leaders being slain.   Eteocles and Polynices pierced each other through the body in a hand-to-hand encounter.   The earth, struck by a lightning bolt on the spot where Amphiaraus stood, yawned and swallowed him, from which time forward he continued to exist as a spirit endowed with the gift of prophecy.   Adrastus alone escaped, and that by means of the winged horse Arion.

Creon, the uncle of the fallen sons of Oedipus, succeeded to the throne of Thebes, and, as his first duty, buried Eteocles with great ceremony—a rite which he at the same time denied to the body of Polynices, on pain of death to any one who should perform it. The kindly heart of Antigone could not bear this sentence, which caused her brother's soul to wander forever without rest in the lower world, and accordingly she defied Creon's strict order, and buried the corpse secretly, as she thought, but his watchman having observed the act she was condemned to be buried alive—the fact of her being betrothed to his son, Haemon, and the tears and entreaties of the latter being of no avail to mitigate her doom. Antigone was pent up in a subterranean chamber, in which, to avoid the pangs of starvation, she hanged herself. Haemon, unwilling to outlive her, put an end to his existence, and Creon's inhuman cruelty was punished by the desolation of his house, by which the family of Oedipus became extinct.

Thirty years having elapsed since the expedition of the seven, their sons undertook to avenge the death of their fathers by a second attack on Thebes. This was the so-called war of the Epigoni (that is, "offspring" or sons), which was entered upon with the consent of the gods, and ended in the destruction of Thebes, which for a long time remained a mere open space called "Lower Thebes."

THE TROJAN WAR.

THE CAUSE OF THE WAR.

CONTEMPORARY with the contest of Thebes by the Epigoni, which has been related above, we find on the throne of Troy, or Ilion, a king named **Priamus**, whose chief distinction consisted in his being the father of a noble race of sons. His wife was **Hecuba**. When the time approached for another son to be born to them, their daughter **Cassandra**, on whom Apollo had bestowed the gift of prophecy, announced that the child would grow up to be the ruin of his country. To prevent such a calamity the infant was at its birth exposed on Mount Ida, where it was found and brought up by shepherds, in whose society and occupation **Paris**, or **Alexander**, spent the early part of his life.

On a beautiful day, as he tended his flocks, three goddesses came to him—Hera (Juno), Athene (Minerva), and Aphrodite (Venus), commanding him to decide which of them was the most beautiful. Here we must explain. When Zeus withdrew, as we have already seen, from his proposed marriage with Thetis, on account of a prophecy communicated by Themis, that the issue of such a union would be a son who would surpass his father in might, it was agreed to give the sea-goddess in marriage to Peleus, a young prince of Phthia, in Thessaly, whose piety had endeared him to the

Venus "the most beautiful."

gods. "The gods came to their marriage feast," as they did to that of Cadmus and Harmonia, all but Eris, the goddess of strife. Angry at not being invited, she determined to mar the pleasantness of the company, and to this end threw among them a golden apple, on which was written, "To the most beautiful." Hereupon the three goddesses mentioned above claimed each the prize, and Zeus referred them to Paris, the shepherd on Mount Ida, for a decision

Unwilling at first to take upon himself so much responsi‧bility, Paris was at length persuaded to decide, on being promised the throne of Asia by Hera, immortal fame as a hero by Athene, and the loveliest wife on earth by Aphrodite. He assigned the prize to the last-mentioned goddess, and in so doing drew upon himself and his native country the most bitter enmity of the other two.

In the meantime it happened that a sacrifice was to be offered in Troy, for which oxen were wanted. Two of the king's sons, Hector and Helenus, were sent to the herd on Mount Ida, to select fitting animals. Their choice included one that was a favorite of Paris, who boldly refused to give it up, and followed it to the town, intending to demand its restoration from the king. But a quarrel ensued on the way, and Paris would have fallen at his brothers' hands, but for the timely appearance of Cassandra, who revealed the story of his birth. Then there was joy in the king's palace at the return of the lost son, grown up as he was, to be beautiful, handsome, and brave. The untoward prophecy was forgotten.

The sudden change from the life of a herdsman to that of a prince surrounded by the pleasures of court and town, made Paris oblivious of the visit of the goddesses and the promise that had been made to him of the most beautiful wife on earth. But Aphrodite meant to fulfil the promise, and to this end commanded him to have ships built to sail to Hellas, and proceed to Sparta, where, in the person of Helena, he would find the wife in question. Paris obeyed, and was accompanied on the journey by Aeneas, a son of Anchises and the goddess Aphrodite.

Arriving at Amyclae, he was met and kindly welcomed by the Dioscuri, Castor and Polydeuces (Pollux), the brothers of Helena. To the same family (of which Zeus and Leda were the parents) belonged Clytaemnestra, the wife of Agamemnon, who, like her brother Castor, was mortal, while the other two, Helena and Pollux, were immortal. Of the close attachment of the two brothers to each other there is a fine instance which we shall here relate, though in point of time it did not take place till a little later. Being present, according to invitation, at the nuptials of Lynceus and Idas with Phoebe and Hilaeira, the daughters of Leucippus, they became enamoured of the brides, and attempted

Paris and Helena.

to carry them off. A fight ensued, in which Castor, after slaying Lynceus, fell into the hands of Idas, whom Pollux next slew to avenge his brother's death. Pollux then prayed to Zeus that he might restore his brother to life, proposing as a compensation that both should live only on alternate days. Zeus granted the prayer with its condition. In after times the twin-brothers were regarded as divine beings, and supposed to ride on white horses in the sky, with dazzling spears, and each with a star above his brow. In storms, when a mariner saw a ball of fire in the air, he was assured that the Dioscuri were near to help him.

After spending some time with the Dioscuri, Paris, accompanied by Aeneas, set out for Sparta, where he was received by the king, **Menelaus,** and his wife, Helena, in the same spirit of kindly hospitality as the brothers of the latter had displayed at Amyclae. Of Menelaus we have already mentioned his descent from **Atreus.** The story of his marriage and its consequences is as follows :

Such, it would seem, had been the astonishing beauty and grace of Helena, that even as a young girl she had captivated the hearts of men, and, among others, of Theseus, who carried her off. The Dioscuri, however, soon found and brought her back, taking with them as a prisoner, Aethra, the mother of Theseus, and presenting her as a servant to Helena. As Helena grew to womanhood, so numerous and so pressing were the noble suitors for her hand that **Tyndareus,** her foster-father, became alarmed at the prospect of provoking the hostility of so many by choosing one of them for her. He determined, therefore, to allow her to choose for herself. But first he called upon them all to take an oath, not only that they would be satisfied with her choice, but would assist her husband then and after in whatever danger or difficulty he might be placed. She chose Menelaus, the brother of Agamemnon, her sister's husband, and the marriage was celebrated with great pomp. Tyndareus, however, had omitted to offer a sacrifice to Aphrodite, who, to punish him, made the heart of his foster-daughter readily accessible to unbridled love.

Paris, as has been said, was kindly received by Menelaus, and freely admitted to his hospitality and the society of his wife, Helena, with whom he soon formed an attachment which deepened with time and under the influence of the costly presents of Asiatic wares which he gave her. Menelaus, meanwhile suspecting nothing, prepared to pay a visit to Idomeneus of Crete, leaving his wife under the care of his guest. With her husband safely at a distance, Helena was readily persuaded to elope with Paris to Troy, to become his wife, and there live in oriental luxury and splendor. Reaching the coast under the cover of night they embarked, and after weathering a storm sent by Hera, the goddess of marriage troth, reached Troy in safety, and were married with great pomp and magnificence.

The Dioscuri (Castor and Pollux).

To Menelaus, at the court of Idomeneus in Crete, Iris, the divine messenger, carried the intelligence of the disgrace that had fallen on his house. Returning at once, and having consulted his powerful brother Agamemnon, he proceeded to Pylos, to seek the advice of the aged Nestor, whose reputation for prudence and wisdom throughout Greece had been acquired by his services in many wars in the course of the two preceding generations, such was his great age. His counsel on this occasion was that nothing short of a combination of all the armies of Greece would be sufficient to punish the crime that had been committed and recover the possession of Helena.

Acting on this advice, Menelaus and Agamemnon visited all the princes and heroes of the land, to obtain pledges of their assistance. Those who had been suitors of Helena had been bound by an oath to assist Menelaus whenever called upon by him to do so, and were now ready to carry out their engagement. Others promptly offered their services, from feelings of resentment at the vileness of the act of Paris. Only in two cases was any difficulty experienced, but they were very important cases, as it proved. The first was that of Odysseus (Ulysses), son of Laertes, the king of the island of Ithaca.   His beautiful and faithful wife, Penelope, had borne him a son, **Telemachus**, and being in the enjoyment of perfect domestic felicity, he was unwilling to exchange it for a part in a war the issue of which appeared very dubious. But instead of returning a blunt answer, he pretended insanity, put on a fisherman's hat, yoked a horse and an ox together, and commenced to plough.   But Palamedes, detecting the sham, set the infant Telemachus on the ground in front of the plough.   In saving the child Odysseus revealed the sobriety of his senses, and was compelled to join the expedition.   The other case was that of **Achilles**, the son of Peleus and Thetis, a nymph of the sea.

Ulysses and Telemachus.

Thetis, having been offered by the gods the choice, in behalf of her son, of either a long life spent in obscurity and retirement, or a few years of dazzling martial fame, chose the life of obscurity, and with that view conveyed him, dressed as a girl, to the court of **Lycomedes**, in the island of Scyros.

There he was brought up among the king's daughters, and gained the love of one of them, Deidamia, who bore him a son, Neoptolemus, who afterward took part in the war against Troy.   Meantime it was known to be of the highest importance for the Trojan expedition to discover the concealment of the young son of Thetis and to enlist his services.   For

Ulysses Discovers Achilles.

that purpose Odysseus was sent in the dress and character of a trader to Scyros.   On the pretext of offering his trinkets and wares for sale to the king's daughters, he obtained admittance to the palace, and discovered Achilles, disguised as he was.   Odysseus ordered a magnificent suit of armor to be displayed before the youth and a call to arms to be sounded

on a military horn. The scheme was successful—an impulse
to achieve military glory seized upon Achilles, who forthwith
offered his services to the projected expedition. Peleus sent
Patroclus, the son of Menoetius, to be a companion for his
son.

The harbor of Aulis was where the various contingents of
ships and soldiery were appointed to assemble; and when all
had arrived—more than 1000 ships, each with at least 150
men—it was a sight such as had never been seen in Greece
before. Agamemnon, the most powerful prince in Greece,
was elected to the position of commander of the expedition.

While the fleet lay in Aulis a serpent was observed coiling
itself round a plane-tree, on which was a sparrow's nest with
nine young birds. The serpent devoured the young ones,
but on turning to the mother-bird was instantly changed into
stone. Calchas, the high priest, was summoned to divine
what the strange occurrence might betoken. He replied :
" Nine years we must fight round Ilion, and on the tenth
take the town." Thereafter the fleet sailed, crossed the
Aegean, and landed by mistake in Mysia, which the Greeks
prepared to lay waste. They were, however, stoutly opposed
by the king of the country, Telephus, a son of Hercules. In
the contest Patroclus proved his bravery, fighting side by
side with Achilles. He received a wound, which Achilles—
thanks to his early training under the Centaur Chiron, and
the knowledge of medicine then obtained—was able to cure.
Telephus also had received a wound from a spear of Achilles
in the engagement, and, finding that it would not heal, consulted an oracle regarding it. The reply of the oracle was
that it could be healed only by him who had caused it.
Meantime another oracle was communicated to the Greeks,
to the intent that Telephus should lead them to Troy. How
this came about we shall see presently.

The Greek fleet had returned again to the harbor of Aulis.
While lying there, Agamemnon had chanced to see a beautiful stag, sacred to Artemis. His passion for the chase led

him to draw upon the stag and kill it, while in the pride of
his success he dared to boast that he could excel the goddess
of the chase herself. This was the cause of a series of misfortunes that then befell him. The injured goddess first sent
a calm which detained the fleet week after week. In spite
of Palamedes' invention of the game of draughts and other
means of amusement, the prolonged inactivity began to tell
upon the force and to create serious discontent. At last

Achilles and Chiron.

Calchas, being ordered to discover what the gods desired,
explained that Artemis required, on the part of Agamemnon,
the sacrifice of his daughter **Iphigenia**. His fatherly feelings had to yield to his sense of duty as commander of the
expedition. He sent a message to his wife Clytaemnestra,
to come to Aulis, bringing Iphigenia with her—to be married, he said, to Achilles. They came; but it was as a victim,
not as a bride, that Agamemnon led his daughter to the altar
of Artemis. The goddess, satisfied with his intentions, suddenly appeared on the scene, provided a goat for the sacrifice,

carried off Iphigenia in a cloud to Taurus, and appointed
her to the care of her temple there. Clytaemnestra could
not forgive her husband for the deception he had practised.
How she avenged herself shall be afterward related.

In consequence of the oracle concerning the wound which
he had received from the spear of Achilles, Telephus pro-

The Sacrifice of Iphigenia.

ceeded to Aulis, where the Greek fleet lay, and presented
himself in disguise to Agamemnon, seized his infant son,
Orestes, whom Clytaemnestra had brought with her, and
threatened to slay the child, if healing were refused him.
Odysseus interposed, and scraping some of the rust from the
spear of Achilles, applied it to the wound, and healed it.
Thereupon Telephus offered his services in leading the expedition to Troy, and, the oracle being thus fulfilled, the Greeks

set sail a second time for Troy, landing on their way at Lem-

Iphigenia.

nos, to sacrifice at an altar raised there by Hercules; Philoctetes, who had inherited the bow and arrows of Hercules, was bitten in the foot by a snake, and suffered agony that made him scream continually. Unable to heal the wound, and unwilling to endure his screams, the Greeks left him behind, and proceeded on their journey, reaching at last the Trojan shore.

THE FIRST YEARS OF THE WAR.

The Trojans, having received intelligence of the hostile preparations of the Greeks, prepared on their part also to meet the enemy, assembling in and around the city of Troy all the forces they could obtain from neighbors and allies. Their foremost hero, whom they chose to lead them in assaults, was Hector, the eldest son of the king. The first engagement of the two forces occurred while the Greeks were in the act of landing from their ships, the result of it being that the Trojans were driven back within their walls, but not without inflicting considerable loss on their enemy. The first attempt of the Greeks to take the town by storm entirely failed, and, finding that the Trojans would not surrender Helena to her husband, the Greek commander could see no other means of compelling them to do so than by a siege. Accordingly a well-fortified camp was constructed around the ships, which had been hauled up on the shore, and, with that camp to fall back upon, the Greek army proceeded to lay waste the territory and towns in the neighborhood. The Trojan forces, acknowledging the superiority of the besiegers, did not seek a battle, and excepting such incidents as when Achilles and Hector fought in single combat, or when Troilus, the youngest son of Priam, was captured and put to death by Achilles, nothing of moment transpired.

In the course of the raids made by the Greeks in the neighborhood, it happened that, having taken the town of Pedasus, and come to divide the spoils, Agamemnon obtained as his captive Chryseis, a daughter of Chryses, the priest of Apollo in the island of Chryse, while to the lot of Achilles fell Briseis, a maiden as beautiful as the priest's daughter. Chryses entreated Agamemnon to restore him his daughter, offering a heavy ransom for her, but was met with refusal and contumely. Having one other resource—an appeal to

Ajax Bearing the Body of Patroclus.

the god in whose service he was—Chryses implored the aid of Apollo, who, being for other reasons also hostile to the Greeks, visited them with a plague which carried them off

in great numbers.   Agamemnon called a muster of the army,
and inquired of the high-priest, Calchas, by what the angry
god could be appeased.   Calchas, being assured of the protection of Achilles, boldly declared that the wrath of Apollo
had been caused by the unjust detention of Chryseis, a
daughter of one of his priests.   Upon this, Agamemnon,
who had borne a grudge against Calchas ever since the sacrifice of Iphigenia, rated the priest in reproachful terms,
charging him also in the present instance with being in
league with Achilles—a charge which the latter would have
resented with force had not the goddess Athene interposed.
Agamemnon felt his dignity as king and commander of the
army insulted by the threat of Achilles, and demanded as
satisfaction for this the person of the beautiful Briseis, apparently to take the place of Chryseis, whom he had been compelled to give up.   Achilles, having been warned by Athene
to be calm, confessed his inability to resist the demand, and
from that time withdrew with all his men from the camp.

Thetis, having besought Zeus to take measures to compel
Agamemnon to atone for this insult to her son, obtained a
divine decree setting forth that so long as Achilles held aloof
the Greeks would be defeated in every engagement with the
Trojans.   Emboldened by the intelligence of the step taken
by Achilles, the Trojans sallied from their walls, and after
numerous battles, skirmishes, and personal encounters, always
attended with serious loss to the enemy, drove the Greeks
back to the shelter of their fortified camp beside the ships.
At last, abased and humiliated by disasters, Agamemnon
sent an embassy to Achilles, offering to restore Briseis, and
in addition to bestow on him his daughter's hand, with seven
towns for a dowry.   But the wrath of Achilles would not
relent, and still the need of his countrymen grew worse.

The end seemed to be near when Hector, at the head of
the Trojans, had stormed the wall of the camp, and set several of the ships on fire.   Seeing this Patroclus begged
Achilles to lend him his armor and allow him to lead the

Myrmidons to the fight. The request being granted, Patroclus and his men were soon in the heat of the battle, their sudden reapperance striking the Trojan army with terror, and causing it to fall back. Not content with thus deciding the battle, Patroclus, disregarding the advice of Achilles, pursued the enemy till Hector, turning round, engaged him in a hand-to-hand fight, the issue of which was the death of the Greek hero. Hector stripped him of the armor of

Parting of Hector and Andromache.

Achilles, which he wore, but left the body for the Greeks to take possession of. The grief of Achilles at the loss of his friend was as violent as had been his anger against Agamemnon. He called for vengeance on Hector, and with the object in view of obtaining it, yielded to a reconciliation which all the sufferings of his countrymen could not previously induce him to submit to. With armor more dazzling and superb than had ever been seen before, forged by the god Hephaestus, and brought by Thetis in the hour of her son's need, he went forth to battle, seeking Hector in the Trojan ranks, which everywhere hurried back like sheep before a wolf. The Trojan hero stepped forth to meet his adversary, but not without sad misgivings. He had said farewell to his faithful wife, **Andromache**, and to his boy, **Astyanax**. But even the strong sense of duty to his country which had supported him in this domestic scene deserted him utterly when the young Greek hero approached with the dauntless bearing of the god of war himself. Hector fled; but Achilles, having a faster step, cut off his retreat, and thus imbued him with the courage of despair. The combat did not last long, the victory of Achilles being easily won.

Unappeased by the death of Hector, Achilles proceeded to outrage his lifeless body by binding it to his war-chariot. After dragging it thus three times around the walls of Troy in the face of the people, he returned with it to the Greek camp, and there cast it among dust and dirt. Displeased by such excess of passion, the gods took care of Hector's body, and saved it from corruption, while Zeus in the meantime softened the heart of Achilles, and prepared him for the performance of an act of generosity which was to blot out the memory of his previous cruelty. On the one hand, Thetis was employed to persuade her son to give up the body without a ransom. On the other hand, Hermes was sent to bid Priam go stealthily in the night to Achilles' tent, and beg the body of his son. The aged king of Troy obeyed, and coming to the young hero's tent, besought him, as he valued his own father, to give him leave to take away the lifeless body and pay to it the customary rites of burial. Achilles was touched by the gentleness of his beseeching, raised the old man from his knees, shared with him the hospitality of his tent, and, in the morning, having given up the body, sent him back under a safe escort. In the pause of hostilities that took place then, the Greeks buried the body of Patroclus with great ceremony.

THE DEATH OF ACHILLES.

The loss of Hector had so dispirited the Trojans that without fresh succors they could not face the euemy again. Such succors, however, consisting of an army of Amazons, under the command of the beautiful Penthesilea, arrived in the interval of mourning for Hector in the one camp and for Patroclus in the other. When hostilities commenced again, the valiant Penthesilea, being eager to measure her strength with that of Achilles, and to avenge the death of Hector, led the Trojan army into battle. The leaders of the Greeks were Achilles and Ajax, the son of Telamon. While the latter hero was engaged in driving back the Trojan ranks, Achilles and Penthesilea met in single combat. He would have spared her willingly, and did not, till compelled in self defence, strike with all his might. Then she fell

An Amazon.

mortally wounded, and as she fell, remembering the fate of

Hector's body, implored Achilles to spare hers that disgrace. There was no need of this; for he, to save her still, if possible, and if not, to soothe her last moments, lifted her in his arms, and there held her till she died. The Trojans and Amazons made a combined rush to rescue the body of their leader; but Achilles made a sign to them to halt, and praising her valor, youth, and beauty, gave it to them freely—a kindly act which touched friends and foes alike. Among the Greeks, however, there was one **Thersites**, mean and deformed in mind as well as body, who not only dared to impute a scandalous motive to Achilles, but, approaching the fallen Amazon, struck his spear into her lightless eye. A sudden blow from Achilles laid him lifeless on the ground.

All who saw this punishment inflicted approved of it, except **Diomedes**, the son of Tydeus, a relation by blood of Thersites, who stepped forward and demanded of Achilles the usual reparation, consisting of a sum of money. Feeling himself deeply wronged because his countrymen, and especially Agamemnon, did not unconditionally take his part in the matter, Achilles abandoned for a second time the cause of the Greeks, and took ship to Lesbos. Odysseus was sent after him, and by dint of smooth words, cleverly directed, succeeded in bringing him back to the camp.

What made the return of Achilles more urgent at that time was the arrival of a new ally to the Trojans, in the person of **Memnon**, a son of Eos (Aurora) and Tithonus, who beside being the son of a goddess, as well as Achilles, appeared further to be a proper match for him, inasmuch as he also carried armor fashioned by Hephaestus. When the two heroes met, and were fighting fiercely, Zeus received in Olympus a simultaneous visit from their respective mothers, Thetis and Eos, both imploring him to spare their sons. He answered that the issue must abide the will of Fate, Moera, to discover which he took the golden balance for weighing out life and death, and placing in one scale the fate of Achilles and in the other that of Memnon, saw the latter sink to denote his death. Eos made haste to the battle-field, but found her son dead. She carried away his body, and buried it in his native land, in the distant east.

A Fighting Amazon.

Achilles did not long enjoy his triumph; for, animated by success, he led on the Greeks, and would have captured Troy, however clearly the Fates might have decreed the contrary, had not Apollo given unerring flight to an arrow drawn by Paris. By that shaft from an unworthy source, as far as could be judged, Achilles fell. Ajax, the stout hero, and

Odysseus, clever as well as brave, seized his body, and fighting all the way, carried it back to camp, where its burial was attended with extraordinary pomp and ceremonial, the Muses chanting dolorous lays, and the heroes who had known him personally taking part, as was the custom on such occasions, in athletic competitions. The armor which he had worn in the fight was offered by Thetis to the most deserving. Only two claims were preferred, and those were on behalf of the two heroes who had rescued his body. The award being given in favor of Odysseus, Ajax, from grief at what he deemed neglect, sank into a state of insanity, in the course of which he intentionally fell upon his sword, and died.

A cessation of hostilities was obtained on the death of Achilles and Ajax, the two foremost of the Greek heroes. This period of peace having expired, and the former conditions of war having been resumed, the first event of importance that occurred was the capture of Helenus, a son Priam, who, like his sister, Cassandra, was endowed with the gift of prophecy. Odysseus, who had made the capture, compelled Helenus to disclose the measures by which it was decreed that the siege should be brought to a determination. The answer was, that to take the city of Troy, and thus close the siege, three things were necessary : 1, the assistance of the son of Achilles, Neoptolemus; 2, the bow and arrows of Hercules; 3, the possession of the Palladium (an image of the goddess Pallas Athene), which was carefully preserved in the citadel of Troy. In satisfying the first condition no difficulty was experienced. Odysseus, always ready to be of service for the common good, proceeded to Scyros, where he found Neoptolemus grown to manhood, and thirsting for martial renown. A present of the splendid armor which his father, Achilles, had worn and which Odysseus now magnanimously parted with, fired the youth's ambition, and led him easily to Troy, where he distinguished himself in a combat with Eurypylus (a son of Telephus), who had joined the Trojan ranks.

A more serious matter was the fulfilment of the second condition, seeing that the bow and arrows of Hercules were then in the possession of Philoctetes, whom, as we have already said, the Greeks abandoned at Lemnus, not caring to endure the screams caused by the wound in his foot. His feelings were known to be rancorous toward the Greeks. Notwithstanding that, Odysseus, accompanied by Diomedes (or, as others say, by Neoptolemus), went to Lemnus, and successfully tricked Philoctetes into following him to Troy, where his wound was healed by Machaon, a son of Aesculapius, and a reconciliation was effected between him and Agamemnon. The first on whom his fatal arrows were tried was Paris, after whose death Helena married his brother, Deiphobus. The Trojans were now completely shut up within the town, no one daring to face the arrows of Philoctetes.

There remained, however, a third condition—the seizure of the Palladium. Odysseus, successful in the other two, and undaunted by the greater difficulty of the new adventure, proposed to steal alone within the walls of Troy in the disguise of a beggar, and as a first measure to find out where the Palladium was preserved. He did so, and remained unrecognized except by Helena, who, having felt ever since the death of Paris a yearning for Menelaus, proved to be a valuable ally. Odysseus, in the meantime, returned to the Greek camp to obtain the assistance of Diomedes. The two, having made their way back to Troy, laid hold of the Palladium, and, carrying it off in safety, fulfilled the third and last condition.

The next difficulty was the plan of assault to be adopted. It was proposed by Odysseus, on the suggestion of the goddess Athene, that Epeios, a famous sculptor, should make a great wooden horse, sufficiently large to hold inside a number of the bravest Greeks, and that the horse being ready, and the heroes concealed within it beyond detection, the whole Greek army should embark and set sail, as if making homeward. The plan of Odysseus was agreed to, and great was the joy of the Trojans when they saw the fleet set sail. The people, scarcely trusting their eyes, flocked to the abandoned camp, to make sure. There they found nothing remaining but a great wooden horse, about the use of which various opinions arose—some thinking it an engine of war, and demanding its instant destruction. But the opinion that prevailed most was that it must have been an object of religious veneration, and if so, ought to be taken into the city. Among those who thought otherwise was Laocoon, a priest of Apollo, who had arrived on the scene, accompanied by his two young sons, to offer a sacrifice to the god in whose service he was. Laocoon warned his countrymen in no case to accept this gift of the Greeks, and went so far as to thrust his spear into the belly of the horse, upon which the weapons of the heroes within were heard to clash, and the bystanders were all but convinced of the justice of the priest's opinion. But the gods had willed it otherwise, and, to turn the opinion of the people against Laocoon, sent a judgment upon him in the shape of two enormous serpents, which, while he and his two sons were engaged in sacrificing at an altar by the shore, issued from the sea, and casting their coils round the two boys first, then round the father, who came to their assistance, caused him to die in great agony. The scene is represented in a marble group now in the Vatican. The mysterious fate of Laocoon was readily believed to be a punishment for the violence he had done to the sacred horse.

But to carry out effectually the stratagem of the horse, Odysseus had left behind on the shore his friend Sinon, with his hands bound, and presenting all the appearance of a victim who had escaped sacrifice, which he professed to be. The good king Priam was touched by the piteous story which Sinon told, ordered his bonds to be struck off, and inquired the purpose of the horse. Sinon replied that it was a sacred object, and would, if taken into the city, be a guarantee of the protection of the gods, as the Palladium had been before.

The city gates being too small, part of the wall was broken through, and the horse conducted in triumph toward the citadel. This done, the Trojans, believing that the Greeks had abandoned the siege in despair, gave way to festivity and general rejoicing, which lasted well into the night.

When the town had become perfectly quiet, the inhabitants, exhausted by the unusual excitement, being fast asleep, Sinon approached the horse, and opened a secret door in its side. The heroes then stepped out, and made a fire signal to the fleet, which lay concealed behind the neighboring island of Tenedos, and now advanced quietly to the shore. The troops having disembarked and made their way silently to the city, there ensued a fearful slaughter, the surprised inhabitants falling thickly before the well-armed Greeks. Finally, the town was set on fire in every corner, and utterly destroyed. Priam fell by the hand of Neoptolemus. The same fate befell the son of Hector—not for anything that he had done, but that he might not grow up to avenge his father's death. Of the few Trojans who escaped were Aeneas, his father Anchises, and his infant son Ascanius. Carrying his aged father on his shoulders, Aeneas fled toward Mount Ida, and thence to Italy, where he became the founder of a new race.

Menelaus became reconciled to his now penitent wife, Helena, and took her back with him. The Trojan women of rank and beauty were distributed among the Greek heroes as captives in war, Neoptolemus obtaining Andromache, the widow of Hector, and Agamemnon carrying off Priam's daughter, Cassandra. The extensive booty from the king's palaces having been divided, preparations were made for returning home. While some — as, for example, Nestor, Idomeneus, Diomedes, Philoctetes, and Neoptolemus — had favorable voyages, and reached their respective homes in safety, others, like Menelaus, were driven hither and thither by storms, which delayed their passage for years. But the heroes to whose return the greatest interest attaches were Agamemnon and Odysseus.

Agamemnon, returning after an absence of ten years, found that his wife, Clytaemnestra, had in the meantime accepted as her husband Aegisthus, a son of Thyestes, and, therefore, of an accursed line. These two proposed to compass the death of Agamemnon ; and he, though warned of their designs by Cassandra, whose prophetic power enabled her to foresee the issue, lent himself easily to their purpose, innocently accepting as genuine his wife's expression of joy. He entered the warm bath that had been prepared for him, but on coming out of it, found himself entangled in a piece of cloth which his wife threw over his head. In this helpless condition he was slain by her and Aegisthus, Cassandra and many of his followers perishing with him. His young son Orestes, contriving to escape with the help of his sister Electra, fled to Phocis, where he was received hospitably, and remained several years, during which Aegisthus ruled over Argos on the throne of Agamemnon.

A few years after the murder of Agamemnon an oracle of Apollo was communicated to Orestes, commanding him to revenge that foul deed, and promising the assistance of the god. Without being recognized he arrived at Mycenae, accompanied by his faithful friend Pylades, and there revealed himself to his sister Electra, while to his mother he professed to be a messenger come with intelligence of the death of her son Orestes. Seeing her and Aegisthus rejoice at the news, he was enraged, and slew her, while her husband fell at the hands of Pylades.

The shedding of a mother's blood was regarded as the blackest crime on earth; and though the fact that Orestes had perpetrated the deed to avenge the murder of his father, and at the instigation of Apollo, went far to exculpate him, it did not satisfy the malignant Erinys (Furies), who pursued him from land to land, permitting no peace to his throbbing heart. Arriving, in the course of his wanderings, at Delphi, Orestes complained to Apollo of his sufferings, and was told by the god that he might expect relief if he could fetch the

ancient statue of the goddess Artemis from Taurus. The difficulty of the task consisted in this, that it was the practice of
the Tauric Artemis to secure the immolation of all strangers
that approached her temple. Fortunately for Orestes, as it
happened, his sister Iphigenia held the office of priestess
there, having been carried away, as we have already seen,

Orestes Slaying Aegisthus.

by the goddess at the moment when she was to be sacrificed
by her father Agamemnon. On arriving at the temple,
Orestes, who was accompanied by Pylades, was seized, and
would have been sacrificed by the hand of his own sister
had not an accident revealed the relationship. He told her
all that had happened, and how Apollo had commanded him
to carry away the statue of the goddess. With the assistance
of Iphigenia he obtained possession of the image, and in her
company returned with it to Greece.

The task imposed by Apollo was accomplished, but still
the relentless Furies continued to persecute the unhappy
youth. Apollo then advised him to proceed to Athens, and
there to call for a trial in the Areopagus, a court appointed
to hear causes of murder, especially the murder of a relative.
(See "Ares.") The goddess Athene appealed for justice in
his behalf. Apollo defended him at the trial. The Erinys

appeared as plaintiffs. When the pleadings had been heard, and the votes of the judges came to be taken, they were found to be equally divided for and against. The right of giving the casting vote was reserved on this occasion for Athene, who, stepping forward, took up a white voting-stone, and, placing it among the votes favorable to Orestes, declared his lawful acquittal. The Erinys professed themselves appeased, desisted from persecution, and from that time enjoyed the title of Eumenides. (See " Erinys.") Thus acquitted and purified from the stains of crime, Orestes ascended the throne of his father Agamemnon, in Mycenae, married Hermione, the daughter of Helena and Menelaus, and at their death succeeded to the dominion of Sparta also.

Turning now to Odysseus, we find him, long after the other heroes of the Trojan expedition had reached their homes, still being tossed about by storms, passing through great perils, encountering strange beings, and ultimately succeeding in many unhopeful adventures. He had left Troy with a well-manned fleet richly laden with spoil, and after several adventures of less moment, in which, however, he lost a number of men, reached the country of the Cyclopes— enormous giants with only one eye. In a cave which was the habitation of one of them, Polyphemus by name, a son of the sea-god Poseidon, Odysseus and his fellow-travellers took shelter, while their ships lay anchored beside a neighboring island. Polyphemus, who was absent at the time of their arrival, returned with his sheep to the cave. The first thing he did on entering was to close up the entrance with a great stone, which a hundred men could not have moved. The next thing was, having discovered the strangers, to eat two of them for his supper, after which he slept soundly. The following morning, after driving out his sheep, he replaced the stone at the mouth of the cave, to prevent the escape of his victims and the consequent loss of several suppers. The history of the first day having repeated itself on the two following days, a plan of escape occurred to Odysseus. The giant having had his usual supper, Odysseus offered him some wine, which had the effect of creating a desire for more. His goblet being constantly replenished, Polyphemus at last sank helpless, through sleep and intoxication. Seeing this, Odysseus, with the help of his companions, laid hold of a great pole, and having made the end of it red hot, let it down on the giant's eye, and burned it out. Polyphemus sprang up in great fury, and after groping in vain for his supple enemies, made for the doorway of the cave, removed the stone, and sat down in its place, determined to permit no one to escape. But Odysseus and his companions fastened themselves each under the belly of one of the great sheep within the cave, knowing that the giant would let them pass out unmolested. And so it was; for, feeling the fleece as they passed, he was quite

Polyphemus Hurling the Rock.

satisfied. Odysseus once outside the cave, and with what remained of his crew safe in the ship, shouted jeeringly back to the Cyclopes, telling him also his name. Polyphemus then implored his father, the god Poseidon, to punish Odysseus for what he had just done. It was in answer to this prayer that Odysseus was driven hither and thither, detained here and there, and at last, after ten years' wandering, and the loss of all his men, reached home in a miserable plight. Of the adventures that befell him after leaving the country of the Cyclopes, the most important were the following : After leaving Aeolus, the king of the winds, and suffering the misfortune already related (see "Aeolus"), he reached the habitation of the sorceress Circe (a sister of Medea, it was said), whose first act was to transform his companious into swine. For Odysseus himself her charms had no potency. He compelled her to restore his men to their proper human form. Changing her manner, Circe now exhibited a cordial feeling toward Odysseus, entertaining him and his companions very hospitably for the period of a year, on the expiry of which she advised him to make a journey to the lower world, to question the shade of the seer Tiresias as to the fate in store for him. Acting on her advice, Odysseus penetrated to the region of Hades, saw and conversed with the shades of some of his former companions in the siege of Troy, and then returned to Circe, who gave him good counsel in regard to his future journey. On his voyage homeward he passed the Sirens safely (see " Sirens "), passed Scylla the sea-monster, with loss of six men, and afterward, in spite of the warnings both of Tiresias and Circe, landed on the island of Trinacia, where his companions plundered the sacred flocks of the sun-god. As a punishment for this they were afterward overtaken by a fearful storm at sea, and all perished except Odysseus, who, clinging to a piece of his ship for nine days, was at length driven on shore on the island belonging to the nymph Calypso, who received him kindly, and out of love detained him as her prisoner for seven years.

Despising her love and her offer of immortality, Odysseus sat disconsolate by the seashore, thinking of his home in Ithaca, and yearning to see it again before he died. The gods, taking compassion on him, prevailed on Calypso to let him go. He made a raft, and put to sea; but Poseidon, not yet appeased for the wrong done to his son Polyphemus, raised a storm which shattered the small craft, and would have caused Odysseus to perish but for the timely aid of the sea-nymph Leucothea. Swimming to land, he found himself in

the island of the Phaeacians, was discovered on the shore by
the king's daughter, Nausicaa, and entertained hospitably
by the king, Alcinous, to whom he related his adventures.
After receiving many costly presents, he was conveyed home
to Ithaca in a well-manned ship. There he found his wife,
Penelope, still faithful to him, in spite of the incessant wooing
of all the princes of the neighboring islands in the course of
her husband's long absence.

Circe.

His son, Telemachus, whom he left an infant, had now
grown to manhood, and, having just arrived from a journey
in search of intelligence concerning his missing father, was
staying in the house of a shepherd when Odysseus arrived,
and heard the story of how suitors of Penelope were vexing
her and consuming her husband's possessions. Odysseus
and his son appeared among them in disguise, raised a
quarrel, and, with the help of Athene, slew them all. Then
took place the touching meeting with his wife. After crushing an insurrection raised by the friends of the slain suitors,
Odysseus spent the rest of his life reigning peacefully over
his island kingdom of Ithaca.

ROMULUS AND REMUS.

The Romans had no heroes in the sense in which we have come to regard that word from a study of the Greek legends. Romulus and Remus, it is true, have a legendary character, which may be compared in some respects with that of several

Romulus and Remus.

Greek heroes. They were the offspring of a god (Mars) and a vestal virgin. They were exposed to death at their birth, were suckled by a she-wolf, were preserved and brought up among herdsmen. On arriving at manhood, they returned to claim their inheritance, and founded the city of Rome, Romulus naming it after himself. They instituted festivals —the Palilia and Lupercalia—the latter to commemorate their having been nourished by a wolf. They established the priesthood of Arval Brothers. Remus, less fortunate in his adventures, was slain. His brother Romulus was at last carried up bodily to heaven in the presence of the people and in the course of a storm of thunder and lightning. A simple hut on the Palatine hill was preserved with veneration as the sanctuary of Romulus. But the demand for historical truth, or the appearance of it, was too strong in Rome to permit a poetic embellishment of the story, such as it would have experienced in Greece.

HORATIUS COCLES.

The ancient Roman ballads sang of the brave Horatius, who had fought so well in the old wars raised by the exiled royal family and their partisans. A golden statue of him

"In the Brave Days of Old."

stood in the market-place, and beside it sacrifice was offered in his memory. Such honors were the same as were appointed for Greek heroes. But the story of the deeds of Horatius wanted, nevertheless, the true legendary character, and was probably accepted by the people with more of pride than pious feeling.

NORSE AND OLD GERMAN MYTHOLOGY.

UNLIKE their Aryan kinsfolk, the Greeks, the Teutons were not a literary people. Their mythical tales were preserved not in books, but in memory. And Christianity, as represented alike by the missionaries and by Charlemagne himself, did its best to destroy Teutonic paganism root and branch. Hence it happens that of the myths of the gods and heroes of those great nations who, in pre-Christian times, inhabited the territories now included under the general name of Germany, no complete and systematic account has been transmitted to modern times.

But the old Germans were of the same race with the people of Norway, Sweden, and Denmark. Their speech was essentially the same. They had the same social and domestic customs and the same religion. Further, during the time when Christianity was spreading over Germany and Scandinavia, that exodus of the Norsemen was likewise taking place which ended in the colonization of Iceland—or Snowland, as it was also named by its discoverers in the middle of the ninth century. There, "on the verge," as Dr. Dasent says, "of the polar circle," the Vikings established their little independent principalities or republics; unmeddled with by Christian priests, and disdaining the continental kings who were aping the customs of the new times, the Icelandic Norsemen preserved, for five centuries more, the pure faith of their forefathers.

Lastly, there appears to have been less antagonism, less friction, between the two rival religions—Odinism and Christianity—in Iceland than in other countries. Its Christian priests would seem to have felt the loyalty of children toward their old faith, then dying away. Hence, in a measure, the complete and systematic form in which the Icelanders were able to leave a permanent record of their mythology. It was a Christian priest—Sigmund Sigfusson—who in the middle of the eleventh century, composed the compilation of mythical poems known as the elder Edda. To the succeeding century belongs the younger Edda, which is merely a prose rendering of those portions of the first work which narrate the creation of the world and man, and the generation, adventures, functions, and ultimate fate of the gods. As a cosmogony and theogony this Edda, or, as the word might be paraphrased, "Tales of a Grandmother," is as complete even as its Greek prototype, the Theogony of Hesiod. And as a record and expression of the spiritual life of those Teutons, who also were the progenitors of our English race, it is, or surely ought to be, incomparably more interesting.

THE CREATION.

In the prose Edda, Ginki, the wise king, travels in search of knowledge to the home of the Asia folk—the Norse gods —each of whom supplies the visitor with some piece of special information. The cosmogonic history thus patched up between them closely corresponds in main points with that contained in the Hesiodic poem; while its special details, tone, and coloring are the expression of special climatic conditions. Where the earth now is there was in the beginning, says the Edda, no sand, sea, or grass, but only an empty space (Ginnunga-gap), on whose north side lay the region of mist, ice, and snow (Niflheim), and on its south side the region of warmth and sunlight (Muspelheim). The warm breaths from the sun-land caused the ice to melt and topple over into Ginnunga-gap; and from the matter so accumulated sprang the huge Ymir, ancestor of the Reimthursen, Rime,

or Frost—giants. Ymir fed on the milk of the cow Aud-
humbla, whose name, it may be observed, in the Zenda-
vesta, stands indifferently for " cow " or mother-earth. The
cow herself lived by licking the ice-blocks ; from which, in
consequence of the licking, was produced Bori, who is alike
the fashioner of the world, and the father of Bor, who was
the father of Odin. Odin's brothers were Wili and We;
and just as in Hesiod the deities Zeus, Poseidon, and Hades
supplant Cronus, so the sons of Bori overthrow and succeed
the primitive dynasty of Ymir and the Frost Giants. Also
the dead Ymir is turned to account similarly with the dead
Cronus. His flesh becomes earth; his blood, the sea; his
bones, the mountains; his teeth, cliffs and crags; his skull,
the heavens, wherein his brains float in the form of clouds.
The heavens are supported by four Dwarves—Austri (east),
Westri (west), Nordri (north), and Sudri (south); and the
stars in it are the sparks from the fire-land of Muspelheim.
The new world thus fashioned was called Midgard, as being
placed midway between the lands of frost and fire. To
preserve it and its inhabitants from the giants who dwelt in
Jotunheim, Odin and his brother surrounded it with a fence
made from the eyebrows of Ymir. The inhabitants themselves were said to have been produced from two pieces of
wood which the brothers found floating on the sea, and
changed into a man, whom they named Ash, and a woman,
whom they named Embla.

From this middle world, or Midgard, arose the Norse
Olympus, or Asgard, whereon dwelt the Asa folk—Odin
and the twelve Aesir. It contained two mansions—Gladsheim for the gods, and Vingolf for the goddesses. There
also was Walhalla, wherein Odin placed one-half of the
heroes slain in battle, the other half being received by
Freija, the wife of Odin. Beside those already named there
were, as the Edda says, other homesteads, such as Elfheim,
where the elves dwelt; Breidablick, where dwelt the bright
and beautiful, far-seeing Baldur; Himinbiorg, or the Heaven-

tower of the thunder-god Thor; and Valaskialf, whence Odin could watch all gods and men. These gods also met in daily council beneath the branches of the tree Yggdrasil, one of whose roots grew in Asgard, the second in Niflheim, and the third in the realm of Hela, or death; and their way

Freija.

thither lay over the bright Asa-bridge, or Bifraust, or Rain-bow, which was said to burn all a-fire, so as to keep away the Frost Giants of Jotunheim. Lastly, the

LOWER WORLD

Was ruled by the goddess Hel, and to it were consigned those who had not died in battle. It was so far away that Odin's swift horse Sleipnir took nine nights to reach it. The river Gioll—the Norse Styx—surrounded this lower world on every side. Nastrand was the name of the worst spot in the

Norse hell.   Its roofs and doors were wattled with hissing snakes, ejecting poison, through which perjurers and murderers were forced to wade by way of punishment.

THE AESIR,

Whose thrones were in Gladsheim, were twelve in number. Their names were—Thor, Baldr, Freyr, Tyr, Bragi, Hodr, Heimdall, Vithar, Vali, Ullr, Ve, Forseti. Thus, with Odin, the "All-father," whose throne rose above the other twelve, the great gods of the Norse Pantheon were thirteen in number.

ODIN.

The physical origin of the idea of Odin is evident, first from the meaning of his name, and, secondly, from the various attributes assigned to him. The word Odin is simply another form of Woden, or Wuotan, which Grimm connects with the Latin *vadere*. He is thus the moving, life-giving breath or air of heaven; and as such corresponds to the Hindoo Brahmin—Atman (German, Athem), or ever-present life and energy.   His Greek correlative is, of course, Zeus, who is likewise spoken of as All-father.   The name Zeus is derived from a root signifying " to shine," and thus the King of the Greek Asgard was originally " the glistening ether."   It was but natural that Odin, as the personification of the blue sky, should rule the rain-clouds and the sunlight; hence as Odin the rain-giver he corresponds with Zeus Ombrios (the showery Zeus), while as the light-god he is merely a Norse Phoebus or Apollo, whose spear—the sun rays—disperses the darkness.   As sky-god, and god of the moving air, he was, no less naturally or inevitably, invoked as the protector of sailors.   In this respect he corresponds or is interchangeable with Thor.   But this interchange, or overlapping, of func-

tions is as distinctive of Norse as of Greek mythology.
Finally, Zeus and Odin resemble each other in their development from purely physical into spiritual beings. Odin, the
ever-present ether, becomes the ever-present and ever-know-
ing spirit, the Father of all. And as Zeus is the father of
the Muses, so Odin is the father of Saga, the goddess of
poetry. The two ravens that sat on the shoulders of Odin,

Odin.

and every morning brought him news of what was passing
in the world, were called Hunin and Munin—Thought and
Memory Memory, or Mnemosyne, was the mother of the
Greek Muses. A trace of the worship of Odin survives
even to the present day. In one of the Orkney islands is
an Odin stone, in a hollow of which superstitious people

thrust their hands, by way of testifying on their most solemn oath.   The island of Heligoland is said to have derived its name from Odin, who was also named Helgi (*der Heilige*), or the Holy.   " Charles's Wain," as we now call it, was named Odin's Wain; and the " Milky Way" was also known as Odin's Way.   Unlike Zeus—the Greek All-father — Odin was also a god of war.   Hence it was that, as already observed, he received into Walhalla one-half of the heroes slain in battle.

Frigg.

The two goddesses *Frigg* and *Freija*, who were at different times believed to be each the wife of Odin, appear to be the one simply a development of the other.   Of all the goddesses, Frigg was the best and dearest to Odin.   She sat enthroned beside him, and surveyed the world. She knew all, and exercised control over the whole face of nature. In art she is represented seated with the golden spindle by her side, with which she used to spin. She is attended by her handmaiden *Full* or *Fulla.* Freija was also a goddess who presided over smiling nature, sending sunshine, rain, and harvest. She was further a goddess into whose charge the dead passed. As has been said, half the number of heroes who fell in battle belonged to her. She is represented driving in a cart drawn by two cats.

In art Odin is figured seated on his throne, and attended by the ravens, Hunin and Munin, and the two dogs.

THOR,

Or Donar, simply meant the Thunderer—*der Donnerer ;* and he dwelt in the vault of heaven. As he was likewise said to

Thor.

be the son of Odin, or of Heaven, it is evident that, as in the case of the All-father, he had a purely physical origin. As the god of thunder and lightning Thor resembles Zeus;

and as the thunderbolts of Zeus were forged by the smith-
god Hephaestus, who dwelt below ground, so the hammer of
Odin was smithied by the Dwarves (*zwerge*), or black elves,
who dwelt within the earth.   Thor is represented driving
through the clouds in a car drawn by two goats.   Among

Thor.

the pagan Norsemen Thor's hammer was held in as much
reverence as Christ's cross among Christians.   It was carved
on their gravestones; and, wrought of wood, or of iron, it
was suspended in their temples.   Thor, under the symbol of

the hammer, was invoked as the deity who made marriages fruitful. He was also the god of the hearth and of fire.

As a sky-god Thor is identical with Odin much in the same way as Vishnu is with Indra. While the other Asa folk ride to their trysting-place, Thor goes on foot: he is the striding god, as Vishnu is, who traverses heaven in three steps. Thor is perhaps identical with the Gallic god Taranis, whose name resembles in sound the Scottish Celtic word for thunder. Thor has also been identified with the Slavonic god Perkunes, or Perune, whose name, according to a well-known law of phonetic change, is thought to be connected with the Greek word for thunder—Ceraunos. In art Thor is represented driving in his car drawn by two goats, with his hammer raised to strike.

BALDR

Means the shining god. His son Brono means daylight, in the Anglo-Saxon theogony. His home is called Breidablick —the far or wide-shining; and the name evidently conveys an idea similar to that suggested by such Greek words as Euryphassa, Eurynome, and Eurydice. The story of Baldr —the most lovely and pathetic not only in Norse but in any mythology — leaves no doubt whatever as to its physical origin and significance. The joy of the world in the presence of Baldr means only the gladness inspired by sunlight. The solemn oath sworn by all living things not to hurt the bright god, and their speechless dismay at his death, only mean the gloom of the northern climes during the winter months, when, in the purely concrete language of the primitive race, Baldr, or the sun, was dead.

The myth says that only the mistletoe had not sworn not to hurt Baldr; that Loki discovered the fact, and then directed Hodr—the blind god of the winter months—to shoot him with a twig of it. This mistletoe-bough is

another form of the thorn with which Odin puts to sleep
the spring maiden Brynhild, of the thorn of the Persian
Isfeudyar, or of the boar's tusk which kills the bright,
spring-like Adonis.   Loki, it was said, fled from the wrath
of the gods, changed himself into a salmon, was then caught
by them in a net, and bound fast until the twilight of the
gods—or, in Christian terminology, until the judgment-day.
The unlucky Hodr was killed by Odin's son, Bali, whose
home was among the willows and in the dry grass.

FREYR,

Is likewise named Fro.   The functions ascribed to him are
another instance of that interchange or overlapping to which
we have referred above, and which seems to be accounted
for by the hypothesis that whole groups of mythical beings
are in reality but personified epithets of one and the same
thing.   Thus Freyr, as the cause of fruitfulness, is merely
the sun-lit and air-breathing heaven as represented by Odin.
Like Odin, he is the patron of seafarers.   Not only is Freyr
repeated, so to speak, in Odin, but also—or if not the god
himself, then his servant Skirnir — in the Volsung and
Niblung heroes, Sigurd, Sigmund, and Gunnar.   And as
Sigurd can win the maiden Brynhild only by riding through
the flaming fire which surrounded and guarded her dwelling,
so by the same exploit must Skirnir win Gerda for the
master.   In later times, when the old religion had given
way before Christianity, and its myths were being explained
on the Euhemerist method, it was alleged that Freyr had
only been a Swedish king, whose sorrowing subjects buried
his body in a magnificent tomb, to which, for three whole
years, they continued to bring their presents, as if Freyr
were alive.

   This Euhemerism is, however, inconsistent with the most
authoritative source of all—the Eddas.   In Dasent's *Prose*

Edda Freyr is described as the god of rain, sunshine, and fruits—as Odin, in fact, in another shape. His wife was Gredr, whose beauty—as he saw her leaving her father's house, and shedding a lustre over air and sea—captivated the god, and allowed him no rest till he won her.

Freyr.

In art Freyr is represented riding on a wild boar through the air at a speed greater than that of the swiftest horse. Sometimes he was drawn by it in a car. In crossing the sea he also used a boat.

TYR

Is likewise named Ziu, and Saxnot. Our word Tuesday is
a memorial of his name. Once more, this god seems to be
an instance of personifying an epithet. Ziu is identical with
the root—meaning "shine"—of the Sanscrit *Dynaus,* the
Greek *Zeus,* and the Latin *Deus.* Tyr, therefore, is another
glistening god. He is pre-eminently the god of war and of
athletic sports. "On him it is good for wrestlers to call."
Tyr had only one hand, the other having been bitten off by
the wolf Fenris, into whose mouth the god had placed it as
a pledge of security, when the wolf allowed himself to be
bound in the net that shall hold him fast till the judgment-
day.

BRAGI

Is the god of poetry and eloquence. "He is famous for
wisdom, and best in tongue-wit and cunning speech." A
sort of counterpart of this god was his wife Iduna, who
dwelt in the underworld. She is spoken of in terms that
recall the Hindoo description of Ushas—Eos—or the Daure
goddess. For as Ushas—the Dawn—makes the world young
every new morning, so Iduna is said to preserve in a box the
golden apples which the gods ate, and so made themselves
young again.

HEIMDALL

Was the watchman of the bridge Bifrost, leading to the
underworld. The sound of Heimdall's horn is heard over
the world, and shall be the signal for the great battle between
the gods on the day of their ending, or twilight. The name
of his horse, Gulltopr (Goldropf, or golden mare), connects
him with the sun-gods and sun-horses of classical mythology.
Heimdall was so sharp a watchman that he could even hear

the grass grow on the earth and the wool on the backs of sheep !

Vithar was next in strength to Thor. As the " twilight," or *Götterdämmerung,* Vithar shall destroy the wolf Fenris, the devourer of the gods, by placing one foot on the monster's lower jaw, and pushing up the upper one — thus wrenching them asunder. Ulle is the god of the chase; a skilful bowman and a fast runner on stilts. Like Bragi and Iduna, Mimir is the deity of wisdom and knowledge. He dwelt by the ash-tree, Yggdrasil, beneath whose roots bubbled forth the well of wisdom, Mimir's well, from whose waters Mimir drank his daily draught.

The Wolf Fenris.

Loki dwelt in the land of the dead. He was the son of the giant Farbanti, whose duty it was to ferry the dead over the waters of the lower world. Loki had three children as cruel and hateful as he himself was full of mischief. One was the huge wolf Fenris, who, at the last day, shall hurry gaping to the scene of battle, with his lower jaw scraping the earth and his nose scraping the sky ! The second was the serpent of Midgard—the serpent which Odin threw into the sea, where the monster grew to such length that it embraced the whole world in its folds. The third was the goddess Hel, who was half black and half blue, and lived daintily on the brains and marrow of men.

Hel is, in fact, that dreadful Hindoo goddess Kali, who, in these modern days, has degenerated into a Doorga of quite a pathetic and interesting character. Loki was at the bottom of all the mischief that ever happened in the society of the gods. The character of this god and his close relationship with a personage who figures conspicuously in modern theology are pretty well indicated in the following adage, with its equivalents in German and English : Loki er or bondum —der Teufel ist frei gelassen—the devil is loose.

Of the almost countless beings who figure in Norse mythology we must say but very little. Like the great gods, they appear to be representative of the good and evil powers of nature. Among them are the Elves (Alfen, Elfen) who live in Alfheimr (Elf-home). Their king is the Erlkonig (Elfen Konig). In the night hours they come in troops to dance in the grass, leaving, according to popular belief, their traces in the form of fairy-rings. The dwarves (Zwerge), whose father is named Ivaldr, dwell in the heart of the hills. To them belong precious stones and metals, on which they prove their skill in workmanship. As guardians of hidden treasures they were propitiated by the seekers of the same with a black goat or a black cock. An echo is called by the Icelanders Dwergmaal-Zwergsprache—or dwarf-voice. The evil beings who stole the light every evening, and the summer every year, were called giants. Such were the Reifriesen (Hrimthursen) who brought the winter. The giant Hrungnir had a head of stone and a heart of stone; and a giantess, mother of Gmir, as many as nine hundred heads. Another giant was Thiassi, who slew Thor and cast his eyes up to heaven, where they shone thereafter as stars. In the extreme north dwelt the giant Hresvelgr, the motion of

whose wings caused wind and tempest, in which respect he
resembles the gigantic bird of the Buddhist play, *Naga-*

The Valkyrior.

nanda, who raises the waves of the sea by the flapping of
his wings. On the extreme south was Surtr, whose flaming

sword guarded the bounds of Muspelheim. Besides these
there were the Trollweiber (troll arvis), phantoms from the
land of the dead, who in the dark nights rode to the earth
on a wolf bridled with snakes. The three Nornen were the
Norse Fates. The Valkyrien were fair maidens who hovered
over the field of battle, woke up the dead heroes with a kiss,
and led away their souls to fight and drink ale as of old in
the happy Valhalla.

THE TALE OF THE VOLSUNGS AND NIBLUNGS.

The Volsunga Saga and Nibelungenlied hardly differ in
anything but the name. The one is merely the Norse, the
other the German, form of one and the same nature myth,
or epic. According to the "Solar myth" theorists, this epic
serves the common purpose of all Aryan nations; in India
being known under the names of Ramayana and Mahabharata; in Greece as the Iliad and the Odyssey; in our more
northern lands as the Tale of the Volsungs and the Nibelungen
Lay; and in England as the tale of King Arthur and his
Knights of the Round Table. Whatever objections may
be urged against the "Solar myths" explanation of these
stories, it is quite indisputable that the main incidents in all
of them completely coincide. Indeed, it is not too much to
affirm that fully to appreciate the spirit of any one of these
great epics of the world, the student must possess some
acquaintance with its co-ordinate ones. But not only do the
main incidents in the *Northern Epics* coincide with those in
the *Iliad* and *Odyssey*, but they even contain episodes which
correspond in everything except the name with plots in
Greek tragedy. Gudrun, for example, is only a Norse
Medea. We now proceed to give a slight sketch of the
Volsunga Saga.

Volsung was the son of Rerir, the son of the Sigi, the son

of Odin. Volsung lay for seven years in his mother's womb; and they said the youngling kissed his mother before she died. Volsung had a daughter called Signy, who was married to Siggeir, King of Gothland. During the marriage festivities in Volsung's house, and as the good folk sat round the evening fire, there entered an old man wrapped in a cloak, who drove a sword into a log of wood right up to the hilt, predicted great things of the hero who should be able to draw it out again, and immediately disappeared. The old man was Odin; and the sword was the sword of Gram, which has its counterpart in the sword of Chrysaor, in Roland's Durandal, and in King Arthur's Excalibur. And as only Theseus could lift the huge stone, and none but Ulysses could draw his own bow, so among the assembled heroes only Sigmund the son of Volsung could pull out Gram.

Volsung was afterward murdered in the land of Siggeir; wherefore Sigmund avenged the death of his father by killing the children of his brother-in-law, Siggeir. After that he returned to his own land, and married Borghild, by whom he had two children, Helgi and Hamund. But Sigmund was no more constant in his loves than other heroes of whom we read in classical literature. He fell in love with Hjordis, who was beloved by the son of King Hunding. Between the two heroes there ensued a fight, during which the one-eyed man in a blue cloak, and a bill in his hand, appeared, whereupon Sigmund was slain. The dying Sigmund comforted his wife Hjordis, and entrusted to her charge his sword Gram, wishing her to preserve it for their unborn boy. "And now," said he, "I grow weary with my wounds, and I will go to see our kin that have gone before me." So Hjordis sat over him till he died at the day dawning.

Hjordis after that married Hialprek, King of Denmark, a character who corresponds to the Grecian Laius and Akrisius. At Hialprek's court was born Sigurd, the son of Hjordis and Sigmund—the favorite hero of Norse mythol-

ogy. Sigurd was taught in all the arts and sciences by
Regin, the cunning blacksmith, who was also the brother of
the otter killed by Odin, and the serpent—or worm—Fafnir,
who guarded those golden treasures which, according to the
Solar theory, mean the gladdening and revivifying sunlight,
Fafnir himself being the evil power, the cloud, or the darkness which steals the light.   Regin wished to secure the
treasure for himself, and forged a sword for Sigurd to slay
the worm with.   But it shivered into pieces on its very first
trial; and Sigurd, in contempt at Regin's smithing, procures
the fragments of his paternal sword Gram, and Regin welds
them together.   Gram stood every test.   Sigurd drove it,
right to the hilt, into Regin's anvil; and after that, a lock of
wool, borne on the surface of the stream, divided into two
against the motionless edge.   Sigurd slew Fafnir, and procured the treasure; and next he slew Regin, who wished to
possess the whole of the prize on the plea that his forging of
the weapon had really won the victory.   After that Sigurd
went to free the Valkyrie Brynhild, according to the Solar
myth, the Maiden of Spring, for whom the cold earth is long-
ing.   Brynhild lay in the sleep into which she had been
thrown by the thorn of Odin—that is, by the thorn, or cold,
or frost of winter.

Sigurd, like his mythical relatives in Norse and Greek
stories, was unfaithful in his loves.   He fell in love with
Gudrun, the sister of Gunnar, and that, too, in spite of those
love scenes and speeches of his with Brynhild, for the beauty
of which the Volsung Saga is perhaps unequalled by any
other epic story whatever.   Brynhild had sworn to marry
only the man who could ride through the fire which surrounded her dwelling.   This Gunnar could not do; but
Sigurd did it in Gunnar's shape, whereafter Brynhild agreed
to marry Gunnar.   But Gudrun, in her triumph, revealed
the secret; and just as Oenone procured the death of the
unfaithful Paris, and Deianeira that of the fickle Hercules,
so Brynhild compassed the death of Sigurd.   Brynhild also,

like another Deianeira, dies, in grief, on the funeral pile of
her husband. Next, Gudrun, also grieving for Sigurd,
leaves her home; but she marries Atli, King of Hunland.
It would seem that this Atli must be another name for the
powers of darkness, for he invited his wife's brothers to his
court, in order that he might seize the golden treasure, " the
sunlight," which they had received from the dead Sigurd.
These treasures the brothers buried in the Rhine river, and
went on their way to Hunland, though they well knew they
were destined never to return. The scene in which the
brothers are slain by the treacherous Atli is unsurpassed for
power and terror by any fighting story, except, perhaps, by
that one in the Mahabharata which describes the final struggle on the battle-field of Hastinapur. Next follows Gudrun's
revenge for the death of her brothers; like, as we have
already said, a Norse Medea, she slew her own and Atli's
children.

But we cannot further pursue those final tragedies in which
all the various kinsfolk die by each other's hands and in
obedience to that stern, inevitable fate which in these tales
seems to be personified in Odin, and looms so terribly in the
background of the dramas of Sophocles and Aeschylus.

We would, in conclusion, recommend the student to read
the translation of the *Volsung Saga*, recently published by
Morris and Magnusson, as also Dr. Dasent's translation of the
Prose Edda. Those who know German may also consult
Wilhelm Mannhardt's *Die Götter der deutschen und nor-
dischen Völker*. For an exhaustive exposition of the " Solar
myth" theory, alike of the subjects embraced in the fore-
going sketch and of Aryan myths in general, we recommend
the student to the work of George W. Cox on *The Mythology of the Aryan Nations*.

THE MYTHOLOGY AND RELIGION OF THE HINDOOS.

In the *Veda*, the earliest record of the Sanscrit language, many of the myths common to the Aryan nations are presented in their simplest form. Hence the special value of Hindoo myths in a study of Comparative Mythology. But it would be an error to suppose that the myths of the Greeks, Latins, Slavonians, Norsemen, old Germans, and Celts were *derived* from those of the Hindoos. For the myths, like the languages, of all these various races, the Hindoos included, are derived from one common source. Greek, Latin, Sanscrit, etc., are but modifications of a primitive Aryan language that was spoken by the early "Aryans" before they branched away from their original home, wherever that may have been, to form new nationalities in India, Greece, Northern Europe, Central Europe, etc. The Sanscrit language is thus not the mother, but the elder sister of Greek and the kindred tongues : and the Vedic mythology is, in like manner, only the elder sister of the other Aryan mythologies. It is by reason of the discovery of the common origin of these languages that scholars have been enabled to treat mythology scientifically. For example, many names unintelligible in Greek are at once explained by the meaning of their Sanscrit equivalents. Thus, the name of the chief Greek god, Zeus, conveys no meaning in itself. But the Greek sky-god Zeus evidently corresponds to the Hindoo sky-god Dyaus, and this word is derived from a root div or dyu, meaning " to shine." Zeus, then, meant originally " the glistening ether;" and the Sanscrit devas, Greek

theos, and Latin **deus,** meaning " god," are from the same root, and signify " shining" or " heavenly." Similarly

The Incarnation of Vishnu.

other Greek names are explained by their counterparts, or cognate words in Sanscrit. Thus, the name of Zeus's wife, Hera, belongs to a Sanscrit root **svar,** and originally meant the bright sky, the goddess herself being primarily the bright air; and Erins is explained by the Sanscrit **Saranyu**. In India there have been two dynasties, as it were, of gods— the Vedic and Brahmanic. The Vedic gods belong to the very earliest times, appear obviously as elemental powers, and are such as would have been worshipped by a simple, uninstructed, agricultural people. The Brahmanic religion was, in great part at least, a refined development of the former; and was gradually displacing the simpler worship of Vedism many centuries before the birth of Christ. Five or six centuries before the last event, Dissent, under the name and form of Buddhism, became the chief religion of India; but in about ten centuries Brahmanism recovered its old position. Buddhism now retains but comparatively few followers in India. Its chief holds are in Burmah, Siam, Japan, Thibet, Nepaul, China, and Mongolia; and its nominal followers at the present day perhaps outnumber those of all other religions put together.

THE VEDIC GODS.

DYAUS

Was, as we have already indicated, the god of the bright sky, his name being connected with that of Zeus through the root *div* or *dyu*. That the god-name and the sky-name were interchangeable is evident from such classical expressions as that "Zeus rains" (*i. e.*, the sky rains). In such expressions there is hardly any mythological suggestion ; and the meaning of the name Dyaus—like those of the names Uranus and Cronus in Greek—always remained too transparent for it to become the nucleus of a myth. Dyaus, however, was occasionally spoken of as an overruling spirit. The epithet, Dyaus pitar, is simply Zeus pater—Zeus the father; or, as it is spelled in Latin, Jupiter. Another of his names, *Janitar*, is the Sanscrit for genetor, a title of Zeus as the father or producer. *Dyaus pitar*, "father sky," and *prithus matar*, "mother earth," are generally spoken of together.

VARUNA

Is also a sky-god : but in later times he becomes god of the waters. The name is derived from the root *var*, to cover, or envelop : and so far Varuna (accent Váruna) means the vault of heaven. Here, then, we seem to find a clue to the meaning of the Greek Uranus, whom we already know to have been a sky-god; Uranus means the coverer; but, as observed above, the name would have remained unintelligible apart

(379)

from its reference to the Sanscrit name. The myth of Varuna is a wonderful instance of the readiness and completeness with which the Hindoo genius spiritualized its sense-impressions. From the conception of the thousand-eyed (or starred) Varuna, who overlooked all men and things, the Indian Aryans passed to the loftier conception of Varuna as an all-seeing god or providence, whose spies, or angels, saw all that took place. Some of the finest passages in the Vedic hymns are those in which the all-seeing Varuna is addressed, as in the following verses, translated by Muller from the Rigveda :

" Let me not yet, O Varuna, enter into the house of clay ; have mercy, Almighty, have mercy !

" If I go along trembling like a cloud driven by the wind ; have mercy, Almighty, have mercy !

" Through want of strength, though strong and bright god, have I gone to the wrong shore ; have mercy, Almighty, have mercy !

" Thirst came upon the worshipper, tho' he stood in the midst of the waters ; have mercy, Almighty, have mercy !

" Whenever we men, O Varuna, committed offence before the heavenly host, whenever we break thy law through thoughtfulness ; have mercy, Almighty, have mercy ! "

INDRA.

The connection, or identity, between Zeus and Dyaus seems to be chiefly limited to the names. There is greater resemblance between Indra and Zeus than between Zeus and Dyaus. Indra, as the hurler of the thunderbolts and as a " cloud compeller," coincides with Zeus and Thor.

The myth of Indra—the favorite Vedic god—is a further instance of that transition from the physical to spiritual meaning to which we have referred, though Indra is by no means so spiritual a being as Varuna. It is also a good instance of the fact that, as the comparative mythologists express it, the further back the myths are traced the more " atmospheric " do the gods become. First, of the merely

physical Indra. Indra shatters the cloud with his bolt, and
releases the imprisoned waters. His purely physical origin
is further indicated by the mythical expression that the
clouds moved in Indra as the winds in Dyaus—an expression implying
that Indra was a
name for the sky.
Also, the stories
told of him cor-
respond closely
with some in
classical my-
thology. Like
Hermes and
Hercules he is en-
dowed with pre-
cocious strength;
like Hermes he
goes in search of
the cattle, the
clouds which the
evil powers have
driven away;
and like Hermes

Indra.

he is assisted by the breezes—though in the Hindoo myth
by the storm-winds, rather — the *Maruts*. His beard of
lightning is the red beard of Thor. In a land with the
climatic conditions of India, and among an agricultural
people, it was but natural that the god whose fertilizing
showers brought the corn and wine to maturity should be regarded as the greatest of all.

" He who as soon as born is the first of the deities, who has done
honor to the gods by his exploits; he at whose might heaven and
earth are alarmed, and who is known by the greatness of his strength;
he, men, is Indra.

" He who fixed firm the moving earth; who tranquillized the in-

censed mountains; who spread the spacious firmament; who con
solidated the heavens; he, men, is Indra.

" He who, having destroyed Ahi, set free the seven rivers; who
recovered the cows detained by Bal; who generated fire in the clouds;
who is invincible in battle; he, men, is Indra.

" He under whose control are horses and cattle, and villages, and
all chariots; who gave birth to the sun and to the dawn; and who
is the leader of the waters; he, men, is Indra.

" He to whom heaven and earth bow down; he at whose might
the mountains are appalled; he who is the drinker of the Soma juice,
the firm of frame, the adamant-armed, the wielder of the thunderbolt;
he, men, is Indra.

" May we envelop thee with acceptable praises as husbands are
embraced by their wives! "

The first verse in the preceding hymn from the Rigveda
perhaps refers to Indra as a sun-god, and to the rapidity with
which, in tropical climates, the newly born sun grows in
heat-giving powers. The Ahi, or throttling snake, of the
third verse, is the same as the Greek Echidna, or the Hindoo
Vritra; and is multiplied in the Rakshasas—or powers of
darkness—against which the sky-god Indra wages deadly
war. He is likewise spoken of in the same hymn in much
the same kind of language that would naturally be applied
to the creator and sustainer of the world. But so is almost
every Hindoo deity. Absolute supremacy was attributed to
each and every god, whenever it came to his turn to be
praised or propitiated.

SURYA

Corresponds to the Greek Helios. That is, he was not so
much the god of light as the special god who dwelt in the
body of the sun. The same distinction exists between Poseidon and Nereus; the one being the god of all waters, and
even a visitor at Olympus, the other a dweller in the sea.
Surya is described as the husband of the Dawn, and also as
her son.

SAVITAR

Is another personification of the sun. His name means the " Inciter or enlivener," and is derived from the root *su*, to drive or stimulate. As the sun-god he is spoken of as the golden-eyed, golden-tongued, and golden-handed; and the Hindoo commentators, in their absurd attempts to give a literal prosaic explanation of a highly appropriate poetic epithet, say that Savitar cut off his hand at a sacrifice, and that the priests gave him a golden one instead. Savitar thus corresponds to the Teutonic god Tyr, whose hand was cut off by the wolf Fenris. Like other gods in the Hindoo and Norse mythologies, Savitar is regarded as all-powerful. That Savitar is a sun-god appears from the following passages, among many others, from the Rigveda :

"Shining forth he rises from the lap of the dawn, praised by singers; he, he, my god Savitar, stepped forth, who never misses the same place.

" He steps forth, the splendor of the sky, the wide-seeing, the far-shining, the shining wanderer ; surely enlivened by the sun do men go to their tasks, and do their work.

" May the golden-eyed Savitar arise hither !

" May the golden-handed, life-bestowing, well-guarding, exhilarating, and affluent Savitar be present at the sacrifice ! "

The second passage seems to identify Savitar with Odin, who was also " the wanderer " — *Wegtom*, and who was one-eyed, as Savitar was one-handed.

SOMA.

In some respects the myth of Soma is the most curious of all. Soma, as the intoxicating juice of the Soma plant, corresponds to that mixture of honey and blood of the Quoasir, which, in the Norse mythology, imparts prolonged life to the gods. In the Rigveda the Soma is similarly described, as also the process by which it is converted into intoxicating liquid. But in the same hymns Soma is also described as an all-powerful god. It is he who gives strength to Indra, and enables him to conquer his enemy Vritra, the snake of darkness. He is further, like Vishnu, Indra, and Varuna, the supporter of heaven and earth, and of gods and men; thus it would seem as if the myth of the god Soma is but an instance of that fetishistic stage in the history of the human kind during which men attributed conscious life and energy to whatever hurt or benefited them. The following passages from the Rigveda are adduced to show in what terms Soma was spoken of as a god and as a mere plant:

"Where there is eternal light, in the world where the sun is placed, in that immortal, imperishable world, place me, O Soma

. . . .

"Where life is free, in the third heaven of heavens, where the worlds are radiant, there make me immortal."

And again:

"In the filter, which is the support of the world, thou, pure Soma, art purified for the gods. The Usijas first gathered thee. In thee all these worlds are contained.

"The Soma flowed into the vessel for Indra, for Vishnu; may it be honeyed for Vayu!"

AGNI

Is the god of fire, his name evidently being connected with the Latin *ignis*. He corresponds to the Greek Hephaestus. Of this god Mr. Wheeler, in his introduction to his *History of India*, thus writes: "To man in a primitive state of existence the presence of fire excites feelings of reverence. Its powers raise it to the rank of a deity whose operations are felt and seen. It burns and it consumes. It dispels the darkness, and with it drives away, not only the imaginary horrors which the mind associates with darkness, but also the real horrors—such as beasts of prey. . . . It becomes identified with the light of the sun and moon;

with the lightning which shoots from the sky and shatters the loftiest trees and strikes down the strong man; with the deity who covers the field with grain and ripens the harvest; with the divine messenger who licks up the sacrifice and carries it to the gods."

Agni.

As another curious instance of the sort of fetishism to which we have referred, the Veda describes Agni as being generated from the rubbing of sticks, after which he bursts forth from the wood like a fleet courser. Again, when excited by the wind he rushes amongst the trees like a bull, and consumes the forest as a raja destroys his enemies. Such expressions, of course, prove the purely physical origin of the god Agni; and it is hardly necessary to observe that, like Indra, Varuna, Soma, Vishnu, etc., he is an all-powerful god, and supporter of the universe.

VAYU

Is the god of the winds, or of the air. Allied to him are the Maruts —the storm-gods or "crushers," whose name has been derived from a root meaning to grind, and regarded as connected with such names as Mars and Ares. The same root appears in Miolnir, an epithet of Thor, conceived as the crashing or crushing god. The Maruts are the Hindoo counterparts of the Norse Ogres—the fierce storm-beings who toss the sea into foam, and who in the *Norse Tales* are represented as being armed with iron clubs, at every stroke of which they send the earth flying so many yards into the air. The primary meaning of the name is clear from the Vedic passages which describe the Maruts as roaring among the forest trees and tearing up the clouds for rain.

Among all the personifications of Hindoo mythology, one of the purest and most touching and beautiful is

USHAS,

Whose name is the same as the Greek Eos—or the Dawn. The name Ushas is derived from a root *us,* to burn. The language in which the physical Ushas was spoken of was especially capable of easy transformation into a purely spiritual meaning. The dawn-light is beautiful to all men, barbarous or civilized; and it did not require any great stretch of poetic fancy to represent Ushas as a young wife awakening her children and giving them new strength for the toils of the new day. It happens that the word which in Sanscrit means "to awake," also means "to know;" and thus, like the Greek Athene, Ushas became a goddess of wisdom. The following passages show how Ushas was regarded by the Vedic worshippers :

"Ushas, daughter of heaven, dawn upon us with riches; diffuser of light, dawn upon us with abundant food; beautiful goddess, dawn upon us with wealth of cattle.

"This auspicious Ushas has harnessed her vehicles from afar, above the rising of the sun, and she comes gloriously upon men with a hundred chariots.

"First of all the world is she awake, trampling over transitory darkness; the mighty, the giver of light, from on high she beholds all things; ever youthful, ever reviving, she comes first to the invocation."

Had we space for discussion of so interesting a subject, it would be easy to show how naturally monotheistic conception would grow out of the polytheism of the Vedic religion.

Meantime we content ourselves with the following monotheistic hymn, translated by Max Muller :

" In the beginning there rose the source of golden light. He was the only lord of all that is ; he established this earth and this sky : who is the god to whom we shall offer our sacrifice ?

" He who gives life, he who gives strength ; whose blessings all the bright gods desire ; whose shadow is immortality ; whose shadow is death : who is the god to whom we shall offer our sacrifice ?

" He who through his power is the only king of all the breathing and awakening world. He who governs all, men and beasts : who is the god to whom we shall offer our sacrifice ?

" He whose power these snowy mountains, whose power the sea proclaims, with the distant river. He whose these regions are as it were his two arms : who is the god to whom we shall offer our sacrifice ?

" He through whom the sky is bright and the earth firm. He through whom the heaven was established—nay, the highest heaven ; he who measured out the light in the air : who is the god to whom we shall offer our sacrifice ?

" He to whom heaven and earth, standing firm by his will, look up, trembling, inwardly ; he over whom the rising sun shines forth : who is the god to whom we shall offer our sacrifice ?

.   .   .   .

" May he not destroy us, he the creator of the earth ; or he the righteous, who created heaven ; he who also created the bright and mighty waters : who is the god to whom we shall offer our sacrifice ?

THE BRAHMANIC GODS.

Of the later Hindoo religion the chief deities are Brahma Vishnu, and Siva—forming the Hindoo Trinity, or Trimurti. These are not regarded as separate, independent gods, but merely as three manifestations or revelations or phases of the spirit or energy of the supreme incomprehensible being Brahm. This trinity is a comparatively late formation.

Trimurti, or Hindoo Trinity.

The trinity of the later Vedic writings is composed, rather, of the representative gods of earth, air, and sky—Agni, Vayu, and Surya. Again, no such trinity as the Brahmanic appears to be known in the Mahabharata, which represents Brahma, Vishnu, and Indra as being the sons of Mahadeva, or Siva. Perhaps, however, the reason of this is to be found in the mutual jealousy of the two great sects, Vaishnavas and Saivas, into which the Hindoo religion came to be divided. To Brahm as the self-existent—of whom there is no image—there existed neither temples nor altars. As signifying, among other things, the principle of divinity, the name Brahm is of the neuter gender, and the divine essence is described as that which illumines all, delights all, whence all proceeds, that of which all live when born, and that to which all must return.

BRAHMA

Is that member of the triad whose name is best known to us, and most familiar to the Hindoos themselves. Images of him are found in the temples of other gods, but he has neither temples nor altars of his own. The reason of this is that Brahma, as the creative energy, is quiescent, and will remain so until the end of the present age of the world—of the *Kali Yuga*, that is—only a small portion of whose 432,000 years has already passed.

Brahma and Saraswati.

It appears, however, that an attempt was made to represent even the divine spirit of Brahm; for the god Narayana means the spirit moving on the waters. Narayana is figured as a graceful youth lying on a snake couch which floats on the water, and holding his toe in his mouth.

Brahma is figured as a four-headed god, bearing in one hand a copy of the Vedas, in another a spoon for pouring out the lustral water contained in a vessel which he holds in a third hand, while the fourth hand holds a rosary. The rosary was used by the Hindoos to aid them in contemplation, a bead being dropped on the silent pronunciation of each name of the god, while the devotee mused on the attribute signified by the name.

Brahma, like each god, had his *sacti,* or wife, or female counterpart, and his *vahana* or vehicle, whereon he rode. Brahma's *sacti* is **Saraswati,** the goddess of poetry, wisdom, eloquence, and fine art. His *vahana* was the goose—*hansa*—in Latin, *anser,* in German, *gans.*

VISHNU

Is the personification of the *preserving* power of the divine spirit. The Vaishnavas allege that Vishnu is the paramount god, because there is nothing distinctive in the act of annihilation, but only a cessation of preservation. But of course

Vishnu.

the argument would cut all three ways, for it might as well be said that creation, preservation, and destruction are at bottom only one and the same thing—a fact thus pointing to the unity of God. Of the two Hindoo sects the Vaishnavas are perhaps the more numerous. Vishnu is represented as being of a blue color; his *vahana* is Garuda, the winged half-man, half-bird, king of birds, and his *sacti,* or wife, is the goddess Lakshmi. He is said to have four hands—one holding a *shankha,* or shell, the second a *chakra* or quoit, the third a club, and the fourth a lotus. Our illustration represents Vishnu lying asleep on Ananta, the serpent of eternity. At the end of the *Kali Yuga* Vishnu will rest in that position ; from his navel will spring a lotus stalk, on the top of which—above the surface of the waters, which at that time will cover the world—Brahma will appear to create the earth anew.

SIVA

Is the destroyer—the third phase of Brahm's energy. He is represented as of a white color. His *sacti* is Bhavani or Pracriti, the terrible Doorga or Kali, and his *vahana* a white bull. Sometimes Siva is figured with a trident in one hand, and in another a rope or *pasha,* with which he or his wife Kali strangles evil-doers. His necklace is made of human skulls ; serpents are his ear-rings; his loins are wrapped in tiger's skin; and from his head the sacred river Ganga is represented as springing.

Siva.

Among the minor deities may be mentioned Kuvera, the god of riches; Lakshmi, being the goddess of wealth; Kamadeva, the god of love, who is represented as riding on a dove and armed with an arrow of flowers, and a bow whose string is formed of bees; and thirdly, Ganesha, the son of Siva and Prithivi, who is regarded as the wisest of all the gods, is especially the god of prudence and policy, and is invoked at the opening of Hindoo literary works.

Kamadeva.

AVATARS OF VISHNU.

The word *avatar* means, in its plain sense, Descent—that is, from the world of the gods to the world of men. In these descents, or incarnations, the purpose of Vishnu has always been a beneficent one. His first avatar is named Matsya, wherein, during the reign of King Satyavrata, Vishnu appeared in the form of a fish. For the world had been deluged by water for its wickedness, and its inhabitants had perished, except the king and seven sages, with their families, who together with pairs of all species of animals, entered into an ark prepared for them, and of which the fish took care, by having its cable tied to its horn. In the second, or Kurma avatar, Vishnu appeared in the form of a tortoise, supporting Mount Mandara on his back, while the gods churned the sea for the divine ambrosia. In the Varaha, or third avatar, Vishnu appeared as a boar to save the earth when it had been drowned a second time. The boar went into the sea and fished the earth out on his tusks. In the fourth he appeared as Narasingha, the man-lion, to free the world from a monarch who, for his austerities, had been endowed by the gods with universal dominion. In this shape Vishnu tore the king to pieces. Subsequently he

appeared as a dwarf, then as Rama, the hero of the Ramayana, who likewise was a beneficent being.   His chief incarnation appears in Krishna, the
god who is most loved by the
Hindoos.   Buddha, the founder
of the Buddhist religion, was
also said to be an incarnation of
Vishnu.   Nine of these avatars
have already passed.   In the
tenth,   or **Kalki Avatara**,   he
will appear armed with a scim-
itar, and riding on a white horse,
when he will end the present
age; after which he will sleep

Buddha.

on the waters, produce Prama, and so inaugurate a new
world.

THE MYTHOLOGY AND RELIGION OF EGYPT.

EGYPTIAN myths undoubtedly originated and were developed similarly to the myths of all other nations with which we are acquainted. Yet an indication of the various stages of that development, and an understanding of the system as a whole and as it is now known to us, are far more difficult in the case of Egyptian than of Greek, Norse, Germanic, or Hindoo mythology. The reason of this is very evident. The Egyptian religion seems to have reached its abstract or metaphysical stage long before any of the religions to which we have referred; and as its records belong wholly to that stage, there are no means of enabling the student to bridge over the gap between its earliest and its latest formations.

Indeed, it would appear as if precisely the same kind of differences existed between the Egyptian and the Greek genius as between the Greek genius and that of the Hindoos. The temperament of the Greek was open, joyous, sensuous; that of the other two races was self-repressive, brooding, and mystical. The bias or mental bent of these was not so much toward what was artistically or logically preventable, as toward the elusive, mysterious spirit of which they imagined all things visible and tangible to be merely the veil. The Greek was artistically sensuous; the Hindoo was mystically religious. Or, the difference between them may be said to resemble that between form and color. The contrast in intellectual bias between the Egyptians and their adversaries, the Greeks, is sufficiently indicated in what Herodotus says of the Egyptian contempt for the claims made by the Greeks of descent from the gods. The priests of Egypt could only laugh at the absurdity of the belief according to which a god was said to be the sixteenth ancestor of Hecataeos. *Our* gods, said they, never lived on earth.

However, it appears as if a comparison of it with other systems shows that the mythology of Egypt is, in great measure at least, explicable by the general doctrines implied in the title "Solar Myth." Even that very readiness with which the Greeks identified the Egyptian gods with their own affords, if not proof, at all events some countenance, to the supposition that both Pantheons were, so to speak, peopled after the same manner. Again, the functions and characters of the Egyptian gods interchange like those of the Greek and Norse gods. Their names have in both cases similar physical meanings. In both cases also the birth and genealogy of the gods appear to be but an expression of physical, visible sequences. We find in both cases the same confusion, or identity, between a god's mother and his sister; and what appears to be the same conflict between the light-giving and the light-stealing powers of nature. The old German religion is, perhaps, of a more spiritual character than that of Egypt. Yet there is no doubt that the idea of the contest between the purely spiritual powers Ormuzd and Ahriman was originally only the idea of the contest between the sunlight, Indra, and the clouds or darkness, Vritra. This seems a strong indirect proof that Osiris and Typho are the same as Indra and Vritra. The idea of dynastic overthrow and succession common to the Aryan religions, and presented with such weird and pathetic grandeur in Norse mythology, is, if at all, but faintly defined in the religion of Egypt. Yet it seems to be implied in such phrases as "Osirian divinities," and "three orders of the gods." Lastly, it appears that many of the Egyptian deities are only personified attributes of one and the same thing or person.

The great gods of Egypt were **Neph, Amun, Pthah, Khem, Sati, Maut,** and **Bubastis.**

NEPH

Is also named Num, Nu, Nef, Cnouphis, and Cenubis. Now Nef means spirit or breath, in which sense it is still retained in Arabic. He is " the spirit of God moving on the face of the waters." Therefore, in this special, physical sense Neph corresponds to the Teutonic Woden, or Wuotan, as also Brahma and Zeus. Neph was worshipped in Aethiopia and the Thebais. He is represented as having a ram's head with curved horns. His wife, or in Hindoo phraseology *sacti*, was named Auka.

Pthah.

PTHAH

Is only Neph under a new name; or, to express it otherwise, he represents a special energy of that god. He is the creator, or the universal life in *action*. Jamblichus calls him the *demiourgos*, or artisan of the world; and the Greeks regarded him as the counterpart of their own artisan god, Hephaestus or Vulcan. As the creator he was thought of as the father and sovereign of the gods. He was worshipped chiefly in Memphis. He appears as a mummy-shaped male figure; also as the pigmy-god.

KHEM,

Like the former god, is only a special energy or activity of the universal life. He is a personified attribute, or epithet.

Amun.

He is the god of generation and reproduction, and was identified as Pan by the Greeks, who called his chief city—

Chemmis, in the Thebais—by the name of Panopolis. But Khem not only merges into the god Num or Neph, he also usurps the functions of, or is the same as, the garden-god Ranno. It was but natural that the god of reproduction should also be a garden-god. This garden-god, Ranno, was represented under the form of an asp, whose figure is found on wine-presses and garden and agricultural implements. It should here be observed that Priapus, the classical counterpart of the procreative Khem, was the tutelary deity of gardens.

AMUN

Was the chief god of Upper Egypt. From the signification of the name—" hidden "—it would appear that Amun was a deity of a highly spiritual character. As in the preceding instances, he is identified or connected with various other gods, e. g., he is named as Amun-ra (Ra being the sun-god), and Amun-num (Num, the living breath or spirit). His companion goddess was Mut or Maut; and the two deities, with their son Khuns, formed the Trinity of Upper Egypt.

SATI

The Greeks imagined to be the same as Hera. As such she would be the queen of heaven; but a distinction was made between her and

NEITH,

Who was said to be the goddess of the upper heaven (or ether), whereas Sati was the goddess of the lower heaven (or air). If Neith be a sky-deity, and if she be also the mother of the sun-god, the facts are another instance from Egyptian mythology of that same process through which the Greeks peopled their Olympus and the Norsemen their Asgard. But further, the functions attributed to Neith seem to show that the idea of this goddess was developed much in the same way as that of the Greek Athene. As Athene in Greek, and Ahana in Sanscrit, meant originally the light of the dawn, and finally, moral and intellectual light, so we find that Neith also came to be a deity of wisdom. This goddess was worshipped especially at Sais in the Nile delta.

MAUT,

To whom we have already referred as the second person of the Theban Trinity, meant the Mother—Mother Nature—and thus corresponded to the Greek Demeter.

BUBASTIS

Was chiefly worshipped in the town of Bubastus in Lower Egypt. She was said to be the daughter of the great goddess Isis. She was represented with the head of a cat, the animal specially sacred to her.

RA

Comes first in the second class of deities. The Greeks identified him with their own sun-god, Helios, and called the city in which he was principally worshipped Heliopolis. He is represented with a hawk's head, over which is a solar disc. His purely physical origin seems to be proved by the myths that Neith, or the upper air, was his mother; and that he married Mut (Demeter), this merely signifying the interaction of earth and sunlight in producing vegetation. But again, Ra was said to have for children Athor, Mu, and

Mat. Athor was identified with Aphrodite, who was originally the goddess of light; while Mu means physical light, and Mat moral light. Precisely the same transition in meaning happens in the story of Neith, and in that of Athene, Ahana, Ushas, and Eos. The wide prevalence of this god's worship shows in what importance he was held, an importance naturally attaching to the sun-god among all nations given to elemental worship. From Ra, with the prefixed syllable Pi, was derived the name Phrah, or, in Old Testament spelling, Pharaoh. Every Pharaoh was thus entitled son of the sun. All this suggests that Sabaeism, or fire-worship, was originally practised in Egypt. Ra is also identical with Baal, a name implying " lord," and applied to the sun. Baalbeck means " city of the sun," and was so named by the Greeks —Heliopolis.

SEB

Is said to be the son of Ra. He is a sort of Egyptian Cronus, being represented in the hieroglyphics to be the father of the gods. Here again we have an interchange of functions; for it has been seen that Neph, Pthah, etc., have been similarly described. Also, like other gods in and out of Greek mythology, Seb marries his own sister, Nutpe. These two were at the head of the " Osirian divinities "— Osiris, Isis, Seth, Nephthys. Nutpe or Nepte has been identified with Rhea. She is supposed to coincide with Lucina, and to preside over births and nursing. As being the mother of Isis and Osiris, she was called the mother of the gods.

OSIRIS,

The great deity of the Egyptians, has been by some identified with the sun, or sunlight, or the vivifying powers in nature. According to this view the sleep or death of Osiris means the sleep of the spring-maiden Brynhild, or the imprisonment of Persephone in the dark realm of Hades. His contest with Seb (by the Greeks called Typho) would certainly seem to be another instance of the plausibility, at least, of this view. At any rate, Osiris, being restored to life, became the judge of the under-world. There he listens to Thoth's tale of the character of the disembodied souls, who are introduced to the judge by Horus (the son of Osiris), after their good and bad deeds have been weighed by Anubis in the scale of truth.

Osiris.

These trials in the under-world were attended by forty officers, called Assessors of the Dead, who are thus described by Gardner Wilkinson : '' These assessors were similar to the bench of judges who attended at the ordinary tribunals of the Egyptians, and whose president, or arch-judge, corresponded to Osiris. The assessors were represented in a human form with different heads. The first had the head of a hawk, the second of a man, the third of a hare, the fourth of a hippotamus, the fifth of a man, the sixth of a hawk, the seventh of a fox, the eighth of a man, the ninth of a ram, the tenth of a snake, and the others according to their peculiar character. . . . They are supposed to represent the forty-two crimes from which a virtuous man was expected to be free when judged in a future state; or rather the accusing spirits, each of whom examined if the deceased was guilty of the peculiar evil which it was his province to avenge.''

The worship of Osiris was universal throughout Egypt,

where he was gratefully regarded as the great example of self-sacrifice, as the manifester of good, as the opener of truth, and as being full of goodness and truth. As Osiris was the personification of physical and moral good, so his brother Seb (Typho) was the personification of all evil. Of the analogy between these two on the one hand, and the old Persian deities of good and evil, we have already spoken.

Osiris.

Another explanation of the Osirian myth has thus been given : Osiris was the Nile god. The river, in its periodical inundations, was said to have married the earth (Isis, Rhea), and in its retreat to have been killed by the giant of Sterility (Seb, or Typhon), who was jealous, perhaps, of the wondrous fruitfulness of the marriage between the soil and the great river.

APIS

Was the great beast-god of Egypt. This sacred bull was known as Apis at Memphis, and as Mnevis, or

Onuphis, at Heliopolis. His worship was so prevalent and popular, because he was regarded as an avatar, or incarnation, of the favorite deity Osiris, whose soul had transmigrated into the body of a bull. The sacred bull was allowed to live for no more than twenty-five years, at the end of which it was taken to the Nile, and drowned in one of the sacred wells. His death was followed by national mournings, which, however, gave place to national thanksgivings, as soon as a new Avatar, or sacred bull, discovered himself by the following

Procession of the Royal Bull, Apis.

marks : a black coat, a white triangular spot on the forehead, a spot like a half-moon on its right side, and under its tongue a knot like a beetle. The following quotations from *Aelian*, as given in *Wilkinson*, narrate the ceremonies consequent on the rediscovery of Osiris :

"As soon as a report is circulated that the Egyptian god has manifested himself, certain of the sacred scribes, well versed in the mythical marks, known to them by tradition, approach the spot where the divine cow has deposited her calf, and there, following the ancient ordinance of Hermes, feed it with milk during four months, in a house facing the rising sun. When this period has passed the sacred scribes and prophets resort to the dwelling of Apis, at the time of the new moon, and placing him in a boat prepared for the purpose, convey him to Memphis, where he has a convenient and agreeable abode, with pleasure grounds and ample space for wholesome exercise. Female companions of his own species are provided for him, the most beautiful that can be

Serapis.

found, kept in apartments to which he has access when he wishes. He drinks out of a well, or fountain of clear water: for it is not thought right to give him the water of the Nile, which is considered too fattening. . . . The man from whose herd the divine beast has sprung is the happiest of mortals, and is looked upon with admiration by all people." Cambyses, it is said, found a set of villagers rejoicing over a new sacred bull, and fancying they were making merry over his recent defeat in Aethiopia, the king of kings at once ran the bull through the body and had the priests flogged. It was considered a good omen if the bull ate food offered to it. Men also listened at the ears of Apis, then put their hands to their own ears to prevent the escape of the secret, which they interpreted according to the nature of the first words they chanced to hear uttered.

SERAPIS

Was another name of Osiris, although the Greeks said that his worship was not known in Egypt until the time of

Ptolemy Philadelphus, when it was introduced from Sinope, under the name of Serapis. Serapis was known as the judge of the under-world.

Serapis Throned.

ISIS

Was the wife of Osiris, also a counterpart of him; for, as he was judge of the dead, so she is described as the giver of death. She is identified with Ceres and Persephone, and, in this view, the grief of Isis for her husband may be regarded as an Egyptian version of the myth representing Demeter as mourning for the loss of her daughter. Apuleius makes her declare : "I am nature, the parent of all the gods, mistress of all the elements, the beginning of all the ages, sovereign of the gods, queen of the manes, and the first of the heavenly beings." But as the mother of all she is convertible with Mat and Nutpe. And then Apuleius proceeds : "My divinity, uniform in itself, is honored under numerous forms, various rites, and different names. . . . but the sun-illumed Aethiopians, and the Egyptians renowned for ancient

Isis.

lore, worship me with due ceremonies, and call me by my real name, ' Queen Isis.' '' Plutarch considers Isis to be the earth, the feminine part of nature, while Diodorus says that the Egyptians, considering the earth to be the parent of

all things born, called her Mother, just as the Greeks called
earth Demeter.

ANUBIS,

With Hor, or Horus, and Har-pi-chruti, or Harpocrates,
were the children of Osiris and Isis. The first was a jackal-
headed god; and, according to another myth, was the son of
Osiris and Nephthys, a sister of Isis, who, fearing the jealousy of Isis, concealed the child by the seashore. The office
of Anubis was to superintend the passage of souls to their
abode in the unseen world. As such he corresponded to the
Greek Hermes Psychopompos. Anubis presided over tombs;
and he is frequently introduced in
sculpture as standing over a bier on
which a corpse is deposited. Horus
was a hawk-headed god. As the
avenger of his father Osiris, who
was slain by Typhon, he was identified by the Greeks as Apollo. He
also corresponded in some degree to
the sun-god Ra, and was worshipped
by the Egyptians as representing the
vivifying power of the sun. Harpocrates seems to be merely another
version of Horus—he is a personification of the sun. He is represented as a child sitting on a lotus
flower, with his finger on his lips.
Under this figure he was thought of
as the god of silence. Perhaps in
placing a representation of him in

Thoth.

front of each of their temples, the wise Egyptians meant to
symbolize the fact that worship ought to be conducted with
silence.

THOTH

Was the god of letters, the clerk of the under-world, and the keeper of the records for the great judge Osiris. He is represented with the head of an ibis, and bearing a tablet, pen, and palm-branch. So great was the respect in which the sacred ibis was held—on account, no doubt, of its usefulness in destroying venomous reptiles—that any one guilty of killing it was himself punished with death.

ANOUKE

Was the third member of the trinity of Northern Aethiopia, the other two members being Sati and Neph.

THE SPHINX,

Unlike her Greek representative—who was a cruel monster born of the evil powers Typhon and Echidna—was a beneficent being who personified the fruit-bearing earth, and, like the sun and sky powers we have named above, was a deity of wisdom and knowledge. Her figure—lion-bodied, with the head and breast of a woman—was placed before every temple. The Egyptian Cerberus, or hell watch-dog, must have been a more forbidding and strange-looking animal than his Greek brother. He had the trunk and legs of a hippopotamus, with the head of a crocodile.

INDEX.

A CATALOG OF SELECTED DOVER
BOOKS IN ALL FIELDS OF INTEREST

100 BEST-LOVED POEMS, Edited by Philip Smith. "The Passionate Shepherd to His Love," "Shall I compare thee to a summer's day?" "Death, be not proud," "The Raven," "The Road Not Taken," plus works by Blake, Wordsworth, Byron, Shelley, Keats, many others. 96pp. 5³⁄₁₆ x 8¼.　　　　　　　　　　　　　0-486-28553-7

100 SMALL HOUSES OF THE THIRTIES, Brown-Blodgett Company. Exterior photographs and floor plans for 100 charming structures. Illustrations of models accompanied by descriptions of interiors, color schemes, closet space, and other amenities. 200 illustrations. 112pp. 8⅜ x 11.　　　　　　　　　0-486-44131-8

1000 TURN-OF-THE-CENTURY HOUSES: With Illustrations and Floor Plans, Herbert C. Chivers. Reproduced from a rare edition, this showcase of homes ranges from cottages and bungalows to sprawling mansions. Each house is meticulously illustrated and accompanied by complete floor plans. 256pp. 9⅜ x 12¼.
　　　　　　　　　　　　　　　　　　　　　　　　　　0-486-45596-3

101 GREAT AMERICAN POEMS, Edited by The American Poetry & Literacy Project. Rich treasury of verse from the 19th and 20th centuries includes works by Edgar Allan Poe, Robert Frost, Walt Whitman, Langston Hughes, Emily Dickinson, T. S. Eliot, other notables. 96pp. 5³⁄₁₆ x 8¼.　　　　　　　　0-486-40158-8

101 GREAT SAMURAI PRINTS, Utagawa Kuniyoshi. Kuniyoshi was a master of the warrior woodblock print — and these 18th-century illustrations represent the pinnacle of his craft. Full-color portraits of renowned Japanese samurais pulse with movement, passion, and remarkably fine detail. 112pp. 8⅜ x 11.　0-486-46523-3

ABC OF BALLET, Janet Grosser. Clearly worded, abundantly illustrated little guide defines basic ballet-related terms: arabesque, battement, pas de chat, relevé, sissonne, many others. Pronunciation guide included. Excellent primer. 48pp. 4³⁄₁₆ x 5¾.
　　　　　　　　　　　　　　　　　　　　　　　　　　0-486-40871-X

ACCESSORIES OF DRESS: An Illustrated Encyclopedia, Katherine Lester and Bess Viola Oerke. Illustrations of hats, veils, wigs, cravats, shawls, shoes, gloves, and other accessories enhance an engaging commentary that reveals the humor and charm of the many-sided story of accessorized apparel. 644 figures and 59 plates. 608pp. 6 ⅛ x 9¼.
　　　　　　　　　　　　　　　　　　　　　　　　　　0-486-43378-1

ADVENTURES OF HUCKLEBERRY FINN, Mark Twain. Join Huck and Jim as their boyhood adventures along the Mississippi River lead them into a world of excitement, danger, and self-discovery. Humorous narrative, lyrical descriptions of the Mississippi valley, and memorable characters. 224pp. 5³⁄₁₆ x 8¼.　0-486-28061-6

ALICE STARMORE'S BOOK OF FAIR ISLE KNITTING, Alice Starmore. A noted designer from the region of Scotland's Fair Isle explores the history and techniques of this distinctive, stranded-color knitting style and provides copious illustrated instructions for 14 original knitwear designs. 208pp. 8⅜ x 10⅞.　0-486-47218-3

Browse over 9,000 books at www.doverpublications.com

CATALOG OF DOVER BOOKS

ALICE'S ADVENTURES IN WONDERLAND, Lewis Carroll. Beloved classic about a little girl lost in a topsy-turvy land and her encounters with the White Rabbit, March Hare, Mad Hatter, Cheshire Cat, and other delightfully improbable characters. 42 illustrations by Sir John Tenniel. 96pp. 5⅜₆ x 8¼.	0-486-27543-4

AMERICA'S LIGHTHOUSES: An Illustrated History, Francis Ross Holland. Profusely illustrated fact-filled survey of American lighthouses since 1716. Over 200 stations — East, Gulf, and West coasts, Great Lakes, Hawaii, Alaska, Puerto Rico, the Virgin Islands, and the Mississippi and St. Lawrence Rivers. 240pp. 8 x 10¾.	0-486-25576-X

AN ENCYCLOPEDIA OF THE VIOLIN, Alberto Bachmann. Translated by Frederick H. Martens. Introduction by Eugene Ysaye. First published in 1925, this renowned reference remains unsurpassed as a source of essential information, from construction and evolution to repertoire and technique. Includes a glossary and 73 illustrations. 496pp. 6⅛ x 9¼.	0-486-46618-3

ANIMALS: 1,419 Copyright-Free Illustrations of Mammals, Birds, Fish, Insects, etc., Selected by Jim Harter. Selected for its visual impact and ease of use, this outstanding collection of wood engravings presents over 1,000 species of animals in extremely lifelike poses. Includes mammals, birds, reptiles, amphibians, fish, insects, and other invertebrates. 284pp. 9 x 12.	0-486-23766-4

THE ANNALS, Tacitus. Translated by Alfred John Church and William Jackson Brodribb. This vital chronicle of Imperial Rome, written by the era's great historian, spans A.D. 14-68 and paints incisive psychological portraits of major figures, from Tiberius to Nero. 416pp. 5⅜₆ x 8¼.	0-486-45236-0

ANTIGONE, Sophocles. Filled with passionate speeches and sensitive probing of moral and philosophical issues, this powerful and often-performed Greek drama reveals the grim fate that befalls the children of Oedipus. Footnotes. 64pp. 5⅜₆ x 8 ¼.	0-486-27804-2

ART DECO DECORATIVE PATTERNS IN FULL COLOR, Christian Stoll. Reprinted from a rare 1910 portfolio, 160 sensuous and exotic images depict a breathtaking array of florals, geometrics, and abstracts — all elegant in their stark simplicity. 64pp. 8⅜ x 11.	0-486-44862-2

THE ARTHUR RACKHAM TREASURY: 86 Full-Color Illustrations, Arthur Rackham. Selected and Edited by Jeff A. Menges. A stunning treasury of 86 full-page plates span the famed English artist's career, from *Rip Van Winkle* (1905) to masterworks such as *Undine, A Midsummer Night's Dream,* and *Wind in the Willows* (1939). 96pp. 8⅜ x 11.	0-486-44685-9

THE AUTHENTIC GILBERT & SULLIVAN SONGBOOK, W. S. Gilbert and A. S. Sullivan. The most comprehensive collection available, this songbook includes selections from every one of Gilbert and Sullivan's light operas. Ninety-two numbers are presented uncut and unedited, and in their original keys. 410pp. 9 x 12.	0-486-23482-7

THE AWAKENING, Kate Chopin. First published in 1899, this controversial novel of a New Orleans wife's search for love outside a stifling marriage shocked readers. Today, it remains a first-rate narrative with superb characterization. New introductory Note. 128pp. 5⅜₆ x 8¼.	0-486-27786-0

BASIC DRAWING, Louis Priscilla. Beginning with perspective, this commonsense manual progresses to the figure in movement, light and shade, anatomy, drapery, composition, trees and landscape, and outdoor sketching. Black-and-white illustrations throughout. 128pp. 8⅜ x 11.	0-486-45815-6

Browse over 9,000 books at www.doverpublications.com